Angelina Grimké

Rhetoric, Identity, and the Radical Imagination

Rhetoric and Public Affairs Series

Angelina Grimké

Rhetoric, Identity, and the Radical Imagination

Stephen Howard Browne

Michigan State University Press
East Lansing

Printed and bound in the United States of America.

Michigan State University Press
East Lansing, Michigan 48823-5202

04 03 02 01 00 99 1 2 3 4 5 6 7 8 9

Library of Congress Cataloging-in-Publication Data

Browne, Stephen H.
Angelina Grimké : rhetoric, identity, and the radical imagination / Stephen Howard Browne.
        p.   cm. — (Rhetoric and public affairs series)
Includes bibliographical references and index.
ISBN 0-87013-530-9 (alk. paper)— ISBN 0-87013-542-2 (pbk. : alk. paper)
1. Grimké, Angelina Emily, 1805–1879—Oratory. 2. Grimké, Angelina Emily, 1805-1879—Language. 3. Rhetoric—Political aspects—United States—History—19th century. 4. Radicalism—United States—History—19th century. 5. Antislavery movements—United States—History—19th century. 6. Women's rights—United States—History—19th century. I. Title. II. Series.
    E449.G865 B76 1999
    322.4'4'092—dc21

                                                                                    99-006955

Book and cover design by Michael J. Brooks
Cover engraving by J. Sartam

Visit Michigan State University Press on the World Wide Web at:
    www.msu.edu/unit/msupress

This book is dedicated to Margaret,
Jessica, Maria, Emily, and Elizabeth,
rebels all.

Contents

Acknowledgements

The merits of this book are owing chiefly to the company I have been fortunate to keep through the past several years. My approach to interpreting Grimké's texts has been deeply informed by the work of Michael Leff, and I wish to thank Michael for his personal encouragement and leadership in the field of rhetorical studies. I also wish to thank Karlyn Kohrs Campbell, whose leadership in the recovery and critical analysis of women's rhetoric has opened up untold opportunities for a generation of scholars; we will remain in her debt for a long, long time. I fear I shall never be the writer she hoped I might become, but I have learned much otherwise from her example. That Lori Ginzberg and I work at the same institution I count as just good luck on my part; she has been and remains a valued colleague whose work continues to inspire. Charles Morris was, throughout the early and late stages of this book, a ready confidant, a source of encouragement and insight, and a friend to both the project and its author. Thank you, Chuck. Anne Demo, Bernard Armada, Brad Vivian, Andrew Hansen, Susan Zaeske, and Alisse Theodore have in their distinctive ways contributed more than perhaps they know to the inception, research, and development of the arguments presented here. Thanks, as well, to Jeff Kurtz and Carmen Heider for their research assistance. The Research and Graduate Studies Office and the College of Liberal Arts provided research funds, for which I am grateful, as I am to the William C. Clements Library of the University of Michigan. As editor of the *Quarterly Journal of Speech,* Barbara Warnick oversaw the first publication of the chapter on Grimké's letter to Garrison. I appreciate her active role in seeing the piece into print.

For his sharp eye, steady hand, and tireless commitment to scholarship in rhetoric and public address, I thank emphatically Martin Medhurst. Robert Abzug provided a thorough reading of the manuscript, as did David Henry, Margaret Michels, and Karlyn Campbell, and I greatly appreciate their efforts. The book is, no doubt about it, better as a result. Still, it must be said: I alone bear responsibility for the book's shortcomings. I wish to thank, finally, my colleagues in the Department of Speech Communication for their many years of friendship and support.

Encountering Angelina Grimké

Angelina Grimké lived her life in the spaces between, in the gaps and fissures that separated her from what was left behind and from a more perfect future. Her biography may well be read as a series of repudiations, as a coming to conviction and so to action. Yet these repudiations—of home, slavery, patriarchy, sectarianism, of the world she knew—far from crippling Grimké, gave to her character its strength, its edge and range. Such coming to conviction was usually done in silence, prayer, reading, and reflection. Acting on it never was. "I will lift up my voice like a trumpet," Grimké declared, "and show this people their transgressions." And when she did, when she lifted her voice in public on behalf of the public, she found that in creating herself she might transform the world. In the process, Grimké crossed the wires of race, gender, and power, and by the explosion produced lit up the world of antebellum America.[1]

This book is one account of the ways in which identity—Grimké's public self, her *ethos*—was symbolically fashioned and put to the purposes of moral reform. Neither Grimké nor her contemporaries used the word "identity," of course, but it is a word I find I cannot do without. So much that was significant about her rhetorical practice pressed on questions of self, being, and being-with-others that I am willing to risk using a word more familiar in our time than hers. Who, then, was Angelina Grimké? The question may be answered biographically, and has been, by historians and critics as diverse as Catharine Birney, Gerda Lerner, and Katharine Du Pre Lumpkin. I wish to raise it again as being critical to our understanding of the relationship between human agency and the art of rhetoric. The question is further complicated by the difficulty of fixing Grimké very firmly within any given cultural grid. Religion? Episcopalian-Presbyterian-Quaker-non-denominational mystic. Regional affiliation? Charleston-Philadelphia-New York Massachusetts. Gender roles? Unmarried Public Speaker-Author-Debater-Married Mother-Women's Rights Activist-Educator. Class? Carolinian slave-holding aristocracy-Northern urbanite benevolence worker-utopian visionary![2]

Consider: in 1837, Grimké insisted to Catharine Beecher that "the present arrangements of society on these points [separate moral spheres for men and women] are a *violation of human rights, a rank usurpation of power*, a violent seizure and confiscation of what is sacredly and inalienably hers. . . ." Eight years earlier, however, in a diary entry she confided these sentiments: "When I say that all men are brothers, I am far from desiring to level the walls of separation which exist between different ranks of society, for I believe the distinctions are right, and tend to the happiness and advantage of the human family at large. Experience has adamantly taught me that a person of high rank cannot put themselves on an equality with one of low life, without injuring both, and vice versa, and yet I fully approve the exhortations of the Apostle, 'condescend to men of low estate.'" Withal, concluded this soon-to-be-equalitarian, "There is a beautiful order in the arrangements of Providence which cannot be disturbed without occasioning confusion."[3]

The point is perhaps obvious, but Grimké simply does not fit into any ready narrative or taxonomy of reform types. In part this is because, as the diary, correspondence, and public statements indicate, her convictions were seldom allowed to sit still for long. She subjected her beliefs to an unrelenting personal and public scrutiny, as if only through such pressure could she remain confident of her commitment to them. In part, too, this may be an artifact of history itself: Grimké entered into public life at a time when virtually every standard, expectation, and practice defining that life was undergoing dramatic changes. Such change is characteristic of every generation, of course, but to be a young female orator from Charleston, come North to lecture against slavery and for human rights during the mid-1830s? That is singular by any standard.

We accordingly have at least two ways of answering the question as to Grimké's public identity. The first is to inscribe her into prevailing and often self-composed narratives of reform, to make of her what she obviously was to many, a "holy warrior," in Stewart's happy phrase. Here she is explicable as a type, a virtuoso who was able, by virtue of her distinctive background and eloquent voice, to advance the vanguard of immediate abolitionism and women's rights. She was, in this view, a particularly effective transmitter for currents already under way, adept at deploying the discursive resources of scripture and early republicanism—what else, after all, could she have done?—for the sake of the enslaved. To ask after her public identity in this case is to consider first the identity of the movement into which she was drafted and from which she drew her strength, support, and notoriety. She was peculiar, yes, but peculiar only in a way that made her above all useful; more peculiar than most of the other peculiar characters making up the radicals of the decade, perhaps, but scarcely alien.[4]

A second approach to the question of Grimké's public identity might stress instead how distinctive she truly was, what a strange, formidable, and subversive voice she turned out to be. Unfettered by institutional politics, religion, reform, gender conventions, institutionalized *anything*, Angelina went forth alone, without precedent, criticized by friends and foes alike, pushing down barriers, absorbing the consequences, and creating new possibilities for those who followed. Far from being a recruit to the movement, she, like Frederick Douglass later, constituted its identity almost singlehandedly, an autonomous and dangerous force unleashed on the plains of antebellum America.

There is, in these caricatures, some appeal to the image of Grimké as either a front person for abolitionism and the woman's rights movements or, more romantically, as the free-ranging, free-fighting, free agent exemplified in the letters to Catharine Beecher and Theodore Weld. It is not necessary or desirable that we choose either model for understanding Grimké's public identity, but it may be worth the effort to find a more satisfying approach to the question. The thesis of this book has been posed as a claim bearing on just this issue; I have tried to account not so much for the ways in which Grimké made herself of service to abolitionism and woman's rights; nor for the ways in which she exploited her unusual background in order to create some autonomous Other. I have sought rather to trace some of the ways in which Grimké crafted herself publicly for the purposes of activating collective moral action. I have assumed throughout that she meant what she said; that she did not come to the work of abolition and women's rights out of anxieties about class displacement, social control, or any other round-about motives. It is possible, after all, that some abolitionists and woman's rights supporters undertook the risks of social reform because they "simply" hated slavery and sexual oppression. Grimké was one of these individuals.

If the analysis offered in this book has been at all plausible, we should have at least one set of responses to the question of Grimké's identity. Making no pretensions to psychological explanations or to the workings of culture generally, I have tried to focus on what Grimké said, to listen closely and to base whatever interpretive claims I make on what it was she desired to communicate rhetorically. The Grimké presented here is therefore a resolutely public figure, but never a public fixture; in constant motion, frequently uncertain of what lay ahead, operating without conventional safety nets, sometimes wracked by doubt, assured of her cause if not her abilities. It would exaggerate the point to suggest that she was a natural at public advocacy—although she was more willing than Sarah to undergo its quite real hardships—but it would understate the case to suggest that Angelina merely endured such work as a grim necessity. Grimké labored in public because she knew that therein could be discovered, composed, and deployed means of persuasion not otherwise available. It required no elaborate theory of the public on her part or on our part to see why: from her perspective, that was where the power was, or at least power of a kind, and she meant to make the most of it.

But in what did this public consist, in what forms did this power shape and present itself? Again, the answer could not have been for Grimké far to seek: the public she looked upon in that summer of 1835, when she first acted on her will to be of service to the world, consisted of a volatile mix of good and evil, of constraints and opportunities, of energies latent and kinetic. Desiring to enter and change that public world, Grimké in effect committed to changing herself, if only to give her purchase on it, to ensure that she would, upon so entering, remain an actor and not acted upon. This commitment, to change herself by way of changing the world, represents at least one important feature of Grimké's public identity. Well aware of the proscriptions against female advocacy, she had to make of herself an "available means of persuasion," had to so compose her own ethos as to command a hearing from those, in a phrase dear to her, who "hath ears to hear."

Among the most remarkable features of Angelina Grimké's rhetorical career—hence the rationale for this book and the approach it contains—was her ability to stage public contests for the soul of America. Her art was to bring opposing ideas into proximity, to give them voice, depth, and range, and by their contact to create new and more compelling visions of social change. The essays making up this book explore various dimensions of that art, particularly as it gave purpose, form, and effect to Grimké's public address. Whatever its limitations, my treatment of Grimké is the result of taking her seriously as a thinker, writer, and orator. I mean by this no condescension, for anyone familiar with Grimké's legacy will know that she was an extraordinary force in the early abolitionist and women's rights movements. The following essays are offered as a means to see the work of such a mind up close, to foreground the structure and detail of her arguments, to recover, in the end, something of the rich texture and rhetorical power of her ideas. To this end I ask rather a lot of the reader: the analysis remains close to the ground, where a good deal of description, quotation, and glossing take place. At this point I can only plead for patience, hopeful that in thus reading Grimké we can open up avenues of inquiry for those more suited to the bigger picture.

Although I do not aim here at a comprehensive synthesis of all the extant speeches and tracts, I do examine most of her public works and, in one instance, a private exchange with Theodore Weld. For better or worse, I do not try to make a case for perspectives already well-established by historians of the period—on the interplay of public and private life in antebellum America, for example, or on the dynamics of class, race, and gender during the 1830s. We are the beneficiaries of a substantial, sophisticated, and expanding scholarship on these and related issues, and I have sought only to rely upon it here. We are in any case well beyond the point when the Grimké sisters merited but a mention or two in histories of moral reform. Two thirds of a century have past since Gilibert Barnes and Dwight Dummond published their two-volume collection of the letters of Angelina, Sarah, and Theodore Weld. That collection, although slighting the sisters' correspondence in some important ways, helped usher in a new and invigorating set of primary source materials and, consequently, new perspectives on the role of the sisters and Weld in the antislavery movement. If nothing else, their letters demonstrate an acute sensitivity to the assumptions and implications driving moral reform, including many uneasy questions about the viability of reform organizations, the role—or lack of role—of African Americans in the movement, and what all this entailed by way of women's rights and political action. I have relied heavily on this correspondence and on the holdings at the Clements Library at the University of Michigan from whence it came. In particular, I have sought through the letters to give a sense of range and depth to the ideas of Angelina Grimké, to stress, that is, the intersection of experience and principle, the proximity of the private and the public, that so marked her rhetorical career.

The single most important contribution to the study of Grimké is the work of Gerda Lerner, whose publication in 1967 of *The Grimké Sisters from South Carolina: Pioneers for Woman's Rights and Abolition* culminated years of research and writing on the subject. Lerner has recently observed that her biography appeared at a time when "women's history was of interest to fewer than a dozen historians in the United States." That number may be a little on the small side, but Lerner reminds us forcefully how far scholarship on women has advanced in a single generation. Students of Angelina Grimké, consequently, have much to be grateful for. Thanks to Lori Ginzberg, for example, we now have a much more complicated and enriched understanding of how Grimké and other "ultraists" fought to expand the scope of political action to include women's issues—even as they fended off narrowing conceptions of the political. Thanks to such studies as those included in Jean Fagan Yellin and John C. Van Horne's edited volume on the political culture of women during the period, we now have comprehensive accounts of the organizational dynamics shaping the range of opportunities available to and created by women reformers. And thanks to Robert Abzug, we have a more clear and detailed picture of how such "religious virtuosos" as Grimké drew from and expanded the religious imagination fueling American reform. Again, my debt to this scholarship is evident; I hope to repay it in small amounts by providing systematic readings of Grimké's key texts, as if in this way we can move toward yet greater detail in accounting for the discursive and rhetorical forces at play in the fields of moral reform. For all these debts to the established scholarship on Grimké and her milieu, no one will mistake what follows as the work of a professional historian. It represents the efforts of a critic to interpret texts of a kind, the point of which is to account for the ideational density, moral ambitions, and rhetorical art that go into the making of public discourse. Within the broader terrain of rhetorical criticism, this work will be identifiable as a form of textual criticism, historically informed and focused on the dynamics of discrete rhetorical productions. Critics within such disciplines as communication and rhetoric will note that I share in this stress on textual dynamics an orientation frequently associated with the work of Michael Leff, Stephen Lucas, and Edwin Black. Although we differ in some important respects, Karlyn Kohrs Campbell has developed a substantial and impressive body of work over the years that has informed this book in many ways. Campbell's recovery and interpretation of early feminist texts has greatly expanded our perspective on the sources, contexts, and implications of women's rights in the nineteenth century. It is not too much to say, I think, that for rhetorical critics at work in departments of communication, Campbell's efforts have set in place the possibility of our own.

Given the rhetorical sensibilites of Ginsberg, Yellin, Abzug, Campbell and many other historians and critics, what I offer in the following may be notable only as a matter of degree and not kind. Part of my relentless stress on the texture of Grimké's thought, in either case, is meant to suggest what is gained by pressing hard on textual details. If we want to talk about voice, about agency, power, and resistance, then we need to squint closely at *what* Grimké and others are saying and *how*. Now as never before, we have available to us textual resources that promise to deepen our understanding of how women availed themselves of the rhetorical capital at hand to change their world. Now would seem the worst time, conversely, to dissipate these voices and their textual embodiments into the ether of theory or grand generalization.

◆   ◆   ◆

This book is about the ways in which Grimké fashioned for herself and others a rationale for public moral action. The materials she used were symbolic, the resources of a culture deeply indebted to received vocabularies by which social, political, and religious ideals were given practical expression. Grimké's speeches and writings are accordingly recognizable for what they are, and need not be transfigured or mystified in order to make them interesting or important. The assumptions which ground the interpretive work of this book—loosely, its method—are similarly straightforward. In general, I ask a set of questions about the conception, composition, delivery, and meaning of key texts in the public life of Angelina Grimké. Together, these questions in turn establish a fairly systematic set of reflections on her rhetorical practice. "Rhetoric" is taken here to designate the process through which individuals avail themselves of such symbolic resources as culture may be said to provide. This view of the art—a little old-fashioned, to be sure, but

I hope not implausible—allows me to address specific issues in particular: how does the form of the public letter negotiate the apparently competing demands of self and community? How can the past be refashioned into a warrant for reconstituted community? What is the relationship between the public sphere and human rights? How could violence be reimagined into an available means of persuasion? This stress on Grimké's rhetoric as a strategic response to the pressing realities of antebellum culture is not meant to suggest that she was reacting simply or without constraint to a set of situational givens. On the contrary, I try to suggest how Grimké created from those very realities the means of their own—and her own—transformation. This is rhetorical work of a powerful and curious kind. If my account is at all useful, then, it will not be owing to such modest methodological grounds as are evident here, but because its gives us reason, as she gave her own audiences reason, to strain toward words that ought not be forgotten.

A great deal of what follows has to do with the ways in which Grimké fashioned from the resources available to her specific kinds of interpersonal relationships, through which she was able to build a platform for public advocacy. Indeed, it is no small part of Grimké's legacy that she so readily assumed prominence among the abolitionist and woman's rights select; that she was able to do so was neither incidental nor merely a function of her distinctive background. Grimké formed these relationships for a reason, rhetorically through acts of solicitude and confrontation, morally to activate collective will. In the process, she leveraged herself into public life, there to stand as an exemplar for generations of human rights activists. As wrenching and intensely spiritual as her journey was, Grimké fortunately had the benefit of extraordinary companionship. These supporters constituted a kind of avant garde for the new moral order. From them Grimké drew strength in a reciprocating process of support and assertion; but above all, they encouraged Grimké in her efforts to recreate the conditions under which radical change was possible. A glance across her audience on the evening of her last major public address, on May 16, 1838 in Pennsylvania Hall, would note among these friends the following:

Maria Chapman, who had just sat down after a frustrating attempt to capture the attention and quiet of the Hall. She had loudly prayed "for the strength which will enable one on such an occasion to speak forth the truth," but seemed not able to command it. This was, indeed, Chapman's first major public speech, a true baptism by fire, and it may have reminded her of the relative calm of her editorial office. There she had led the Boston Female Anti-Slavery Society and edited its *Right and Wrong in Boston*. Chapman, who was nurtured from birth in the ways of reform politics and agitation, was hardly innocent of its excesses: she had witnessed first hand the mobbing of William Lloyd Garrison in 1835, and soon was to be at the center of the schism in abolitionist ranks. In her role as a leader of the New England abolitionists, she recognized just how valuable was Grimké's rhetorical cachet: writing in June of 1837 to the "Female Anti-Slavery Societies throughout New England," Chapman urged the abolitionist community to accept Angelina and her sister Sarah "as eminently qualified for the promulgation of Anti Slavery principles," the more so because of their "elevated and Christian point of view from which they behold the condition of woman; her duties and her consequent rights." Angelina, in turn, had found her equal in Chapman's indefatigable commitment to the abolitionist and woman's rights causes.[5]

Grimké could find support, too, in the deceptively placid aspect of *William Lloyd Garrison*, by consensus one of the most obdurate and morally compelling figures of the movement. Garrison, whose range of moral energies seemed to know no bounds, had long been a supporter of the Grimkés and of female advocates generally. His career virtually defined New England abolitionism: as the founding editor of *The Liberator* in 1831 he gave to the movement its most incendiary medium; as a founding member of the New England Anti-Slavery Society, he helped organize and promote the aims of immediate abolitionism; a year later he helped compose the charter principles of the American Anti-Slavery Society. Like most prominent abolitionists, Garrison forged his beliefs in the crucible of public opinion; more than most, he courted, relished even, its violent expressions, and in 1835 found himself at the end of a rope, dragged unceremoniously through the streets of Boston. He survived, to the dismay of some, no doubt, to lead his followers in 1840 against New York-based proponents of political reform. Garrison's speech tonight was characteristically pointed but unusually short. "There are other speakers to follow me," he said, referring to Chapman, Grimké, Abby Kelly and Mott, "gifted in intellect, and capable of pleading the cause of the bondmen and BONDWOMEN in our land far more effectually than myself." That fact did not keep Garrison from launching into a withering attack on the American Colonization Society, but he did aver that "The slave system in this country will find in the women of America most formidable antagonists. What astonishing effects have already been wrought upon the public," Garrison gestured to the Grimké sisters, "by the labors of only two of their number?"[6]

Grimké's community of reformers included as well the renowned poet and abolitionist *John Greenleaf Whittier*. Whittier had been present just two days before during Grimké's marriage to Theodore Weld, although, as a practicing Quaker, he was obliged to step outside during the actual ceremony. Whittier's relationship to Angelina was intimate but qualified; earlier he had warned her against introducing women's rights issues into her abolitionist addresses, and she had responded, to use a term of the day, in a wrathy way. He was in any case the movement's muse and an avid supporter of Angelina's. On first hearing her during a speech at Haverhill, Whittier wrote that Grimké, though "impetuous," was "at times *very* eloquent and impassioned—and her whole soul kindles with indignation at the wrongs and crimes of which she speaks of . . . Angelina moves the spirit like a trumpet-peal."[7]

Of all the dominant personalities housed in Pennsylvania Hall that night, none commanded such uniform regard as *Lucretia Mott*. The diminutive Hicksite Quaker wielded enormous power as an abolitionist, and was in some sense the spiritual beacon of the movement. Mott had managed in her quiet way to insert herself into the leadership of nearly every important reform campaign of the time, including temperance, peace, and women's rights. Nearby she had attended and played an active role in the founding of the American Anti-Slavery Society as well as the Philadelphia Female Anti-Slavery Society. Mott's spirit was to animate and inspire the young Elizabeth Cady Stanton at the World's Anti-Slavery Convention in 1840; and she later helped pioneer the woman's rights movement throughout the decade. Her home with husband James was a sanctuary for runaway slaves: soon, it was to shelter some of those with whom she shared the stage tonight. In any event, she sought now to remind her audience that this was not, in fact, a meeting of the Anti-Slavery Convention of American Women, inasmuch as certain of its members still proved reluctant to meet and speak before such a promiscuous audience as was present tonight. Exasperated, Mott could only again announce her "hope that such false notions of delicacy and propriety would not long obtain in this enlightened country."[8]

And there was, of course, the two people closest to Angelina and with whom she was to share the rest of her life. With sister *Sarah* she had worked intimately and well, indeed had learned at her feet at an early age and had been greatly influenced by Sarah's decision to leave South Carolina and enter Philadelphia's Quaker community. Sarah's career so closely parallels Angelina's that their stories are often conflated. There are reasons for this approach, but for the purposes of this study Angelina is singled out because she, more than any other figure, exemplified the drama, the tensions, and the artistic character evident in antebellum America's reform movements. Sarah's reputation, to be sure, can stand on its own: she wrote the highly regarded *Epistle to the Clergy of the Southern States* (1836) and the classic feminist text *Letters on the Equality of the Sexes and the Condition of Woman* (1838). Sarah had worked in tandem with her sister during the New England Tour, and although she soon retired from the podium, her contributions were widely heralded. Whittier found her "serious, solemn—as if her heart lingered amidst the crushed and sorrowful tenants of the slave cabins of Carolina—full of sympathy for wronged—of compassion for the wrong-doers." Like her sister, Sarah was intensively introspective and even more given to those internal dramas that seemed all her life to drive, point, and shape her sense of self and the world. "My life, what has it been," she wrote to Weld during the speaking tour, "the panting of a soul after eternity—the feeling that there was nothing *here* to fill the aching void. . . . The world, what has it been? A waste howling wilderness. I seem to be just now awakened," Sarah confided, "or rather awakening to a true perception of the end of my being, my duties, my responsibilities, the rich and perpetual pleasures which God has provided for us in the fulfillment of duty to Him and to our fellow creatures."[9]

In *Theodore Weld* Angelina had found her strongest and most challenging supporter. In a reform community that prided itself on commitment, oratorical energy, and personal piety, few could hold a candle to the enigmatic Weld, who emerged in the 1830s to become the movement's de facto leader for matters strategic as well as spiritual. It is no small measure of his relationship to Angelina that they attended the Pennsylvania Hall convention in the first place. Married but two days, Angelina and Weld could think of no better way to move forward—and, not incidentally, to assure friends that marriage would not silence their legendary voices. In this, of course, the hope was illusory: while it would be simplistic—and inaccurate—to suggest that marriage ended their respective careers in reform, it certainly introduced a drastically new dimension to lives previously unencumbered by relational duties. Like Whittier, Weld had worried that Angelina's concern for "the woman question" muddied waters turbulent enough; their exchange on the matter the year before had precipitated an intense and telling exchange of letters. Weld deeply respected Angelina's talents and commitment, and explained his position by stressing its strategic rather than principled motives. "You may rely upon it," he wrote, "your *specimens* of female speaking and praying will do fifty times as much to bring over to women's rights the community as your *indoctrinating* under your own name thro' the newspapers those who never saw you."[10]

It does nothing to diminish Grimké's singular achievments to observe that she took life from these relationships and that, in return, she defined for herself a unique and compelling identity. This orator, so long traumatized by moral isolation and the loneliness which commitment entails, found her voice amongst these friends, and in being heard she discovered how that identity could be at once constituted through language and given its optimal expression. This study in Grimké's rhetorical craft, however, is not so much about the psychology of commitment as it is about what commitment looks like when it has gone public.

By the white hot summer of 1835 Grimké's anguish could no longer be tolerated. Privately she had been nurturing the prospects of committing to the antislavery cause, but the way before her seemed at times impossibly complicated. The Quaker community to which Grimké had fled five years before was proving more resilient than expected to the idea of independent action; Sarah's support could be halting; Angelina herself was wracked by anxiety. She needed, in effect, a way out, a prompt that would move her from a position of spectatorship into a different and more spiritually compelling world of public action and principled argument. Angelina Grimké needed to go public.

On August 22 of 1835, William Lloyd Garrison published in his *Liberator* an "Appeal" to the citizens of Boston. Things had been going badly, as usual, for the editor, whose cultivated notoriety was beginning to wear thin the patience of his fellow New Englanders. After a particularly hostile series of reactions to the abolitionist George Thompson, on loan from England for a lengthy lecture tour, Garrison took his case once again to the columns of his paper. A copy of his "Appeal" fell into the hands of Grimké, and when it did, her life was changed for good. Grimké's response was to become the first in a series of staged encounters that would literally rewrite the language of antislavery. Published without her permission—and without demand for retraction—the Letter functioned as Grimké's entree into public life. It is thus significant as the best record available of this pivotal moment in her life and for the light it sheds on antislavery rhetoric in its still formative years. In the context of this study, the Letter is particularly interesting for the way in which it announces and constructs a public relationship between author and reader. Fundamental to our understanding of this process is the manner in which Grimké avails herself of the symbolics of violence, persecution, martyrdom, and redemption. I hope to suggest in what follows how deeply her rhetorical work was invested in this logic: most conspicuously in the Letter and later in her speech at Pennsylvania Hall, Grimké dramatically transforms violence into a catalyst for change. The persecution of the abolitionists, likened to that of Christ's, is finally made redemptive through their willingness to sacrifice. Thus what might be viewed as a check on social change—violence—is rhetorically transformed into a specific and highly charged rationale for collective action.

Whatever spiritual or psychological forces are at work when private desire becomes public display, the process is bound to be heavily pressured by the competing demands of individual will and collective tradition. So much was certainly the case with Grimké, whose Letter may be taken as a kind of multicultural transgression. Stressed as it was by the expectations of patriarchy, class, and church, the text makes dramatic the stakes involved: the relationship she seeks to establish had to be public, but not simply so. Grimké needed rather to assert herself into the discourse of antislavery in a distinctive and stylized way, to speak around the various inhibitions which threatened to block or usurp her voice. She had, in short, to reconstitute the conditions under which an authentic relationship could be made possible. This is why it is not enough to say that with the Letter Grimké went public: more accurately, with this letter she went public by rewriting its very terms of ingress.

My exploration of Grimké's Letter, in any case, encourages such a perspective. By stressing the author's mode of address and the formal means through which she inscribes Garrison into the text, I hope to exhibit one way that public relationships get rhetorically crafted. The analysis is driven by the premise that Grimké warrants herself into public life by positioning author and reader equally before a transcultural code. The self-fashioning which takes place in the letter is evidence of this process; more broadly, however, Grimké puts on display a way of reading that code, and in its performance she creates a compelling rationale for collective and equitable action. Grimké's Letter speaks to Garrison, yes, but to Garrison as a member of a greater community and with the expectation that others will themselves be prompted to speak with her. The text, by direct implication, can be reduced neither to its sheerly formal enactments nor to the level of cultural production. Like Grimké herself, it thrives in the spaces between.

Grimké's letter to Garrison is evidence of, among other things, a powerful impulse that might usefully be defined as rhetorical. In this regard rhetoric was at once means and ends: expression was itself a form of realization; speech a sign of emancipation, eloquence of validation. Rhetoric became for Grimké the medium through which relationships were created; and through their creation was born the possibility of authentic community and shared moral responsibility. More than many, however, Grimké understood that community was not, even for radical ends, enough. She spoke with her face to the future, but she knew too that community was born of tradition, and her own relationship to that community she had damaged badly. A year after her epistle to Garrison, Grimké sought to re-create that relationship in her *Appeal to the Christian Woman of the South*. The *Appeal* is a thickly-layered and provocative text, at once subtle and imposing. And although articulated in many voices, they all sound the same and unmistakable message: "Have not women stood up in all the dignity and strength of moral courage to be the leaders of the people, and to bear a faithful testimony for the truth whenever the providence of God has called upon them to do so?"[11]

Grimké's 1836 *Appeal* represents for this study a second critical encounter. It shares with the letter to Garrison that peculiar mix of the hortatory and the solicitous, and we may be tempted at first glance to class it as a monologue under different cover. To do so would be to deny its art, the way in which it rhetorically orchestrates and puts on display the symbolic process by which public relationships are established. Unlike her Letter, the *Appeal* is much longer, more allusive, and, for the first time, engages at length the issue of woman's moral agency. It is, above all, an act of sympathy, a willed effort to embrace others not as they are but as they might become. Grimké had by 1835 found in persecution a vocabulary through which all voices could be equalized in a community of suffering. Now she struggled to repair relationships that had been ripped apart by her own hand.

In that struggle as before, Grimké searched for a way of speaking, a language of commitments, that would not so much transcend differences as reconstitute them into a greater order.

Grimké knew herself to be the cause of one problem and solution to another. Having been obliged by duty to "break those outward bonds of union" which kept her connected to false community, she pled the case of a new union, a sisterhood of the spirit that promised at once to restore old ties and to create new ones. Here was an encounter with friends, enemies, and strangers alike, called together through her *Appeal* because, in her own words, "I feel an interest in you, as branches of the same vine from whose root I daily draw the principle of spiritual vitality—Yes! Sisters in Christ I feel an interest in you, and often has the secret prayer arisen on your behalf, Lord, 'open thou their eyes that they may see wondrous things out of thy Law.'"[12]

My reading of Grimké's *Appeal* asks how relations once traumatized get restored through the act of public address. It extends to the process of public identity formation, I shall argue, by stressing the recuperative powers of language; in this instance, I ask how and to what effect Grimké positions author and reader within epistolary constraints, and how by virtue of that positioning the conditions of community are rehabilitated. The answers, I believe, are important for the way in which we assess Grimké's craft, especially as it shaped her role within the abolitionist movement and established her significance to early nineteenth-century feminism.

Grimké offered to the abolitionist movement a way to *see* differently, to *hear* voices not previously acknowledged, ultimately to *speak* to a broader range of experience. Such a promise was in a sense outrageously bold, reckless even. Certainly it seemed so to Catharine Beecher, whose *An Essay on Slavery and Abolitionism* prompted Grimké into one of the richest and most provocative exchanges of the antebellum era. Beecher's challenge, like her social status and family background, is not easily reduced to simple description. A prominent leader in female education, a writer, and religious disputant, Beecher was every bit Grimké's equal in the arts of public debate. Beecher's deep ambivalence about abolitionism could not, accordingly, be treated as simply racist, because she in fact held slavery to be abhorrent; neither could her attack on the role of women within the movement be chalked up to a particularly articulate version of false consciousness—Beecher had proven herself on too many occasions to be deeply committed to the welfare and development of her sex. She posed to Grimké a genuine challenge: too important to be ignored, too complex to be dismissed, too "right" to be left alone.

Grimké launched her encounter with Beecher on June 12, 1837 with the first of thirteen letters. Together they were to appear in the pages of *The Liberator, The*

Emancipator, and the *Friend of Man*; they appeared in book form a year later as *Letters to Catherine* [sic] *E. Beecher, in Reply to an Essay on Slavery and Abolitionism*. Within the familiar constraints of the public letter, Grimké brings to her encounter the opportune mix of reflection and spontaneity the form affords. In this it shares with the letter to Garrison and the *Appeal* that conspicuous sense of risk that marks the major texts generally. Collectively the letters to Beecher represent perhaps the fullest exposition of the author's convictions; more so than even the *Appeal*, these layer allusion upon appeal, learning upon image, fact upon figure. They suggest something in the way of total response, as if her interlocutor had demanded the most and the best from her.

Here, indeed, lies a key to their reading. As an encounter with one of the foremost voices of the time, Grimké's *Letters* put on display what such an engagement ought to look like. They may be interpreted as a series of exemplary encounters, functioning rhetorically as they invoke an optimal relationship with the putative reader. That is not, of course, to say that such a relationship need be based on the expectation of ultimate conversion. The encounter works, rather, to promote a model of how principled disagreement ought to be managed. Such a display must have been difficult to prepare: the author was by this time fully integrated into the volatile world of abolitionism, where moderation on either side was becoming a rarity. From this context Grimké needed to pull out again the possibility of productive debate, to work toward the horizons of shared meaning. Her *Letters* provide a discursive medium wherein the conditions of debate and honorable exchange are put on exhibit and made rhetorically compelling.

Grimké's exchange with Beecher put her on the vanguard of the abolitionist-feminist movements. It did nothing to convert her interlocutor, of course, but through the process Grimké was able to forge a powerful link between the cause of the slave and the necessity of women's rights. This too was the final and cumulative phase of her career as a writer of public letters. The epistles to Garrison, to the Christian women of her homeland, to Beecher: these were the texts of a private figure becoming public. The form proved itself ideal as a way of asserting herself into public consciousness, even as she retained its posture of privacy as a way of protecting herself from the hostile glare of that world. By early 1838, however, the imperatives of moral reform coaxed Grimké into a full scale assault on Northern intransigence.

But of course Grimké's speaking tour was not, could not be limited to the work of abolitionism alone. Beecher had provoked fundamental questions about moral agency and woman's rights, and Grimké's response made clear that the pandora's box was in fact open. Among those paying very close attention to what lay in that box was Grimké's new friend, Theodore Weld. Observing from afar the course of the sisters' tour, Weld was growing increasingly anxious about their ability to keep the focus on the slave; what he could not discern from that distance was the fact that many women in the movement could no longer ignore certain parallels between the slave's condition and their own. Angelina's unabashed observations on this score alarmed Weld, to the point where, in August of 1837, he felt it necessary to try to bring her up short. There followed a spirited and poignant correspondence, an exchange of opinions, feelings, and principles that can tell us much about the thinking of both interlocutors. In the course of their debate, Grimké was able to elaborate upon views featured in her confrontation with Beecher; in particular, she provides an insightful account of human rights *and* the public contexts and responsibilities through which those rights are accorded. The correspondence was private, but only after a fashion; more to the point, it was about what it meant to act publicly on behalf of the rights of others.

We are brought finally to what is for many Grimké's signature oration, indeed the climactic moment of her public career. Oratory was for Grimké a kind of performance art, a definitively public mode of address through which she could put on display the drama of human relations. Increasingly, that drama was calling into play the question of woman's role in the work of converting the world, and Grimké was becoming more and more insistent that her answer be heard. When Grimké took to the platform of Pennsylvania Hall, she was about to complete what was to be the most extraordinary public speaking tour of the century.

From Monday through Wednesday, Pennsylvania Hall hosted one of the greatest concentrations of rhetorical talent in American history: its register of members and speakers was quite literally a roll call of the reform elite. At the top of that list was Angelina Grimké. Her public life, like that of Pennsylvania Hall itself, was short and splendid, and like it she was at once eloquent, notorious, and dangerous. Bearing witness as the daughter of a slave holding Southerner, she provided a means for others to see differently, to hear voices not previously acknowledged, ultimately to grasp a broader range of experience from which the movement could draw and take on greater moral appeal. Grimké's journey to the stage of Pennsylvania Hall was thus written and spoken along the way, and her speech on the night before its burning proved a consuming statement on the transformative powers of language itself.

Grimké's Pennsylvania Hall Address was an address to friends, but to friends that she could not, in a very specific sense, trust. She could not trust, more accurately, that proclivity in human nature to speak truth and will evil: she had, therefore, to orchestrate an encounter that would turn commitment from a given into a problem. Hence the first words of her address: "Men, brethren and fathers—mothers, daughters and sisters, what came ye out to see? A reed shaken with the wind? Is it curiosity merely, or a deep sympathy with the perishing slave, that has brought this large audience together?" That question in place, Grimké could begin the yet more basic work of reestablishing the terms by which community and collective action were possible. Grimké's was, in this regard, a deeply skeptical text, at least to the degree that its force is subversive of liberal piety; this was, too, a speech about commitment, about how one comes to commitment, acts on it, and retains it in the face of a dangerous and doubting world.[13]

◆   ◆   ◆

The aim of this book is to move past generalities about Grimké's eloquence and her pioneering work for human rights and toward a more specific account of *how* she did what she did. I hope in the process to demonstrate the underlying thesis of the book, that *Grimké so managed the resources of her art as to create from the limitations of her world new possibilities for collective moral action.* She did this by establishing publicly compelling relationships between Self and Community, five key instances of which represent the body of this study. Each in effect places a primary resource between these principles and asks how Self and Community get transformed thereby into an imperative to act. Thus I examine how *violence* is construed through the spiritual logic of sacrifice and redemption into a motive for public action; how the *past* is reconfigured into a warrant for repairing damaged relationships; how an Enlightenment inheritance of *rights* is woven into a scriptural case for women's work of reform; how the *public* may be understood as a site of free moral agency; and finally how *violence*, again, gets reimagined from a problem into a means for renewal and moral purpose. The result, I hope, is a more detailed and nuanced understanding of this most distinctive of reform careers.

CHAPTER 1

Beginnings: Rhetoric and Identity in the Journal of Angelina Grimké

Charleston, South Carolina. 10 January 1828. In the twenty-fourth year of her life, Angelina Grimké decided that the time had come for change. It would not be easy for this heir to the eminent Grimké name, nor would it come readily, for such change as she contemplated meant rupturing old ties, putting away habits that had long defined who she was and who she might become. The first order of business was to eliminate all sources of pride and idleness, all those superfluities that seemed now to make Angelina other than herself. The social rituals, the tiresome parlor talk, the fashionable clothes: she wanted an end to it all. And so, she recorded in the first entry of her diary on the tenth day of the new year, "I have *torn up my novels.*" Her mind had "long been troubled about them," Grimké noted, but "I did not dare either to sell them or to lend them out, and yet I had not resolution to destroy them until this morning when in much mercy strength was granted." Other fineries and foolish things would soon follow, but the books had to go *now.*[1]

The gesture is telling, and in dwelling on it for a moment we get a glimpse of a personality undergoing profound and lasting transformations. Effected in private, to private ends, a silent testimony to the force of spiritual resolve, the destruction of her novels was nevertheless a declaration, a rhetorical act that announced to its own author what conviction requires. It is an act, moreover, the intentions, character, and form of which we shall see recurrently in the years ahead: decisive but the result of long deliberation; dramatic but purposeful; both an ending and a beginning. As simple as it was, the deed was understood to be a provocative reminder that real change was difficult, complex, affirming. It was above all a perfect conflation of physical act with symbolic meaning, where the destruction of one way of life is made prerequisite to the creation of the new.

Grimké's record of personal devotion and reflection is suffused with such gestures. Written during the final months of her residence in Charleston and the early years in Philadelphia, her journal provides us with a rich repository of ideas, images, arguments, and anxieties. Not at all incidentally, it was composed at a time when past and future were colliding before Angelina's very eyes. Its pages offer a glimpse—though only a glimpse—into a mind just coming to conviction, where loyalties are tested, resentments aired, doubts confessed, and resolve strengthened. Familiar as we are with Grimké's later public life, there can be little surprise that her journal would contain such rich stock as this; more surprising is how little it has been availed of by historians and critics. The oversight may be owing in part to the uncertain status of journals as a literary, biographical, or rhetorical text; in part due to the heavy and seemingly narrow emphasis such journals placed on trials of faith; perhaps in part due to the enduring privilege accorded to more overtly public productions over and against the private ruminations of, say, a young woman of the antebellum South. This chapter seeks to recover Grimké's journal as an interesting text in its own right, indicative alike of her thinking as it was being composed and of what lay ahead.[2]

I am mindful that not every figure is a prefiguration, not every statement a hint. Still, I approach the text as an unmistakably rhetorical effort: not explicitly public, but frequently about public affairs; self-directed but outward turning; reflective but no less concerned with arguing, persuading, deliberating, and judging. The journal is, I wish to demonstrate, a compelling account of how its author came to envision herself as a force in the world. After establishing its contextual determinants, I pursue this claim by highlighting three pivotal encounters in the diary, each of which gives convincing evidence of a rhetorical consciousness in the making. We thus see Grimké as she confronts her brother Henry over his treatment of a family slave; as she defends herself before a council of Presbyterian elders; and as she comes finally to persuade herself to leave Charleston and begin life anew in Philadelphia. These three encounters exhibit, in turn, Grimké's rapidly developing capacity to create from the contact between self and world a rationale for moral action; this would be a talent, developed now, that would guide her public and private lives for years to come.

Angelina took up journal writing first in 1826, but the resolves she then recorded were scarcely the first such portents of change. By her midtwenties, Grimké had experienced sufficient turmoil and effected enough major decisions to make us wonder that she had not picked up her pen earlier. The fourteenth—and youngest—daughter of the esteemed jurist Thomas Faucheraud Grimké and Mary Smith Grimké, Angelina came of age at a time of considerable unrest, both in and out of the family circle. Following her sister Sarah's lead, she had as a teenager resolved against confirmation in the Episcopal church and learned a year later of her father's death. Not long after, the beloved Sarah left for Philadelphia, where she joined the Society of Friends in 1823. Angelina's spiritual path continued to wind uncertainly, leading her in 1826 to Presbyterianism and several years later to Charleston's fledgling Quaker community. Sarah's ministrations and Angelina's restless soul took her to Philadelphia to visit Sarah in 1828; that journey, as her diary clearly shows, proved transitional and accelerated one of the first major crises of her adult life.

When Grimké turned to her journal at day's end, she thus had considerable matter for reflection, debate, and evaluation. Of one thing she was certain, however, and that was that great things lay ahead. There was, she firmly believed, "a work before me to which all my other duties and trials were only prefatory. I have no idea what it is," Angelina admitted, but "it does seem that if I am obedient to the still small voice of Jesus in my heart that he will lead into more difficult paths and cause me to glorify Him in a more honorable and trying work than any in which I have yet been engaged."[3]

The journal is by far the best record we have of Angelina's early search for the "difficult paths" that would take her from Charleston to Philadelphia, and from there to New York, Boston, and places as yet unimagined. Taken together, the accumulated entries constitute a text of spiritual ruminations, of complex and poignant struggles to define, direct, and activate an emerging self. Like untold diarists before and after, Angelina availed herself of conventions at once loose and demanding, her writing unsupervised and unread by anyone but its author. To the extent that the form constrained expression, it asked only that the words set therein be marked by simplicity, candor, and humility. At the same time, the devotional tradition warned away from subjects other than explicitly spiritual, encouraging rather a habit of daily prayer and reflection on the meaning and import of Scripture. If there was to be a plot, it told only of the diarist's journey to grace, unflinching in its self-criticism but grateful for the hand there to grab and follow to final salvation and peace. Although she began writing before her conversion to the Society of Friends, Angelina in some ways exemplified the norms of the Quaker diary; indeed, she charted her development in ways very close to the unfolding drama so dear to that tradition: from the innocence and joy of pious youth, to the anguish and spiritual conflict of early adulthood, and ultimately to the serenity of the truly saved.[4]

But of course the way is never so clear, the story never so seamless, as tradition holds. Grimké had no real script before her, and if her journal tells us anything, it is that she grew just as she departed from the imperatives of religion, family, and culture. There is in fact rather little in the way of sustained contentment in its pages; the journal is instead a record of relentless searching, questioning, contesting, and sometimes renouncing much of everything given to her by virtue of place and name. The story is told, accordingly, not as a journey toward contentment as such but as a series of engagements, transformations, and lessons; the path runs finally from the enclaved and privileged world of slave-holding Charleston to the dangers, hypocrisy, and possibilities of the "free" North. The dominant themes and preoccupations found in the journal are thus not surprising: Angelina dwelt recurrently on the interplay of faith and doubt, grace and works, appearances and reality, suffering and redemption. That much is enough for any soul, to be sure, but we will have missed an added dimension to the journal if we leave it at that. For weaving in and out of its meditations is a persistent struggle to define her spiritual prospects and to act on the principles then coming into focus. If there is a plot to her story, then, it takes us, looking over her shoulder though we are, from faith to action, from self to community, from prayer to persuasion. In the process, she forged a new understanding of *who* this Angelina Grimké was, of what she consisted and to what end. This, too, is the rhetoric of her journal, three key instances of which I examine as follows.

In the spring of 1839 Angelina sat down to a desk in her Fort Lee, New Jersey, home and reflected on the experiences of growing up in a slave-holding household. In the decade since leaving Charleston, Angelina had spoken a good deal about slavery, but she had not labored especially to depict graphically its most barbaric features. Few had; so few, in fact, that, along with Sarah and Theodore Weld, she resolved to assemble a compendium of horrors so explicit, so authentic, as to startle awake the complacent North. The result was *American Slavery As It Is: Testimony of a Thousand Witnesses*, the largest selling antislavery tract of its time, a point-blank assault on the soul and sensibilities of its many readers. Angelina's own contribution to *American Slavery* constitutes her most sustained and detailed recollection of a childhood indelibly imprinted by the system. Explaining why she felt moved to bear witness again after a decade of abolitionist labor, Grimké noted pointedly that she bore in mind not only the slaves but "the deep yearnings of affection for the mother that bore me, who is still a slave holder," as well as "my brothers and sisters (a large family circle)," and "my numerous other slave holding kindred in South Carolina constrain me to speak; for even were slavery no curse to its victims," Angelina concluded, "the exercise of arbitrary power works such fearful ruin upon the hearts of *slaveholders*, that I should feel impelled to labor and pray for its overthrow with my last energies and latest breath."[5]

Grimké had by 1839 gained enough distance to testify at length and in moving detail against a practice that had decisively shaped her youth and moral development. At the time she took up writing the journal, however, Grimké communicated relatively little about the practices of slave-holding families and her relationship to them. Why this may be so I can only speculate: perhaps she had not developed a fully conscious and principled resistance to the system; maybe she saw no point in conveying to herself what she already strongly and unequivocally felt; or perhaps she feared unleashing the full fury of resentment for having been born into such a family. Still, the journal is suggestive of the problem, and one event in particular stands out as evidence of her struggle to confront and transform the day-to-day realities of slavery in her household. Angelina's decision to challenge her older brother Henry's treatment of his slave John affords us a rich opportunity to view the formative stages of a radical consciousness, and to see in her own words what she believed to be possible through the arts of resistance, argument, and moral action.

As read through her journal, Angelina was seldom anything except restive. This much is evident, as we have seen, in her continuing struggle to come to terms with her religious commitments, her family, and herself. After her first trip to Philadelphia, where she stayed with Sarah and her host family from July to November of 1828, this sense of unease and longing seemed to take on chronic dimensions. Philadelphia at least offered momentary relief, and Grimké appears to have found genuine peace in "this delightful land which has been an Eden unto my soul and body." The return to Charleston had been disturbed, ominously enough, by no less than three storms, and a grateful Angelina vowed to herself that she had arrived back safely where she belonged, but confided all the same that "I see nothing to do here but it is comforting to reflect that 'they also serve who stand and wait.'" Angelina was not, even by her own reckoning, predisposed to stand and wait very long, admitting that "I almost always speak inadvisably with my lips and feel the burden of a condemned conscience and heavy heart after being in company." Unavoidably, such discontent was to make itself felt within the dynamics of the Grimké household, where the stresses of intergenerational relationships, sibling rivalry, class expectations, and especially master-slave tensions all conspired to make of that house a virtual metonymy of southern life in general.[6]

However the baby girl of the Grimké family might have been indulged in years past, Angelina by early adulthood was pressing hard on the patience of her siblings. Brother Charles she found disappointing in several respects: parasitic on his mother's resources, lazy, intemperate. Taking it upon herself to remind him at regular intervals of these shortcomings, Angelina finally if unintentionally drove Charles from the household altogether. But if Charles was in her view a lout, Henry was something more, a perplexing combination of brutality and restraint, passion and reason, love and hate. All of these traits came together and presented themselves in the form of his treatment of slaves and, especially, of his personal "servant" John. Certainly Henry's behavior impressed Angelina enough that, when recalling life in Charleston for *American Slavery*, she featured it as an exemplary instance of the slaveholder's depravity. Angelina had intervened before on a slave's behalf; in only her second entry in the diary we learn of her efforts to put a stop to the abuse of a family slave, "thinking it really sinful to subject her to such treatment. I therefore determined to go out and get her a place in some religious family," Grimké wrote, and finally "succeeded in my design and placed her with a friend."[7]

One year later Angelina found occasion again to confront a family member on the treatment of slaves. This time, however, we find her commenting on the system that made such behavior routine and acceptable. Henry's slave John, she learned, had run away for fear of being flogged by his "master." John had been subject to this business before and knew full well what lay ahead: Henry had once whipped him so hard and for so long that his assailant's arm had hurt for a week. On 6 February 1829, Angelina noted in her diary the effect of this treatment on her state of mind; sleepless for several nights, she wondered to herself, "who can paint the horror of slavery and yet so hard is the natural heart that I am continually told that their situation is very good[,] much better than that of their owners. . . . How strange," Grimké thought, "that any one should believe such an absurdity or try to make others credit [it]." At age twenty-four, then, Angelina was grasping in the most immediate circumstances a problem that would plague opponents of slavery for decades. *American Slavery As It Is*, indeed, was conceived as a rhetorical strategy to effectively portray slavery to Northerners and to combat the "positive good" arguments launched from southern presses. Grimké's problem, of course, lay not in being too far from slavery to see it clearly but in being so close she could not, would not, ignore it. In bed at night, listening to Henry administer another flogging to John, Angelina knew it was to be another "night of agony," not only for the slave but for her as well, "for it was not only dreadful to hear him beating him[,] but the oaths and curses he uttered went like daggers to my heart[,] and this was done too in the house of one who is regarded as a light in the Church."[8]

Enough can be enough, above all to a slave, and off John went, his whereabouts unknown but his return fully expected. When he did come back to the household, John could expect from Henry "such a whipping as would cure him of doing the same thing again," a beating so fierce and so well-deserved, the older Grimké imagined, that the slave would be unable to stand at its conclusion. Angelina, finding the prospect unbearable, decided she must act. Going to Henry's room, she gingerly brought up the subject of John's treatment and remarked that such whippings "would be treating him worse than he would treat his horse." Henry apparently found the analogy unconvincing, angrily insisting that, if anything, "he considered his horse[,] no comparison[,] better than John and would not beat it so[.]" As the exchange grew more heated, Angelina found herself so physically agitated that she had to sit down for fear of falling down. Still, she remembered, "I pled the cause of humanity" and explained to her uncomprehending brother that "I could not but lift up my voice against the manner of his beating John." Henry thought other motives were at work behind his sister's moralizing, and observed pointedly that she seemed to have returned from Philadelphia for the express purpose of making his and everyone else's lives miserable. So trying had she become that there was no way out except to leave the house altogether. In all, it was an unsatisfying argument by any measure: Angelina nevertheless was pleased to see that Henry "readily acknowledged that he felt something within him which fully met all I asserted and that I had harrowed his feelings and made him miserable[.]"[9]

In the event, John returned soon after the confrontation between sister and brother. Much to Angelina's surprise, Henry did not punish the boy, but simply sent him to work. As she pondered the whole experience and examined its portents, its meaning and significance, Angelina considered the matter of timing, when duty and advantage so cohere as to create an imperative for moral action. With John relatively safe for the moment, she could see now that her efforts had been in fact successful; she had argued Henry out of one practice and into another. She had through the force of her words transformed cruelty into restraint. It was all, Angelina thought, "renewed proof to me how necessary it is for me to watch for the right time to do things in, for if I had not spoken just when I did, I could not have done so before his return." Several days after the episode, Angelina reasoned that her heightened spirits were the result of having intervened so effectively as to have saved one human being from physical assault and another from committing such an act. These moments did not come frequently for Angelina, and she found herself praying desperately "for a release from this land of Slavery." For now, at least, she could enjoy "the sweet testimony of a good conscience toward God, the reward of obedience," Angelina surmised, "in speaking to H[enry]." As obstinate as he was, and as heated and personal as their exchange had been, Henry had proven himself capable of being persuaded. The lesson was for this reason alone important to Angelina's development as an advocate for race and sex reform: it showed ultimately that however hard the "natural heart," or however adamantine the system, change was possible and it could be made the result of language use. As a type, brother Henry was characteristic of most slaveholders, the effect rather than the cause of a pernicious and deeply entrenched structure. Angelina was not yet prepared to take on the system, but she could take on its practitioners and transform them from beasts into men. Henry, she observed, "has good tender feelings naturally," but noted that "education has nearly destroyed them and his own false judgment as to what is manly and what is necessary in the government of slaves." Perhaps it was, under the circumstances, enough to ask only that God "open his eyes and may thy gentleness make him great."[10]

Angelina's encounter with Henry, brief as it was, helps lay down the first layers of a more general account of her moral and rhetorical development. I see in it, for example, the characteristic movement from crisis to action, from anguish to intervention; typical, too, is the utter (and no doubt annoying) confidence with which duty is finally exercised. Similarly, it is worth noting the course taken when she does act—always directly to the source of the problem, where confrontation is made necessary to resolution. Inevitably, here is where relationships are strained, sometimes broken, and recuperate under different terms. The nature of that confrontation is definitively rhetorical, in that it is structured through an exchange of arguments and views, where both parties grasp the stakes involved in the debate. Angelina could be a scold; she could lecture, profess, and demand; but she always gave reasons for her beliefs, and preferred persuasion to coercion at all times. These traits, as much markers of character as her rhetoric, remained indelible for the rest of her life.

On 8 April 1826 Angelina turned her back on the church of her youth and family. Three years after leaving St. Philips' Episcopal Congregation, she was moved to observe again the strange concatenations of nature and spirit so prevalent in the unfolding drama of her life. Angelina had fervently prayed through the rainy night that she might be allowed to attend the following day's Presbyterian meeting. Even now she could not forget "the delightful feelings which clothed my mind as I rose in bed and my eye caught the glittering leaves of the wild orange tree waving with the gentle breeze in the Sun beams." Surely here was a sign that her discontent with the family church had been justified, that the future was hers to choose, and she felt, if possible for this grave young woman, quite nearly giddy. "This was," Angelina recalled, "the beginning of a glorious dispensation to my soul in which I rejoiced with joy unspeakable and full of glory." Portents of weather aside, Angelina's departure from one church into another had not been wholly unexpected by others, mother Mary included. In large part it had been superintended by Charleston's young Presbyterian minister, William McDowell, who in addition to helping her through a conversion experience had taken a keen personal interest in the spiritual welfare of his new friend. Angelina had, initially as least, found in McDowell and his flock a degree of liberality and ecumenicism not evident in the Episcopalian practice. Clearly, she aimed to make the most of her new association, teaching classes, making friends, and even organizing an inter-faith prayer group for local women. Looking back on that time of spiritual regeneration, Grimké admitted to many trials, "many deep baptisms to pass thro," but remembered, too, that "so rich and full and constant were the cups of consolation which were administered . . .

enjoyed so large a foretaste that at times I scarcely knew whether I was in the body or out of the body."[11]

Here was the first of several transformations in the practice and allegiances of faith that would define in important ways the future of Angelina Grimké. Indulging the luxury of retrospect, we can see in her embrace of (and eventual departure from) Presbyterianism but the first instance of a long and intense search for spiritual fulfillment. It was, necessarily, a search, too, for the kind of community that would serve best as a medium for that fulfillment, and it would take her ultimately from Charleston to points north and east. The chapters ahead will treat various expressions of this search, particularly as they helped fuel a deep and abiding skepticism over the rule of clerics she saw standing in the way of radical social change. In the end, Angelina's path led her out of organized religion altogether, and while she seems never to have despaired so intently as Sarah in the process, nor pushed her convictions to such mystical limits, she was to turn from the established church, and for good.

Angelina's struggle with faith and its formal expressions, needless then to say, bore heavily on the person she was to become and the ways in which she sought to transform others and the world. For this reason it is worth peering briefly into a key series of passages in the diary, recording as they do a dramatic confrontation over who she claimed really to be. In some ways, the defense of her conduct before a council of Presbyterian officials reproduced the confrontation with brother Henry: here, too, she appeared at once anxious but also ready and willing to act in a situation of crisis; she evinced no qualms about entering into disputes where the playing field, as we would now call it, was decidedly uneven; and she demonstrated a precocious ability to attack and defend in rhetorically sophisticated ways. But there is enough in the diary to suggest even more about the emergence of Grimké as, to use a phrase of her maturity, a free moral agent..

Angelina found the Presbyterianism she had so ecstatically embraced not all that she had thought it might be. Granted, the church's members were open, gracious, and altogether an attractive lot, but the limits of their tolerance seemed to stop at interfaith participation. Beyond that, beyond the point where real differences might be entertained and welcomed, she found only the familiar and all-too-prevalent prejudices at work. Nowhere was this more evident than in the church's (predictable) refusal to engage seriously the issue of slavery and color prejudice. That the elders were themselves slaveholders did not seem to enter Angelina's mind as an insuperable barrier, and she continued to plead that they—and especially McDowell—speak against the system. Discouragement was inevitable, and at length Angelina came to a decision: in "time of great agony" she resolved to "leave the Presbyterian Society and unite [herself] with Friends." Her meditations on the matter are fully recounted in the diary, expressed almost entirely in scriptural arguments and imagery; indeed, it would be impossible to read these ruminations and not conclude with her that the decision to leave the "Society" should be permanent.[12]

Pastor McDowell was not without resolve himself, and labored to retain his friend and charge. His efforts proved to no avail, and by order of the Third Presbyterian Church, he drew up a list of "charges" and requested of her that they be answered in person before the Session members. The letter, dated 14 May 1829, listed the charges as follows:

A neglect of the publick worship of God in his house[;]
A neglect of the ordinance of the Lord's supper[;] and
A neglect of the means of grace and the ordinance of
the Gospel generally contrary to your engagement when you became a member of that Church.[13]

Grimké was at first mortified. Absent Sarah's certain sympathy, Angelina wept and wondered at how "desolate the feeling" was "under such trying circumstances to have no friend on whose bosom to repose, no human, no sympathizing heart to tell my trials to." By nightfall she had regained her composure, and set about preparing for the meeting. She insisted during the weekend that "I had no idea at that time of being brought before the Session [of] ruling elders," but expressed no regrets. "I am calm, My heart is fixed, O God! my heart is fixed, fixed to serve thee in any way thou *pleaseth*." [14]

By Monday morning, when she was scheduled to appear, Angelina had put together her defense. In one respect, to be sure, the entire event was somewhat moot, and she could easily have conceded the charges and gone on her predetermined way. As this was not Angelina's approach to such serious matters generally, however, she was bound not only to acquit herself but to give a complete and systematic rendering of her decision. The result was a forensic opportunity fully realized, and although but a brief and passing moment, it suggests much of the disputant who later would so forcefully promote her cause before critics far less kind or accommodating. For now she could appreciate the combination of good will and authoritarian stricture that suffused the occasion. "On entering the room (to me it seemed almost like a judgment hall)," Grimké recollected, "I felt the flowings of love to all around and offered my hand in token of fellowship[.] I stood like a statue in the middle of them, speechless and almost trembling with agitation as they came forward one by one and took my hand. . . . I took my seat and lifting my eyes saw my seven judges seated around the room (for I could not but regard them as such)[,] tho' I was well convinced they had none but feelings of tenderness and kindness towards me."[15]

To the first charge, that Angelina had neglected public worship in church, she responded briefly and unequivocally. In language and sentiment, the response is suggestive of Sarah's rejoinder to the notorious Pastoral Letter that would be leveled against the sisters in the summer of 1837; for now, she insisted simply that

> I believe the Supreme Being to be a spirit who is not worshiped by the multitude of words or the parade of ceremony, but in the Spirit and in truth no offering of the lips can be acceptable to Him (however good the words may be) unless it is offered in the Spirit[.] The Apostle tells us that even that pure and spotless sacrifice which was offered upon the Cross for the sins of the whole world was offered thro' the eternal Spirit[.] [H]ow much more necessary than our poor offerings and prayer and praise. If He is a Spirit and he is worshiped not by our bodies but by our Spirits, then the worship certainly may be performed without the intervention of words.[16]

In October of 1827, Sarah had returned to Charleston, a recognized member of the Fourth and Arch Street Meeting of the Philadelphia Society of Friends. At least part of her business back home was to press upon her youngest sister the virtues of the Quaker faith; this effort, together with Angelina's visit north early in the following year, seems to have quickened the process of (re)conversion. In any case, Angelina's defense of herself before the Presbyterian elders gives strong evidence that she had already adopted the basic tenants of her newfound community of believers, not least in her emphasis on the power of the spirit over mere words. Sarah would have been proud: the charge was confronted directly, simply, and with absolute confidence in the rectitude of conviction. Angelina professed no more concern for Presbyterian houses of worship than for Friends' meeting places; neither, she stressed, were to be found in Scripture, and neither could represent a standard for judgment. "I cannot find my place in the New Testament," Grimké concluded, "where any house built of wood and brick is called the 'house of God.'" The only sanctified place of worship was in "a spiritual house, where we may worship at any time and in any place[.]"[17]

In time, the relationship between human place and God's Word would be the object of contentious debate for the Grimkés and those ministers who would insist upon their own version of "the spiritual house." Here are early indications of Angelina's abiding distrust of such forms of organized practice which displaced rather than facilitated the nurture of self and others. Like all "primitive" Christians, she was vigilant against the tendency to mistake the ritual for the real: hence her defense against the charge of "neglect of the ordinance of the Lord's supper." Angelina insisted that, to begin with, she had never promised to observe this particular ordinance as an ordinance of man, but as God's only. Once she had come to believe that it was merely a requirement of the former, she no longer felt herself obliged to meet it. For that matter, Grimké reasoned, the Covenant to which she agreed when joining the church bound her in no other regard except to follow Christ. Whatever may be said of the theology at work here, or of the apologetics in play, Grimké's resistance to organized authority—authority in fact as it was assembled immediately before her—is striking. It is also resolute: not only did she not agree to adopt no other principles, but she also did not "promise to follow either their Minister or their Elders, in their religious faith"; Angelina's only promise was, in effect, to herself—that is, to "take the Lord Jesus Christ to be my prophet to instruct me, and the Holy Ghost to be my guide to whom alone I want to look for light, holiness and peace."[18]

Angelina could not then have known, of course, that one day the refusal to attach this final promise to any human imposition would cost her her membership in the Society of Friends itself. Furthermore, though it is not appropriate to read the future into these words, we cannot ignore the evidence thus presented: behind all the anguish, the confrontations and shifting allegiances, is a set of convictions that holds the ground firm. We observe in this encounter, in short, no spasms of late adolescence, no arbitrary and desperate search for something that will at once indulge anxieties of self and satisfy the expectations of others. Angelina was rather quickly coming to a kind of faith that, while still challenging to herself, could never be transformed by the conventions of others. She had not yet found reason to develop that faith fully into a rationale for changing those conventions, but she demonstrably proved strong enough to have it put to the test and to come out stronger as a result. Thus, to the third charge, of neglecting "the means of grace and the ordinance of the Gospel generally," she had merely to extend the position already expressed. When the prayer meetings and lectures were productive, she attended faithfully; when they were not, she did not. When she realized that such ordinances were unfounded by the Gospel, she looked elsewhere for the means to grace. It was as simple as that. And as real. The "Spirit we all know is as uncertain as the wind that blows," Grimké concluded, and "therefore I must regard all forms of worship however good in themselves, to be contrary to the mind of Christ as being established in the will of man."[19]

In the end, Grimké held no grudge. The whole episode, it was true, had been unsettling, "strangely mysterious," and she admitted in her diary that it was "humbling indeed thus to be brought before seven men to give an account of Principles and Practice into which I believed nothing but the Spirit of all Truth had led me." It is doubtful Angelina ever really got used to giving such accounts of herself, but they would become a routine part of her public career as an abolitionist and women's rights advocate. In addition to the qualities displayed in her confrontation with Henry, we see in the defense before the Session an acute sense of herself as a free moral agent. Even if it was a vision still coming into focus, it was unmistakably that of a being possessed of specific rights, above all of the expressed right to dissent from structures of authority. Although entered into voluntarily, these structures imposed only those duties to which she could accord the status of divine will. It is possible, and perhaps appropriate, to emphasize in her encounter before the elders the anti-institutionalism, the "come-outerism" and anticlericism that would be so conspicuous in later years. More positively, however, the diary records the steady progress of an individual coming to terms with who she is and therefore how she must act. The Angelina Grimké we see therein is resistive but also steadying herself, reacting against the pressures of tradition and discovering the wellsprings of conviction that give to her work its staying power. Put another way, we see in these pages a highly personalized record of how one comes to see oneself as a moral agent, embodying both rights and duties, strengthened and not weakened by the world into which one must assert oneself.[20]

Angelina's encounters with brother Henry and the Presbyterian elders suggest how unwise it is to separate her moral development from the rhetorical skills by which it is given expressive force. She did not undertake systematic study of the principles of eloquence; that would in any case have been literally impossible in view of the cultural proscriptions then firmly in place. Rather, as Angelina set about changing herself, she found that she desired to change others. That is always a risky and frequently a disastrous business, but it is nonetheless to be expected, and in her case was almost inevitable. Certainly Angelina had plenty of opportunities, issues, and people against which to test her newfound convictions, and she seldom failed to act on them. Brothers, sisters, in-laws, mother, friends, and Friends found themselves regularly confronted by this young aspirant to better ways. As might be expected of one so intent on persuading others, she came quickly to realize that the toughest interlocutor of all was herself. In Angelina, she met her match. Coming to conviction would be for her a long and arduous process, painful and fraught alternately with the acute and chronic anxiety with which she struggled during a great deal of her young life. No more explicit and illuminating example of this is available in the diary than in her resolve to return north to Philadelphia.

Grimké's relationship to her Carolinian past came in time to be a key, indeed defining, feature of her public career as an abolitionist and women's rights activist. She knew, perhaps too well, that much of her cache in those roles was rooted in her experience as the daughter of a slave-holding family. The diary provides a revealing record not of how others would eventually see her, but of how she came to view herself, past, present, and future. So much of what we know and understand of Grimké comes by way of reconstruction and rhetorical retrospect that we are apt to forget that this Grimké-*from*-South Carolina once struggled intensely to remain Grimké-*in*-South Carolina. We have reason, then, to examine at least briefly the internal journey that took her from Charleston to the "Eden unto my soul" she imagined Philadelphia to be. Thus the final encounter to be observed in the diary is with herself, and from it we may learn something further of the dynamics of self and community that drove this Southerner to new lands and new worlds of possibility.

Angelina's first trip to Pennsylvania was motivated by no other desire than to visit Sarah and restore her ailing health. She was apparently very busy on both scores, for we do not get an entry until 29 July 1828, three weeks after her last. Yet however she intended the visit, it is telling that in this entry she immediately set to wondering about the meaning of her joy. Should the peace that settled on her literally during the journey be interpreted as a sign for her to stay? On her passage, she had "felt a delighted peace and when tossed on the waves" felt like nothing less than "a little baby rocked to Sleep by the kind hand" of a gentle Providence. Perhaps it was the proximity of the waters, perhaps relief from the Carolina heat, surely the warmth with which she was embraced by Philadelphia friends: in any case, her diary fairly sings of contentment, of nature and the rivers that seemed to bear her to realms of peace she had not known existed. "Is there no more lovely object in nature," she rejoiced, "than the lucid stream whose bosom glistens with the rays of the Sun[?]" With no clouds on the horizon now, "how calm are its waters and thus it is with the believer in Jesus," Angelina reasoned, for he, too, "enjoys a peace which the world can neither give nor take away."[22]

But of course clouds did inevitably reappear, at least for this temporary exile. In what would become a recurrent pattern in the diary for days and months on end, such reveries are followed literally as the night follows the day, and soon she mused that such peace would not last, not yet, not here. How different becomes this scene of contentment when clouds and darkness return, "and the Sun no longer shines upon the river and the winds of heaven are let loose upon it[.]" Soon "all is confusion and O! how like those hours of darkness which sometimes come over the soul when the Sun of righteousness hides his glorious face and our hearts are no longer cheered by the light of his countenance." For the next four months Grimké would vacillate between similar poles of peace and dread, and if she could summon anything with confidence, it was that she would be sent a sign directing her to stay or return. The important point here is that this occurred to Angelina as a question at all; she seems not to have left Charleston in order to test foreign waters. It is indicative of the growing ambivalence, as yet largely submerged, with which she considered her prospects in a land that seemed already far distant.[23]

When she sailed for Philadelphia, Angelina had felt herself rocked gently, "like a little baby." On the return passage she endured, as we have noted previously, no fewer than three storms, casting her about first in alarm, then into a suspicion that "the tempest which howled around us then was typical of what I was to encounter in Charleston," and finally into submission to divine intentions. The symbolic potential of the respective journeys did not escape Angelina; in fact, they seemed perfectly suited to describing the tumultuous year that lay ahead. In that time, she would press into her diary pages tightly packed but prolonged arguments for and against returning to Philadelphia; more so even than in previous entries, these rehearse in the most careful fashion the need ultimately to so silence the soul as to ready oneself for the sign when, and only when, that sign was due.[24]

For the most part Angelina was able to thus still herself. Not always, however, and in the diary we can read periodic eruptions of desire no longer repressible by force of will alone. Significantly, the voice prompting Grimké northward is heard in terms grown increasingly common to her discourse generally, in the language of freedom and slavery, capture and release, bondage and emancipation. The vocabulary is not inevitable; not *everyone* considering removal to northern ports rationalized their motives in words befitting a slave narrative. For Grimké the language was fitting: "when shall I be released from this kind of Slavery?" she asked, referring not to chattel servitude but to the inextricable pull of the human mind to doubt its own resolve. In February of the following year she felt herself free to ask "for a release from this land of bondage, to pray that my work here might be cut short, and that all the suffering I have to endure before I leave Carolina may be laid upon me this winter, and strength to bear it." In April, despair: "I see no way at all open for me to escape thro'."[25]

That Angelina should come to see the internal drama of her struggle to leave Charleston in terms familiar to emancipation narratives is scarcely surprising. She no doubt felt bound to the commitments of place, family, and cultural inheritance. The more general point is that this sense of herself as straining toward a different world intensified as her consciousness of the plight of slaves intensified; increasingly, she saw any justification for remaining in the South disappearing in proportion to the frequency with which the evils of slavery were revealed. Nothing in the diary suggests that she saw herself literally—or figuratively, for that matter—as a fellow slave. There is a good deal to indicate that what she saw around her was sufficiently appalling to destroy whatever bonds of commitment may have heretofore obtained. Several passages appear, in this context, highly suggestive, and describe her growing awareness that to live amongst slavery was, in some sense, a self-contradiction. This was not who she was, or at least not who she wanted to be—a free person among slaves.

Four months after her return from Philadelphia, Grimké noted at length a particularly alarming encounter in the streets of her ancestral city. Walking home after a meeting, Angelina's meditations were interrupted by the noise of two white male teenagers whose charge it apparently was to escort a slave woman to the Work House. Their paths crossed and Angelina heard the woman cry out to her. She did nothing, could do nothing, to intervene, but the episode clearly worked its effect. "How long O lord how long wilt thou suffer the foot of oppression to stand on the neck of the Slave?" Grimké wrote in her diary afterward. "None but those who know from experience what it is to live in a land of Bondage can form any idea of the weight of exercise which is endured by those whose eyes are open to the enormities of Slavery and whose hearts are tendered so as to feel for these miserable creatures." In her full maturity Grimké would be less inclined to dwell on the harm done to the witness to slavery and more on the victims themselves. Nevertheless, she strove to interpret the meaning of the event and, characteristically, was unable to settle on any simple conclusion. Perhaps it was a sign that she must "fly from Carolina, let the consequences be what they might," or perhaps she ought to stay and suffer under the system, thus to become a more powerful "means of exposing the cruelty and injustice which was practiced in this initiation of oppression and of bringing to light the hidden things of darkness[.]"[26]

The ambivalence found in the passage reflects precisely the kind of maybe-I-should, maybe-I-should-not turmoil besetting Angelina for the duration of her stay in Charleston. Angelina seemed clearly to see *herself*, whatever she did and wherever she went, as an agent for change. Increasingly, too, she represented herself to herself as acting against slavery and those within her family who would defend it. This is not to say that she had yet developed anything like a will to public action, but it does suggest an ever-growing awareness of the scale and depth of the system. Among those she most vehemently challenged on the subject was the one person strong enough to keep Angelina in Charleston—her mother. Mary Grimké refused to her dying day to concede the evils of slavery, much less to agree to her daughter's wish that she emancipate the family "servants"; in the final months of Angelina's residence in the South, however, Mary did indulge her youngest child's pointed attacks on the treatment and possession of slaves within the household. Angelina's relationship with her mother was complex, at once strongly affectionate and disturbing, and both strove sincerely to reconcile their obvious differences. At the same time, Angelina seems to have seen her mother's intractability on the subject of slavery as a barrier to leaving the family home. If, on the other hand, Mary Grimké might be made receptive to her arguments, the daughter might then leave Charleston knowing that change was at least possible. Once again, convincing herself of this reasoning proved to be the most difficult of rhetorical tasks.

For all of Angelina's much-lamented tendencies to make family members miserable, she held it as a rule never to provoke but only to respond. If others introduced a subject on which she held opposite opinions, as Mother was alleged to do frequently, Angelina insisted that "it would be wrong for me to withhold the truth." The diary gives no sure answer as to how faithfully she abided by the rule, although it appears unlikely that she did so unswervingly. Angelina, it must be said, seldom missed an opportunity to press her views when the situation called for it; and this was especially the case when observing the effects of slavery on the family women. In effect, she argued, the "Carolina Mistress was literally a Slave driver," a fact "degrading to the female character" and proof that white women under such conditions turned out to be "as great slaves to their servants in one respect as [the servants] are to them." Needless to say, Mother listened to such talk with some difficulty, but the diary depicts her as forbearing, indeed maddeningly so. Mother and daughter, it seemed, were going nowhere for the time being.[27]

Angelina continued through the summer and fall of 1829 to seek those providential signs that would open the way for escape. The search was not made any easier by the conflicting letters from Sarah, now encouraging, now discouraging the move. In the meantime Angelina was asserting herself deeper and deeper into the tumultuous interpersonal affairs of the household, as if in preparation for leaving Charleston she needed to intensify her role as daughter, sister, and, by her own reckoning, as household scold. By September the diary indicates that for all practical purposes she was resolved to join Sarah very shortly. Only one obstacle remained, and that was, as we might expect, Mother. Again, the written construction of their relationship is illustrative, in that it so conspicuously links interfamilial commitments to the issue of slavery; thus bound, the family, and especially its maternal head, could only represent an insuperable barrier to leaving. To leave would be to remove an agent of change from the very environment where she was needed most. As Angelina continued to work on her mother throughout the late summer and fall, however, she thought some progress might be evident. But not much. Her regular attendance at meeting gave her plenty of time for reflecting on the question of going north, and still she could not bear the thought of leaving her mother. Indeed, Angelina would never have thought of leaving, "if she had been willing to listen to my remonstrances and to yield to the requisition of duty as shown her by the Light within[.]" Upping the ante and suggesting something of her own self-importance, Angelina imagined that neither "Sister [n]or myself will ever see her again until she is made willing to give up Slavery. . . . [I]t seems to me her happiness will be completely destroyed by it[.]" As if that kind of toll was not enough, Angelina could inflict more: it would be her mother's "painful experience that she has no child here on whose bosom to lay her aching head, so great will be her suffering that I believe she will rather die than live[.]"[28]

As it happened, Mary Grimké managed to keep body and soul together for some time. By early October, Angelina had reached a breakthrough in her own struggle to reason her way out of the South, and it came in the form of a pleasant and very welcome surprise. Her mother, it seems, was less obstreperous than Angelina had thought, and in discovering this the daughter had discovered the way out. On the morning of 5 October 1829, mother and daughter sat down once again to clear the air about their conflicting views of the world. This time, however, Angelina "found her views far more correct than I had supposed and do believe that thro' suffering the great work will yet be accomplished." Mary reminded her that the relentless animadversions from her and Sarah had been hard to take, but acknowledged that the Lord had put wisdom in their mouths to teach others. If they were right and she wrong, then parent might well learn from the children. Did her mother admit to seeing things differently now than in the past? Yes, Angelina reported her mother saying, "I see very differently, for when I look back and remember what I used to do and think nothing of, I shrink back with horror at the tho't." Angelina had gotten what she needed, and soon she was gone. She never returned.[29]

Angelina Grimké's encounters with Henry, the Presbyterian elders, and ultimately herself represent only select moments in her diary. They nevertheless suggest a great deal about a mind rapidly developing in moral reasoning, rhetorical skill, and self-perception. Above all, we see in her diary a record of a woman coming into focus as a thinker and disputant of formidable proportions, a character whose lineaments grew from the give and take of conflict, debate, and moral argument. In each case, we see at work an element of risk that will be featured in virtually all of Angelina's future advocacy. In announcing her entrance into public life by writing to Garrison; by appealing to the very people she now left behind; by debating Catharine Beecher and Theodore Weld; by confronting her supporters and embracing her critics, Angelina put herself on the line by putting others on the line. Their fortunes, she knew, were so woven together that to speak of private and public lives could only, at least at the level to which she aspired, be a fiction. She was thus blessed, in a peculiar way, to have come into being under such circumstances as she did. Pressured by the inexpressible realities of slavery, subject to a family disintegrating from the weight of that system, Angelina nevertheless came to maturity among people who loved her. The people she left behind had granted to her as much support as might be expected, and they challenged her talents in ways that would bear rich fruit in the years to come.

CHAPTER 2

Violence, Identity, and the Creation of Radical Community

I desire to t*alk* but little about religion, for words are empty sounds, but may my life be a *living* epistle known and read of all men.

Angelina Grimké, Diary, 26 December 1828.

The summer of 1835 burned itself deeply into the racial consciousness of America. From Nashville to New Hampshire, violence against abolitionists had taken on a scope and intensity unprecedented in the annals of the antislavery movement. Even in this, "the era of greatest urban violence America has ever experienced," 1835 was to prove singular: abolitionists were subjected in that year alone to no less than thirty-seven mob attacks. "North and South, East and West," the *New York Herald* reported, people everywhere seemed to be "lashing themselves into a fury—searching for conspiracies—hunting out dangers—and manifesting the utmost spirit of alarm, at some impending dispensation of Providence." By summer's end, abolitionists and their critics alike were forced to reconsider the future of what the English reformer George Thompson had described as "this heaven-favored, but mob-cursed land."[1]

Historians as well as contemporary observers have recognized how crucial was violence in shaping the world of antebellum reform. If they have not agreed on the precise meaning, origins, or implications of that role, they nevertheless offer for our purposes certain relevant conclusions. At a minimum, we can say that violence was a pervasive feature of culture, North and South, black and white, urban and rural. We have been shown, too, how certain strains of violence influenced the character and direction of abolitionist activity. Of particular importance in this essay is the realization that violence could be constitutive of discourse itself: it gave to the abolitionists a repertoire of images, arguments, and appeals; and it lent to their campaign a combustible mixture of urgency, risk, and reward.[2]

The interplay between the violent and the symbolic endures as a feature of public life, and critics have long sought to examine its sources, character, and effects. Certain orientations may be readily identified as relevant here. In one sense, rhetoric is taken in specific circumstances to be itself a form of violence. In this view, as Dickson Bruce suggests of southern oratory, violence can be an effective way to express certain assumptions about life and the world. A similar if less stark conception informs the standard account of Robert Scott and Donald Smith, who write of the *rhetoric* of confrontation, not merely of confrontation, because this action, as diverse as its manifestations might be, is inherently symbolic. Historians frequently recur to this view when describing the abolitionists; thus Donald Mathews stresses that their rhetoric was meant to expose rather than conceal, to arouse to action rather than placate, to confront their opponents and to polarize potentially antagonistic positions rather than conciliate differences.[3]

A closely related but distinctive perspective emphasizes not so much the violence of language as the uses to which violence can be put for inventional purposes. In this sense violence gives rise to certain interpretive possibilities, and makes possible ways of reordering collective commitments and shared meanings. Richard Leeman, for example, sees in public responses to terrorism highly strategic uses of language. Counter terrorist rhetoric, he explains, works to interpret the act of terrorism and to prescribe the appropriate reaction, and he concludes that counter terrorists see their rhetoric as a response to terrorism, which is itself largely rhetorical. Taken together, the two views create a kind of ongoing dialogue, one played out for the benefit of a public audience.[4] This stress on the symbolic opportunities afforded by violence represents an important advance on preceding conceptions, and serves as a basis for the following study. I seek therein to specify how violence can serve as a medium not only for public debate, but for the creation of an identity sufficiently powerful to shape that debate.

The very scope and history of violence, its rituals and public displays, the anxieties it bared and concealed suggest that violence was more than something to be endured. The violence to which abolitionists were subjected was also a manifestation of spirit, evidence of authentic if unwelcome desires. To the degree that such violence was publicly performed and culturally sanctioned, it took on symbolic dimensions that might in turn be construed to the abolitionists' advantage. Hence the creative function unwittingly provided by the mobs: they gave to the abolitionists a way of reading their culture and therefore a way of speaking about it. Ultimately, the ability to relocate violence from a condition of brute force into available contexts of meaning and action meant that far from preempting or dissolving communities of reform, violence might well serve their purposes to perfection.[5]

We could not wish for a better illustration of this process than Angelina Grimké's 1835 public letter to William Lloyd Garrison—prompted, she wrote, to express her "sympathy and encouragement in regards to the efforts of Abolitionists and the violent opposition made to them." [6] Itself an act of no small transgression, the letter was composed under circumstances of considerable personal and public conflict. Not surprisingly, then, the text fixes violence as its source and subject; but more tellingly, it puts on display an interpretive process through which violence was to be transformed from a secular problem to a divine solution. The process is hermeneutic in character, a display of reading made rhetorically compelling to the extent that it made public claims on the convictions of its audience and promised to reward those who would, in effect, read as she did.

Grimké understood not only that change required violence, but that desirable change required the ability to read violence in optimal ways. Violence disorders, and in disordering it calls into question the structures of commitment through which communities define themselves. This disordering becomes rhetorically significant when it destabilizes the interpretive communities for which the abolitionist message was constructed. The opportunity that violence affords for the reordering and reconstitution of community is met by offering up a new vocabulary, a symbolic means to transform events and ideas into a new rationale for human relations and collective action. Violence therefore becomes crucial to the transformation of meaning and commitment that abolitionists in general and Grimké especially sought to effect. It could only secure that transformation, however, if it was itself made the object of interpretation. This process defines the rhetorical action of Grimké's text, and is the specific concern of this essay.

Grimké's stock in trade was, like most but not all of the abolitionists, language. She, like her colleagues in the business of moral reform, had little else to go on but the commitment and community that language could bring about. When she sought to achieve certain ends, she did so critically: she developed and used the resources of argument and public debate to create relationships among ideas, values, and people. Grimké's was an agonistic art, and when she exercised it critically she could not help but draw attention to the work and status of language within the movement. Through these critical encounters, then, rhetoric itself was put to the test, its possibilities and limits dramatized in the contexts of public life. [7]

Grimké came to events and people she felt to be important and made them pivotal; there is in the letter to Garrison a powerful sense of timeliness and locality, and with that sense the accompanying anxiety that action must be immediate or all will be lost. Her rhetoric is critical, then, to the extent that it defines what is at stake in the given encounter. The root meaning of critical (*kritikos*), from the feminine "ability to discern," suggests, then, an additional sense in which the term may be applied. We find in Grimké's major public letters and orations an overriding concern with distinguishing properly the relationships that bind and destroy human community. This feature of her rhetoric represents more than a tendency evident across cases: it is rather definitive of her art. To stage an encounter and enter into it critically is in this regard to discern what goes with what, who with whom. Critical judgment of this type remaps a geography of commitments by submitting conventional boundaries to an unforgiving scrutiny. To read Grimké within an encounter is therefore to read a process, the rhetorical function of which is to reconstitute the conditions of authentic community and public action.[8]

Such an approach to Grimké's text draws our attention to the complex and stressed conditions of its appearance. Because those conditions bear so heavily on the form, function, and meaning of the letter, it will be useful at this point to establish the role of violence as a situational constraint and inventional opportunity; to examine Garrison's "Appeal" as the immediate prompt to Grimké's public debut and move then to the work of textual explication.

Garrison's Appeal to the Citizens of Boston

Violence was a normal feature of Grimké's otherwise irregular life. As a child of a slave-holding family, she could hardly have expected otherwise: tensions within the household were chronic and given to periodic eruptions that often cast a pall over her daily routine. Angelina's experiences were anything but unique: "Mistress and slaves," Elizabeth Fox-Genovese explains, "lived in tense bonds of conflict-ridden intimacy that frequently exploded into violence on one side or the other." The daily brutality inflicted on the slaves had driven Angelina into recurrent disputes with family members and in particular with her mother. Some of the consequent wounds were healed over, some not, but one fact remained clear to her: slavery by its very nature, by the false order it imposed and its mimicry of familial and social relationships, could not but result in violence in one form or another. As a youth, Angelina had been in a sense called out by this violence, the sinews of her personality defined and strengthened as she fought, with little success, to challenge the domestic version of the slave system.[9] Grimké searched for and found in Philadelphia a more tranquil home life amongst her Quaker hosts and with sisters Sarah and Ann. Yet whatever relative peace she may have enjoyed within those private circles could not last for long: the immediate and domestic realities of slavery left behind returned in the form of public debate, abolitionist appeals, and anti-abolitionist mobs. For a time, as spiritual doubt and the disapproval of others worked against her, Grimké remained silent; now, five years after her arrival in Philadelphia, the thirty-year-old daughter of the system itself was ready to speak.

The circumstances in which Garrison and Grimké encountered one another could not have been more dramatic. Amidst what he called "the hurricane excitement of the times," Garrison published, on 22 August 1835, his "Appeal to Our Fellow Citizens." He had written similar appeals for the *Liberator* before, and more were to come in the volatile months and years ahead. The "Appeal" bore all the unmistakable features of Garrison's polemical style: the heated prose, the protestations of innocence, the resolutions, and the sheer scale of its righteousness. The timing, however, was singularly apt. Boston and other cities had been the scene of numerous attacks on abolitionists, and, as Garrison personally was soon to discover, the mobs were proving less and less discriminating in their choice of victims. The "Appeal," then, was written ostensibly to clarify the abolitionist position and, in Garrison's words, to save his fellow citizens from "the adoption of measures, and the commission of acts, that may bring lasting disgrace upon this city, and innocent blood upon your heads." As longtime readers of the *Liberator* may have expected, Garrison's statement was something less than conciliatory and more than "self-defence." It was a manifesto designed to make clear the stakes involved, the terms of battle, and the consequences for those obtuse enough not to see the world as Garrison and his followers saw it.[10]

Garrison's genius was to render the world into basic terms, to make clear and simple what was heretofore made falsely complicated. The invention required for such a rendering was itself uncomplicated. Garrison had access to a scriptural logic which defined the relevant issues, identified friends and foes, and insisted that the stakes involved were very high indeed. The issue, Garrison proclaimed, was not the conduct of abolitionists; it was slavery itself. The contest thus unfolding was therefore not between defenders and violators of the public order; it was between "a system of irresponsible and despotic power on the one-hand, and of unprotected and suffering humanity on the other." Slavery, Garrison thundered, was, in reality,

a system of concubinage, incest, and adultery, which threatens to bring the exterminating judgments of an incensed God upon our land—a system of violent, unholy and scandalous AMALGAMATION, teeming with physical as well as moral corruption, and filling our borders with a spurious population—a system that banishes the Bible, desecrates the Sabbath, nullifies the laws of heaven, unhinges the moral government of the universe, tramples upon the blood of the Son of God, and usurps the prerogatives of the Almighty—a system that transforms more than TWO MILLIONS OF AMERICAN CITIZENS into BRUTES, to be branded, maimed, lacerated, plundered, driven, tasked, or murdered, as their proprietors may elect![11]

Slavery was, Garrison insisted, a sin; to speak of it as belonging primarily in political, economic, or any other context was to willfully distort its true character and hence its means of resolution. Understood in this way, slavery was an affair of conscience as much as an objective practice. For this reason, Garrison explained, "We have a moral and constitutional right to cherish and to utter this belief."[12] Slavery thus imposed an obligation to act and speak—if not in Senate chambers then certainly in the streets and halls and newspaper rooms across the nation; it was a matter of conscience, yes, but not private conscience alone. And yet this built-in rationale for public speech carried with it a potential dilemma: without the apparatus of conventional politics, without access to or desire for partisan resources, what means did the abolitionists have for being heard? Newspapers, of course, they had aplenty, and orators and agents, societies and benevolent organizations. Yet all of these outlets in a sense beg a question: their very existence presupposes a collective will to go public and a basis upon which to animate and sustain their reform activities.

The answer, at least in part, may be found in the creative and constructive role that violence was made to serve. Violence, Garrison demonstrated, could work not just as a goad to action, but as a means to suffuse abolitionist performances with a highly symbolic, publicly visible, and morally potent current. By understanding and deploying violence as a kind of cultural code, they could effect a tactical trans-formation, and create thereby an interpretive resource for public action without becoming complicitous in mainstream politics. Put another way, Garrison needed power, but he wanted it pure. He found it in Scripture, appropriated it to the ends of the movement, and exercised it in the form of a rhetorical appeal:

> We acknowledge no earthly leader. God is our strength and shield—our light and defense; and under the banner of the Prince of Peace we rally. . . . We are persecuted, but not dismayed; cast down but not destroyed. If any of us, like Stephen, shall be cruelly stoned to death by those who would gnash upon us with their teeth, and stop their ears, and run upon us with one accord, we trust that in the agonies of a martyr's death his prayer will be ours. . . . If we are nailed to the cross, we pray that the spirit and example of our dying Lord will lead us to exclaim—"Father, forgive them! they know not what they do!"[13]

The markers here are conspicuous: the anti-institutionalism; the persecution motif and its accompanying images of Stephen and Christ, martyrs whose resolve—indeed grace—is only strengthened in the face of violence. These mark-ers will in turn serve to pattern Grimké's response, and allow her to develop from Garrison's text a more elaborate, artful, and compelling rationale for rereading violence.

Garrison's "Appeal" was well timed in at least one other sense. A copy of the *Liberator* in which it was published chanced into Grimké's hands at a most important juncture. Well before she had joined the Philadelphia Female Anti-Slavery Society in the spring of 1835, Angelina had been struggling to articulate a complex new vision of her world and the roles within it of church, state, and slavery itself. Whatever early signals she may have sent about her interest in the cause, they were met with little enthusiasm among most family and Friends. By 1832, however, Angelina could confide to her brother Thomas her anticipation of momentous changes ahead. "I am no politician," she wrote, "but when I look at the progress of the world and the *Church*, I fear the decree has gone forth, and from a higher tribunal than Rome that the city must be destroyed. Slavery is too great a sin for justice always to [sleep?] over, and this, this I believe is the true cause of the declining state of Carolina, this, the root of bitterness which springing up in our Republic has troubled us." Grimké was not at that time prepared to specify just what her place and purpose would be in this scenario, but of one thing she was certain. "I do verily believe," she wrote Thomas, "that there are hundreds, perhaps thousands who carry the spirit of martyrs about them and are now preparing the way for the universal reign of Truth and Righteousness in the earth."[14] Three years later Grimké was ready to join their ranks—and to do so publicly. Grimké noted in her diary that lately she had "become deeply interested in the subject of Abolition." Having overcome her despair that the cause was hopeless, she now thought anti-slavery principles to be "so full of the power of Truth that I am confident not many years will roll over before the horrible traffic in human beings will be destroyed in this land of gospel privileges." Her prayer now was that "the Lord would be pleased to permit me to be instrumental of good to these degraded, oppressed, and suffering fellow-creatures." Grimké concluded the entry with a telling prediction: "Truly, I often feel as if I were ready to go to prison and to death in this cause of justice, mercy and love. . . . If I am called to go back to Carolina, it will not be long before I shall suffer persecution of some kind or another."[15]

As it happened, Grimké never went to prison, died in the cause, or returned home. She did, however, give to these private thoughts their public expression in the form of a response to Garrison's "Appeal." Subsequently entitled *Slavery and the Boston Riot*, the letter represents Grimké's abolitionist debut: with it, she went public, and thus announced the arrival of a new and commanding voice in northern reform circles. The letter was, in the words of Gerda Lerner, "a symbolic act, a public gesture of commitment from one world to another. All the years of floundering and searching had finally brought her to this single moment."[16]

The interpretation that follows takes seriously Lerner's point about the symbolic and public character of Grimké's letter. I am accordingly concerned with examining in some detail the ways in which the text creates for the author an identity of sufficient strength to allow her to enter and help determine the course of public life. This process I take to be rhetorical in its most overt sense. It draws upon and is shaped by available means of persuasion, and seeks to open opportunities for change at just the point when such opportunities seem most distant. More specifically, the symbolic action of Grimké's letter is to recast violence from a negative force working against shared public commitment into the very possibility of such commitments. The rhetorical force of the text is therefore transformative, a formal representation of what it means to change problems into solutions and despair into resolve. As I have hinted previously, Grimké's identity within the text is itself both a source and a result of this process. We have, then, a rather complex interplay of theme, image, and identity at work here. In order to make sense of it, we might see the text as displaying a set of transformations ranging from doubt to faith to action. These internal movements, each one of which enables and exemplifies certain kinds of relationships, function rhetorically by giving the reader both a reason and a means to believe.

Analysis of the Text

My reading suggests that in context, violence may be understood as an optimal means through which public relationships are constructed. This process, I argue, is exemplified by terms established within the text itself; it is therefore wholly explicable as a rhetorical performance. Grimké's letter, that is, is of sufficient artistic density to reward attention to detail, nuance, and internal transformations. Because I wish to dwell at some length on this text, I need at the outset to sketch the interplay of form and function that I think is basic to the rhetorical force of the letter. With these coordinates set, the reader may be in a position to proceed systematically through the text without losing sight of its more general economy of meaning.

The overarching pattern generated by the text is grounded in a process of conversion—of self, of reader, of situation, and ultimately of the world. All claims, each image and every allusion, may be accounted for by reference to the dynamics of conversion. These dynamics are played out in multiple ways and within the course of each of its six paragraphs. The text as a whole may thus be envisioned as one wheel composed of smaller ones, each turning on its own even as it pushes forward and sustains the momentum of the larger structure. The reader's task, then, will rest in identifying the transformations taking place within each paragraph and in explaining how these particular movements contribute to the letter in its entirety.

Like its author, Grimké's letter resists any quick assignment to type, sphere, or mode of address. Composed in private anguish, it wound up an object of public celebration. Is it, then, a public letter, in the manner of eighteenth-century epis-tolary conventions? Not in the sense normally intended, I think, and yet we would not want to ignore its conspicuously public and persuasive features. The letter borrows from epistolary convention to convey a sense of the private, the intimate, the authentic; at the same time, it is patently addressed to a powerful figure, on matters of pressing and public concern. Still again, there is in the letter's theme of persecution and resolve strong echoes of the Quaker diary and spiritual autobi-ography, a centuries-old tradition to which Grimké was heir. Between these pub-lic and private realms Grimké established the terms of her appeal, where artistic range is defined by concrete needs and where individual will is realized through the production of shared meaning. The generic inheritance of the text can be fur-ther specified as Pauline in spirit, if not in rigid detail. Its thematic concern for the conditions for authentic speech, its manifest sense of address, its interweav-ing of doctrine and exhortation—all bespeak a conscious artistry in the service of rhetorical ends.[17]

We will have missed the full impact of that artistry, however, by simply reduc-ing the text to its level of generic production. Its key lies elsewhere. In the sym-bolic interplay of speaker, subject, and audience, Grimké constructed a model of interpretation through which she could reread the text of the world and thus her place in it. This reading, as I have indicated, dramatizes the transformation of its referent from secular to sacred ground, and therefore requires that we look closely at the rhetorical action of the text.

To transform the meaning of violence is first to position it as an object of interpretation. This process in turn presumes an interpretive agent, in this case an author uniquely equipped to superintend the shifting semantics of the text. The key to understanding this process is to trace the ways in which Grimké located violence within a matrix of unfolding relationships. Violence, which for her pur-poses is meaningless in isolation, takes on its significance as it is positioned with respect to the dynamic relationship defining author, reader, and situation. Accordingly, the meaning of violence is contingent on its place within this matrix, and will change as this relationship itself changes. We may trace the semantic career of violence, then, as it is subjected to the pressures imposed by these terms.

Respected friend:

It seems as if I was compelled at this time to address thee, not withstanding all my reasonings against intruding on thy valuable time, and the uselessness of so insignificant a person as myself offering thee the sentiments of sympathy at this alarming crisis.[18]

The author presented herself, first, as a subject acted upon. If not a victim of events, she was driven by them—"compelled at this time"— and what follows was presumably determined for the same reason. The courage to write was thereby modified by the tentativeness of the author's stance; indeed, she even appeared uncertain as to her compulsion: it only "seems as if I was compelled at this time to address thee." This image of the subject being acted upon is further enhanced as it is set in relation to her reader. The author's reticence bespeaks a self-consciousness, an awareness that there is a vertical distance between writer and reader. Her own reason proves unconvincing, even to herself, as to why she should not write: the reader's time is valuable, her time is by counterimplication not; her person is "useless" and "insignificant," his presumably the opposite. At this early moment the posed communicative relationship is based on difference and contrast; it is hierarchical and stressed, where authorial defacement ironically reflects an exalted reader.

Grimké's depiction of events, and of her relationship to them, underscores her status in the text. In viewing violence in conventional terms, she is in turn seen as reacting to events, to "this alarming crisis." Violence in this sense compels; its function is to provoke and bring otherwise distant voices into hearing range. Her response, to write and offer "sentiments of sympathy," may be taken as an assertion, perhaps, but it does nothing so far to address or alter the nature of those events. Outside the text, to be sure, we are reminded that as a woman, a Southerner, an aspiring Quaker with virtually no claim on public convictions, her stance is entirely authentic. To leave it at this, however, is to miss the significance of the text as a form of rhetorical action—not as autobiography, but as an exhibition of how the text of the world might be reread for lasting advantage. This is but the first step in that process, whereby violence mediates the dangerous passage from private anguish to public encounter.

The plaintive lines inaugurating the letter establish a logic that, far from subverting Grimké's aims, gives them reason and direction. This logic is developed in the second paragraph in a way that complicates the basic relationships thus far established. Author, reader, and situation remain foregrounded, but their status changes, and this opens new possibilities for transforming the realities of violence. Because the paragraph is relatively lengthy, and because of its complexity, it is worth considering in detail.

The ritualized defacement marking the text's introduction does not disappear, but it is less obvious and functions to different ends. "I can hardly express to thee," Grimké wrote,

> the deep and solemn interest with which I have viewed the violent proceedings of
> the last few weeks. Although I expected opposition, yet I was not prepared for it so

soon—it took me by surprise, and I greatly feared Abolitionists would be driven back in the first onset, and thrown into confusion. So fearful was I, that though I clung with unflinching firmness to our principles, yet I was afraid of even opening one of thy papers, lest I should see some indications of compromise, some surrender, some palliation.

Grimké retained, to be sure, some of her avowed diffidence. She could "hardly express" herself, and she remained subject to disabling anxieties: in the face of the Boston violence, she confessed to being "not prepared," "surprised," "fearful," "afraid." The author remained, in short, acted upon. If we look closer, however, we find evidence that the posture was only momentary, and tactical at that.

For all of the diffidence, there was an emerging sense of a stronger self, of a speaker who nevertheless clung "with unflinching firmness to our principles." Grimké's resolve and her appeal to principle set in juxtaposition the words "compromise," "surrender," and "palliation," and thus sustained the tension between author and reader. Her commitment to principle was unquestionable, however traumatized, and this commitment allowed her at least to see the dangers that violence imposed upon others. Paragraph two in this way shifts authorial character from a subject acted upon to a perceiving subject. Grimké displayed herself as occupying a space of spectatorship and reflection, a space that, while not optimal, granted her a perspective not available to those in the heat of battle.

As the author underwent transformation, so, too, must her relationship to the reader. It was the reader, indeed, who functioned as the agent of change, where Garrison's strength became her strength and his image her guiding light. Having read Garrison's "Appeal," she realized that her

fears were utterly groundless, and that thou stoodest firm in the midst of the storm, determined to suffer and to die, rather than yield one inch. My heart was filled with thanksgiving and praise to the Preserver of men; I thanked God, and took courage, earnestly desiring that thousands may adopt thy language, and be prepared to meet the Martyr's doom, rather than give up the principles you [i.e., abolitionists] have adopted.

The transformations announced in this passage are clear and basic to the rhetorical action of the text. Where once she was fearful, Grimké now took courage; where she opened the letter solicitously, she now stood as a witness; and where Garrison was a possible problem, he now functioned as a solution. Grimké's injunction that others "adopt thy language" is key to this transformation. The reinterpretation of violence is signalled by a discursive event, a willed assumption of a privileged vocabulary. The rest of the letter confirms what is here promised:

by "adopting thy language," Grimké redefined the terms of the situation from their secular to their sacred contexts. Garrison's status as reader exemplified this process of redefinition. From profane dissident to honored martyr, he was recast within an utterly different language and thus took on a new aspect altogether. Grimké's reconstitution of this author-reader relationship was dramatized by a radical shift in her mode of address. Far from being defaced or solicitous, she now assumed a voice at once commanding and prophetic.

> The ground upon which you stand is holy ground—never surrender it.[19] If you surrender it, the hope of the slave is extinguished, and the chains of his servitude will be strengthened a hundred fold. But let no man take your crown, and success is as certain as the rising of tomorrow's sun. But remember you must be willing to suffer the loss of all things—willing to be the scorn and reproach of professor and profane. You must obey our great Master's injunction: Fear not them that kill the body, and after that, have nothing more that they can do.[20] You must, like [the] Apostles, "count not your lives dear unto yourselves, so that you may finish your course with joy."[21]

The passage is pivotal. Grimké established a vantage point from which she could now make sense of—and hence reinterpret—the events taking place. She could do this only after her relationship to the reader and the historical situation had been so realigned as to identify Garrison with Stephen, at which point he becomes a typological instrument of divine will. Grimké, in turn, echoed the apostolic counsel, associating at once the images of Moses, Stephen, Christ, and Garrison. That accomplished, the issue of violence was positioned within a crucible of relationships, and there it was subject to radical reformulation. Fixed now within the logic Grimké had imposed upon the events of the world, violence could be reread not as a crisis to be feared but as a force to be expected and, ultimately, required for the work of transforming the world.

In sum, we may say at this point that Grimké's relationship to Garrison had evolved into that of an acolyte, the voice impersonal but increasingly exhortative. The immediate issue of violence had undergone a kind of symbolic change as well. If in the first paragraph it carried the weight of an imperative, here violence was rendered indeterminate, a fact not to be dismissed but to which a response was to be a matter of principled choice. Thus Grimké's exhortation: in a variable and contingent world, the word itself must be relied upon to move from fear and doubt to faith and resolution.

Grimké's third paragraph continues to build, strengthen, and transform the terms with which she inaugurated the letter. It represents, however, a distinctive phase of her appeal, wherein the personal and local give way to more global issues.

Thematic concerns about persecution and resolve remain evident, but Grimké here effected a conspicuous shift of scale, where the plaintive tone of previous lines was subsumed by a widening perspective. In this, the central passage of the text, author, reader, and context undergo significant variation: the principled distance achieved with Garrison is expanded into a rationale for community, and mob violence is reconceived as essential to the public constitution of that community.

Grimké's insistence that violence be understood in its public aspect presumed a sense of its historic relationship to the state. She need have looked no further than to the Quaker legacy, of course, for evidence of this relationship, but the tale she tells is older and the lessons enduring.

> Religious persecution always begins with mobs; it is always unprecedented in the age or country in which it commences, and therefore there are no laws by which Reformers can be punished; consequently a lawless band of unprincipled men determined to take the matter into their hands, and act out in mobs, what they know are the principles of a large majority of those who are too high in Church and State to condescend to mingle with them, though they secretly approve and rejoice over their violent measures.

The reflective and relatively abstract tone here is notably different from that of the letter's opening lines; it indicates, however, not a flight from the relationship so far established but the beginnings of its expansion. Far from being subjected to events, Grimké appeared here to surmount them, to perceive and interpret the world through the perspective such distance affords. That perspective, specifically, works here to identify the historical forces through which the abolitionists' efforts would be mediated. In the process, Grimké set in play an unfolding set of oppositions between authentic and false conceptions of community and collective action. Her own experience testified to the power of both. In her struggles with faith, family, and regional culture, Grimké spent much of her adult life trying to discern between and negotiate the claims of true and false relationships. Armed now with that experience, Grimké could see the same patterns at work: mobs were merely the popular counterpart of corrupt government, persecution not illegal but pre-legal expressions of a complicitous church and state. By this reckoning, secular government was in its present state simply controlled and rationalized violence, and the people merely instruments of its will.

Grimké's judgment was severe, but it was not pessimistic. If mobs could be revealed as manifestations of false community, they still had the unwitting power to call out and strengthen convictions, a process by definition public and symbolic, as well as spiritual. For this purpose both Garrison's and Grimké's allusions to Stephen were especially useful. As the typological martyr, Stephen's crown was forged in a crucible of violence and language; his witness was thereby given dramatic force as a public declaration. Indeed, Grimké recalled, "The first martyr who ever died, was stoned by a lawless mob; and if we look at the rise of various sects—Methodists, Friends, &c.—we shall find that mobs began the persecution against them, and that it was not until after the people had thus spoken out their wishes, that laws were framed to fine, imprison, or destroy them." The lesson here, as the reference to sects pointedly makes clear, is that the "rise of various sects" was attended by and often defined against violent opposition.

By implication, then, mobs were to be viewed in the present crisis neither as new—as instruments of religious persecutions, they predated Christ—nor as an aberration or departure from secular law—they were rather preliminary to such law. The appropriate response, then, was not despair or flight, but total engagement. "Let us," Grimké counseled, "be prepared for the enactment of laws even in our Free States, against Abolitionists. And how ardently has the prayer been breathed, that God would prepare us all for all he is preparing us; that he would strengthen us in the hour of conflict, and cover our heads (if consistent with his holy will) in the day of battle!"

The allusion to Psalm 140:7 is, in the context, telling. As an instance of chiasmus, it syntactically reinforces the process of conversion to which it alludes. Through its use, moreover, Grimké sought God's judgment against those who would, in speech, corrupt the holy cause. The battle, then, was to be a war of words, a *logomachia,* wherein good and evil vied for the convictions of the people. The need to come together in and through language was thus again underscored, and recalled Grimké's earlier hope, "that thousands may adopt thy language." The point is further accented by the author's own language, especially the progressively inclusive use of pronouns from the predominant "I" of earlier lines to "you" in designating the specific terms of her relationship with Garrison, to the "we" and "us" which mark the third paragraph. The more general set of transformations suggested by this usage is fully realized as this phase builds to climax. It makes dramatically clear what we have already come to understand—that this letter is not about Grimké and Garrison alone, nor indeed about abolitionists individually or collectively: it aspires rather to a greater conception of community, brought about through persecution and suffering.

> But O! how earnestly have I desired, not that we may escape suffering, but that we may be willing to endure until the end. If we call upon the slave-holder to suffer the loss of what he calls property, then let us show him we make this demand from a deep sense of duty, by being ourselves willing to suffer the loss of character, property—yea, and life itself, in what we believe to be the cause of bleeding humanity.

These, then, were the terms of authentic community—sufferance, duty, faith, perseverance, the unyielding pursuit of a purified world. Within these terms, persecution is made to represent not an impediment to reform but a condition of it. With that premise in place, all the markers of uncertainty and fear, of protocol, hierarchy, and social distinction, are displaced by a superintending code of commitments.

We are at some distance, rhetorically at least, from the tentative lines initiating the letter. This distance has been created and charted by a set of conversions, each one of which modifies certain constitutive relationships, including most importantly those which obtain among author, reader, and situation. At the center of these changes, at once overseeing and a result of them, is Grimké, whose letter we may now see as an exhibition of reading itself, a public display of how the world might be reinterpreted by imposing order on disorder, sanctity upon profanation. As a textual act, the letter writes into itself an image of Grimké productive of her motives and ends, and this image, as we have seen, is itself key to the conversions effected. By the letter's fourth paragraph it has undergone drastic transformation. Here the cultivation of a prophetic ethos, so prominent in later encounters, can be glimpsed in its early stages. The paragraph reminds us too, that the depersonalized voice apparent in preceding lines represents not absence or loss but the traditional emptying of one's self as preliminary to divine fulfillment. The assumption of this office imposes further transformations upon the course of events and the structure of commitment which give them meaning.[22]

The courage of the prophet is the courage to address. Such courage presumes power of speech, of course, but also of perspective, the ability to envision comprehensively those to whom the word must be spoken. Hence the prophet is thought to command both eloquence and wisdom, *Logos,* as prerequisite to the work of transformation. Paragraph four makes conspicuous Grimké's claim to this capacity for privileged insight, through which the public and symbolic nature of violence undergoes further renovation.

> My mind has been especially turned toward those, who are standing in the forefront of the battle; and the prayer has gone up for their preservation—not the preservation of their lives, but the preservation of their minds in humility and patience, faith, hope, and charity—that charity which is the bond of perfectness.

Garrison would have more than one occasion in the months ahead to think of Paul and, having been dragged from temples of his own, to find in the apostle a fellowship of suffering as well as virtue. Here Grimké turned to address the embattled abolitionists everywhere, sustaining as she did the martial imagery that pervades the text. Given the events of 1835, this imagery is neither surprising nor unique, but it does help to dramatize her sense of the conflict and the terms with which it was to be carried out: spiritual perseverance alone could overcome violence, not through defeating it on its own terms, but by literally changing the rules of confrontation.

> If persecution is the means which God has ordained for the accomplishment of the great end, Emancipation; then, in dependence upon Him for strength to bear it, I feel as if I could say, LET IT COME; for it is my deep, solemn deliberate conviction, that this is a cause worth dying for. I say so, from what I have seen, and heard, and known, in a land of slavery, where rests the darkness of Egypt, and where is found the sin of Sodom.[23] Yes: LET IT COME—let us suffer, rather than insurrections should arise.

The peculiar talent of the prophet is to see and thus to speak as others cannot; it is a perspective, Grimké reminded us, born of experience, revelation, and duty. To see as the author does was accordingly to realize that the rules do not hold, that values are subject to reversal and the secular to sacred revision. Thus persecution was a means to divine ends; dependence a sign of strength; life a cause worth dying for. It was a pattern of depiction that would find its most dramatic expression in Pennsylvania Hall near the end of Grimké's public career; for now, she used it to powerful effect by pushing the logic of Christian inversion to its consummate point. "Let it come," Grimké insisted, because the suffering sure to be inflicted was to be read as a sign of victory against the logic of the enemy.

Born in the "darkness of Egypt," Grimké could offer to her readers a vision such as they had never seen, not even from the searching pen of William Lloyd Garrison. The letter gives evidence of an emerging identity, as yet vaguely familiar and patterned from scriptural prophesy, but distinctive, too, for its source and claim on public convictions. At this stage in the letter Grimké offered up new possibilities for thinking about violence, especially in its public and ritualized expressions. By assuming a prophetic voice, Grimké at once set herself apart from her audience—and indeed she was not yet of them—and strengthened her relationship with her audience through a bond of shared symbols and the duties those symbols represented. Above all, the prophetic insight allowed her to see that violence itself was a form of public ritual; it was observable and therefore negotiable within a logic already available to those who would heed her words. Finally, as this mere paragraph from a first production testifies, Grimké understood that even so modest a prophecy as this was itself a public act, ambivalent and stressed, at once a testimony to self, community, and divine will.

Grimké's letter held out to Garrison and all others an identity still under construction. Its readers were invited, in effect, to share in the work of completing that identity by giving it purpose and power. In the image of the prophet Grimké found a means through which her audience might be so induced. This image was, moreover, ideally suited to the process of transforming private experience into publicly resonate expression. Given the contextual and ideological constraints before her, Grimké clearly needed such a symbol, and in fact had struggled for years to craft her unique background to more rhetorically powerful effect. Such craft had not come easily. At times she had found herself "greatly agitated, for so acute have been my sufferings on account of Slavery and so strong my feelings of indignation in looking upon their oppressed and degraded condition, that I cannot command my feelings in speaking of what my own eyes have seen of their suffering, and thus I believe I lost the satisfaction I should otherwise have felt for 'speaking the truth.'"[24]

The language of prophecy promised to return that satisfaction. Yet if Grimké could thereby speak of what her eyes had seen, she had also to recognize the consequences of such speech. Among these, none was so volatile an issue as the fear of slave revolt, an anxiety shared across borders and indeed among some abolitionists. The dramatic misfortunes of Nat Turner had quickened the formation of antiabolitionist sentiment in the North, and by 1835 leaders such as Garrison and George Thompson were being directly accused of inciting rebellion.[25] Thus Boston's *Daily Evening Transcript* anticipated Thompson's impending address in Julien Hall by announcing in its pages a nonpartisan meeting in Faneuil Hall of those "opposed to the proceedings of the advocates for the immediate emancipation of the slaves of the South—and who, however they may regard slavery as an evil, yet look with distrust and abhorrence upon all measures which may tend to instigate the blacks to insubordination and insurrection." There gathered, antiabolitionists hoped to convey to their Southern cousins how greatly they deplored "the unauthorized interference of those who, with a professed zeal for the melioration of the condition of the slaves, are either forging for them new fetters, or placing in imminent peril the lives and property of the white population."[26]

Garrison, of course, was quick to protest innocence, his "Appeal" being one of several efforts to placate a deeply skeptical public. The problem was that Garrison's language—to say nothing of his organizational tactics—seemed to belie any real claim to peaceful motives: "we bring no invidious accusation against the south," runs a characteristic assurance, "but charge the north with being alike guilty of upholding a system of robbery, outrage, and soul-murder." None of this of course was likely to allay concerns that abolitionists would, if unchecked, ignite slave insurrections.[27]

The worry was not, as matters turned out, altogether far-fetched. As Grimké herself confessed in the letter's fifth paragraph, she at one time "thought this system would be overthrown with blood, with the confused noise of the warrior."

But in language familiar now as a logic of sacrifice and redemption, Grimké assured her readers not that blood would not be spilt, but that only the blood of the righteous could destroy the system of slavery. A "hope gleams across my mind," she wrote, "that our blood will be spilt, instead of the slaveholders'; our lives will be taken, and theirs spared—I say a hope, for of all things I desire to be spared the anguish of seeing our beloved country desolated with the horrors of a servile war." The contrast here with Garrison's language has less to do with vehemence or logic than with perspective. Grimké's recurrent emphasis on blood sacrifice imposes on events, past and future, a logic of redemption that is constitutive of community rather than a threat to it.

Armed with this perspective, Grimké gave to the reader an entirely different set of answers to the charge of incitement. This is not to say, then or now, that these answers were necessarily more convincing. The direct relationship between persecution and change is seldom evident in any material sense. Grimké nevertheless saw in the will to suffer not just a principle of perseverance, but of community itself; specifically, such commitment could call people together in bonds of faith, *and* provide a test of that faith. "If persecution can abolish slavery," she reasoned,

> it will also purify the Church; and who that stands between the porch and altar, weeping over the sins of the people, will not be willing to suffer, if such good will be accomplished.[28] Let us endeavor, then, to put on the whole armour of God, and having done all, to stand ready for whatever is before us.[29]

Thus, like Ezekiel's isolators in the temple, there will be those who pretend merely to sympathize and whose faith—or lack of it—will then be exposed under persecution. The allusion is perhaps distant in our time, but Grimké's reader surely would have been reminded of those within the American Colonization Society who, "weeping over the sins of the people," were yet unwilling to suffer for those sins. Persecution, then, might well be used to distinguish false from true community, and thus assist in the ongoing work of purifying the church.

The final paragraph moves quickly from these more universal concerns to more particular issues. The shift is characteristically Pauline. Here the author could return readers to immediate concerns; cite the recent and telling event, perhaps; and offer final words of advice, warning, and encouragement. The effect was to close spaces opened up by the preceding meditations and restore a sense of immediacy appropriate to the epistolary form. At the same time, this return to the particular illustrates how problems may now be interpreted in light of the letter as a whole. The concluding paragraph may thus be seen as serving didactic as well as more formal purposes.

I have just heard of Dresser's being flogged: it is no surprise at all but the language of our Lord has been sweetly revived— "Blessed are ye when men shall revile you, and persecute you, and say all manner of evil against you falsely, for my sake. Rejoice, and be exceeding glad, for great is your reward in heaven."[30] O! for a willingness and strength to suffer! But we shall have false brethren now, just as the Apostles had, and this will be one of our greatest griefs.

These final lines are few, cryptic perhaps, but in the context of the letter they are rhetorically charged. Each of the major appeals shaping this text and the transformations driving it forward are given their final punctuation. Grimké's pointed reference to Amos Dresser, a black abolitionist who had been publicly lashed in Nashville on 25 July, is illustrative. In the early stages of the letter, Grimké had expressed surprise at the opposition and "feared Abolitionists would be driven back in the first onset, and thrown into confusion." The work of the text almost completed, the author could now look with confidence on the scene before her. Such violence occasioned not surprise, but, mediated through the text, a literal reanimation of the spirit. "In the language of our Lord," Grimké concluded, was to be found the possibility of reward, collective identity, and new community. The beatitude that follows is for this reason entirely appropriate, capturing as it does the subversive mix of pacifism and obedience to a higher law to which Grimké was drawn. In it she found a way to uncouple power from its secular basis and yet retain the promise of effecting change in the world. Such change was predicated on an active community of believers, Grimké suggested; and if that community was under threat, it was not through violent opposition but through "false brethren." The proximity of that danger, and Grimké's dark allusion to it, give urgency to the letter's final words, binding author and reader ever more tightly within their mutual profession.

Conclusion

"It is now more than four weeks," Grimké recalled in her diary, "since I tho't I felt right to write WLG a letter of sympathy and encouragement in regard to the efforts of Abolitionists and the violent opposition made to them." Her misgivings had abated for the most part; still, she wrote, "I felt that it might involve me in some difficulty and therefore it was written in fear and after it was written I hardly knew whether to send it or not and therefore again implored divine direction." As the years went by, Grimké could look back on her decision to send the letter—and her refusal to retract it—with considerably more confidence. It was, she wrote in early 1838, "the first long breath of *liberty* which my imprisoned spirit dared to respire whilst it pined in hopeless bondage, panting after freedom to *think aloud*. O! how I suffered for writing that letter, but IT WAS GOOD!"[31] But of course the violence continued. In the month of Grimké's public encounter Philadelphia mobs summarily dumped antislavery literature into the waters of the Delaware; a slave conspiracy was reported underway in Charlestown, Maryland; and an abolitionist was hanged in Virginia for stirring up revolt. The unrest continued well into the autumn months and culminated in Garrison's fittingly dramatic capture in Boston on 21 October— "an awful, sublime, and soul-thrilling scene," Garrison recalled, "enough, one would suppose, to melt adamantine hearts, and make even fiends of darkness stagger and retreat."[32]

Yet, as Grimké's letter of encouragement to Garrison makes clear, she saw in such violence not the repression of public discourse but an opportunity for it. In this she was not unique; the persecuted have always made sense of their condition in ways never intended by their oppressors, and in Scripture Grimké could find a vocabulary already available for this purpose. In the aggregate, however, she must be accorded a distinctive place amongst the early abolitionist host. The spiritual journey, as yet unfinished, which brought her north; the struggle to negotiate competing allegiances; the burst of resolve after prolonged doubt; such experience could be transformed into a rationale for public action. The letter gave to these efforts form and purpose, its rhetoric driving open the gates of reform even as it sought to reshape its very terms of commitment.

This process, I have tried to show, is made evident through a series of textually inscribed transformations. These conversions work progressively through each of the paragraphs even as they cohere into a general pattern of meaning and function. Three key and interacting terms sustain this pattern: the posed relationship between author and reader; the role that violence plays in facilitating this relationship; and the transformation effected thereby. Hence the asymmetrical relationship invoked in paragraph one is by letter's end transformed through the author's prophetic office into a radical egalitarianism; violence is reassigned from a negative force acting against the abolitionist cause into an instrument of divine will; and the historical boundaries of private and public action are ultimately erased by the imperatives of Christ's church. The letter is therefore exemplary, in that it puts on display a conspicuous mode of interpretation—both as a means of addressing urgent situational exigencies and as an assertion of authorial power.

The letter to Garrison is in one sense a record of this private activity, but it is at the same time and for this reason a text of enduring public significance. In its synthesis of arguments and images Grimké offered a compelling rationale for public life that could not—must not—be compromised by constraints imposed artificially by region, race, or gender. She understood, too, that as it was public and persuasive, the letter was a form of enactment; it was a means to an end, a statement about those ends, and a declaration of individual and shared identity.

Theodore Weld, for one, gives evidence that the letter met those ends, that its appeal extended beyond Garrison and his circle, and that its terms of community were in fact compelling. Two years after it appeared in the pages of the *Liberator,* Weld wrote Grimké, the letter "formed an era in my feelings and a crisis in my history that drew my spirit toward yours by irrepressible affinities. I read it over and over and over," Weld continued, "and in the deep consciousness that I should find in the spirit that dictated that letter the searchless power of *congenial communings.*"[33]

For those already familiar with Grimké's antislavery rhetoric, this description seems perhaps perverse. There is in her advocacy that quality of the unyielding and extreme which anti-abolitionists of her time and historians thereafter found so unappealing. It is the rhetoric of the true believer, and to the degree that it disregards the imperatives of time, place, and audience, it may be said to be hardly a rhetoric at all. In this reading Grimké's was an adamantine righteousness, the expression of which is almost always monologic. At a certain level of analysis, of course, this is arguably true; by temperament and experience, faith and commitment, Grimké had little time for policy debates—at least not in public. But to leave it at that is to ignore the greater contexts of her public utterance. Several observations will help illustrate my point.

First, the letter represents the first of a series of encounters characterized by risk—risk to the author, often to the reader, usually to both. In every such encounter—the letter to Garrison, her *Appeal to the Christian Women of the South,* the exchanges with Catharine Beecher, her New England tour, the speech at Pennsylvania Hall—Grimké stood to lose as well as to gain, and it was not always clear to her or to others on which side of the ledger she found herself. Grimké's family reputation, her regional loyalties, her religious affiliations, her marital happiness, her health, her relationship to Sarah, her very life, were at different moments exposed and made vulnerable through her will to public action.

Second, this encounter is characteristic in its staged engagement with well-known individuals or audiences who themselves commanded powerful means of expression. Garrison, Southern clergy, Catharine Beecher, politicians, fellow abolitionists—these are scarcely the gullible or passive audiences upon which monologists train their words. They figure, rather, as highly charged and sometimes skeptical interlocutors. Grimké's audiences were resilient, seldom at a loss for words of their own, and even when sympathetic, held her to exceedingly high standards.

Finally, the letter to Garrison exemplifies what is basic to Grimké's rhetoric generally—its powerful sense of address, the immediacy with which she brings the rhetorical occasion into being. Grimké's voice is never heard from afar, and in it indeed can be detected the strains of proximity and anticipation that bespeak a keen awareness of others. In the face of others, so close as to be felt, she personalized the abolitionist's strident appeal to principle—as if in this way, and in this only, could she summon and then put on display the drama of commitments at risk.

Real Pasts and Imagined Futures in the *Appeal to the Christian Women of the South*

Boston. 14 October 1835. No. 17 Washington Street. The riots that had incited Grimké two months earlier continued apace, and William Lloyd Garrison was predictably in the middle of it all. Here was, he recalled, "an awful, sublime and soul-thrilling scene—enough, one would suppose, to melt adamantine hearts, and make even the fiends of darkness stagger and retreat." The scene of Garrison's rapture was Boston's Anti-Slavery Hall, and from his bench within he was, for the moment at least, party to a glorious confrontation between good and evil. In its fruitless hunt for the English reformer George Thompson, the anti-abolitionist mob had burst in upon the annual meeting of the Boston Female Anti-Slavery Society, disrupted its proceedings, and now threatened to end its business altogether. Mary Parker, president of the society, called instead for Scripture and prayer, but it was not long before its members were obliged to leave. Garrison resolved that he and his fellow abolitionists would not stop speaking until the "scenes from the French Revolution be re-enacted—and men and women, and children even, put to death by human butchers, until the earth be drunk with blood, and the slain cease to find a covering for their mutilated bodies." Garrison, "in the noble company of martyrs," chose to stay behind, locked within an office, and set about to compose the drama unfolding around him. As we know from this familiar story of Garrison's apotheosis, he eventually had to flee as well, was seized by the crowd, and spent the night in protective custody in the Leverett Street jail.[1]

For all its self-promotion and righteous zeal, there is in that image of Garrison, carefully emplotting the moral revolution of the world, much that is telling. Safe for the moment, he knew himself to be at the epicenter of an extraordinary confluence of forces—of violence, community, and language—that in significant ways defined the early abolitionist movement. Much of Garrison's rhetorical art was designed specifically to keep him thus positioned, where he might plan, announce, and implement the end of slavery and race prejudice. Here was no room for equivocation, as he had memorably advertised in the first issue of the *Liberator,* no time for faltering conviction, and certainly there were, whatever Garrison's childhood or whatever his previous colonizationist attitudes, to be no regrets. *Garrison never, ever looked back.* "I will be as harsh as truth," he declared, "and as uncompromising as justice. On this subject I do not wish to think, or speak, or write with moderation. . . . I am in earnest,—I will not equivocate—I will not excuse—I will not retreat a single inch—AND I WILL BE HEARD." And he meant it.[2]

This was a center, too, that Grimké was to occupy in her own fashion and for her own reasons; and like Garrison, she was most alive, most useful, when confronting such storms as this and in her own "noble company of martyrs." Grimké felt herself bound to play a leading role in what Robert Abzug aptly calls the sacred drama of antebellum reform, and like Garrison, she could see what that role required, what words demanded, and what action entailed. Yet for all their mutual commitments and obvious differences, one fact superintended all others and warns against the easy comparison. As the picture of Garrison composing his account of the mob suggests, he took moral energy from the most immediate circumstances, from the clash of will and words he courted and to which he so conspicuously contributed. At the risk of simplifying the point, Garrison's world was always a *present* world; he engaged ideas and ideals as they were revealed here and now, and his rhetoric was simply a means to that end. He kept his eye always on the end, and the end seemed not really far distant; thus "immediatism," however vague as an ideology, describes brilliantly the course of Garrison's mind and imagination. All was *now.*

By contrast, Grimké's encounter with and within abolition was mediated by a much more complex and ambivalent sense of the past. This is not to suggest that she was any less an immediatist than Garrison, nor any less responsive to the demands of pressing circumstances or to audiences hungry for instruction, uplift, and entertainment. Nor is it to deny that Garrison was himself subject to formative, indeed quite painful, forces of his own difficult youth. Like Angelina, Garrison came to moral maturity through a troubling process of conviction, repudiation, and radical recommitment; thus while Grimké found herself struggling against the visibility, wealth, and moral capital of her family background, Garrison sought to free himself from the long psychological reach of obscurity and improvidence. The result of such battles is almost always to damage as well as to strengthen, and these two instances were to prove no exception.

I wish to stress, in any case, how heavily the past bore on Grimké, a past neither private nor public but intractably both. For Grimké the past could never be a foreign country, whatever it was and however she sought to distance herself from it. Her Southern origins, her acute awareness of Carolinian culture and its power in shaping self, family, and community, presented to this spiritual exile an inescapable inheritance. How Grimké managed its claims on who she was, and the possibilities such a past created, are therefore questions basic to our understanding of her rhetorical career. In the effort to discover some answers, we shall find Grimké speaking from, through, and to a past at once oppressive and the source of extraordinary moral energy. From it Grimké fed her imagination, and in reckoning with it was able to re-envision a future that did not so much repudiate that past as reconceive its power to ground the conditions of genuine community. Hence this chapter examines the rhetorical work of her *Appeal to the Christian Women of the South,* the chief function of which, I suggest, was to recover from the ruins of her past a new rationale for collective action; to invest her Southern sisters with a moral agency long forgotten but never gone; and in the process to repair and strengthen herself for the battles to come. To this end, I treat briefly the personal and rhetorical contexts by which the *Appeal* motivated and shaped and turn then to a close reading of this most remarkable text.[3]

As for most of its citizens, life for Angelina in Philadelphia was proving a mixed blessing. There were, on the one hand, the usual outbreaks of antiabolitionism and other objects of urban unrest; on the other hand, Angelina could find in the Philadelphia Female Antislavery Society a robust, diverse, and exciting context for her still-developing antislavery convictions. A rich mixture of Hicksite and Orthodox Quakers, African Americans and whites, speakers and programs, the PFASS composed itself, at least during the 1830s, as one of the most compelling reform organizations in American history. The prominent members Angelina could depend on for moral instruction and sometimes friendship ranged from Lucretia Mott to Sarah Douglass to Jane Smith. Circumstances of a more personal nature, however, seem to have created stresses of sufficient force to make necessary an extended trip, first to the yearly meeting in Providence and then to the Shrewsbury, N.J., home of Mary Parker. Thus removed from the pressing expectations of her Philadelphia hosts, Angelina was able to command a certain space for reflection. Here she undertook various writing projects and here she considered the future before her.[4]

Under different circumstances, perhaps, such pastoral distance might have worked to becalm Grimké's still-restless spirit. If anything, however, the stillness of her surroundings seemed only to amplify her unrest and, at best, to clarify its sources. "My spirit is oppressed and heavy laden," Grimké wrote sister Sarah, "and shut up in prison. What am I to do? The only relief I experience is in writing letters and pieces for the peace and anti-slavery causes, and this makes me think that my influence is to reach beyond our own limits." The words are suggestive, and their layered sense of constraint, creation, and will to public action may be read as an abbreviated version of Grimké's rhetorical career generally. That career was prompted in large part by a crisis of confidence, a deep uncertainty about the possibilities of authentic community and therefore of social renewal. We know that in her past Grimké had speculated in bitter moments about such things. A diary entry of 18 July 1829 is especially stark. "I hear much of the strength of natural affections," Angelina noted, "but when I look abroad in the world I see but little of it and am fully convinced that it is not affection but *interest* and *some* sense of duty which binds the members of most families together." Real love, Grimké confided, could not grow "in a soil whose natural product is thorns and briars," could not grow in man "naturally selfish," for "what he loves, he loves from interest."[5]

Dark thoughts, illustrative, perhaps, only of a young person's passing mood. Still, they indicate a mind acutely aware of how fragile was human community and how compromised could be the bonds that sustained intimate and social relations. If the bitterness that marks these lines were to eventually recede, the ambivalence did not; and as this daughter of the Grimké family and of Charleston and of the South herself tore aware those bonds, we might well expect such sentiments to return in some fashion with dramatic intensity. Now, in the coastal quiet of Shrewsbury, Grimké resolved to repair the damage of which she had been both source and victim. "God has shown me what I can do," she announced to her host. "I can write an appeal to Southern women, one which, thus inspired, will touch their hearts, and lead them to use their influence with their husbands and brothers. I will speak to them in such tones that they *must* hear me, and, through me, the voice of justice and humanity."[6]

Angelina at first thought the task might be met with a dozen or so pages. Certainly the letter to Garrison had demonstrated her ability to compress semantic mass within the requirements of rhetorical form. In the course of two weeks, however, the *Appeal* took on substantively greater weight and complexity than she had expected, and by the end of July Grimké had completed the equivalent of thirty-six pages of printed manuscript. Whatever changes were required in route, Grimké had a steady vision of its course to public consciousness. "My work is to be submitted to the American Antislavery Society of New York," she confided to Sarah. "There revised and corrected," the *Appeal* was "to be published by them with my name attached, for I well know my name is worth more than myself and will add weight to it."[7]

Less than one year after her initial encounter with Garrison, Grimké thus undertook a second, equally dramatic but very different, kind of public engagement. In one regard the rhetorical aims and functions of the *Appeal* were simple: "The plan I am pursuing," Grimké explained, "is first to frame Slavery to the contrary to our Declaration, and to answer the objections that our forefathers were mistaken for the Bible sanctions slavery by showing it to be contrary to the great charter of human rights granted to Adam." The result was less modest than such words imply. In Lerner's judgment, the *Appeal* was to prove unique for its source and audience, and "remarkable also for its simple and direct tone, the absence of fashionable rhetoric and its bold logic which in the name of righteousness advises even lawbreaking with Garrisonean unconcern." Susan Zaeske, who has accorded to the text its most comprehensive and systematic treatment, declares its message to be "nothing short of radical—American women should play an active role in influencing the outcome of the national debate on slavery." Grimké's style—spare but highly allusive, at once pointed but comprehensive—continues to capture the interest of modern observers and allows us to hear the distinctive tones of an emerging public voice. We can detect that voice most clearly as it resonates between private conviction and public appeal, as it speaks to the universal in unmistakably personal ways. For Abzug and others, Grimké's *Appeal*, "demonstrated how quickly Angelina had integrated reform's cosmic vision with her piety as she made the biblical case against slavery, refuted proslavery arguments drawn from the Bible, and argued for invoking higher Christian law against laws establishing and protecting slavery."[8]

At a very basic level of description, we can say that the *Appeal* advances the proposition that slavery is not, was not, and never could be warranted. In pursuit of this conclusion, Grimké structured her case into three parts: the first posed a set of seven propositions refuting popular views on the historical and scriptural bases of the institution; the second proposed that the Christian women of the South were well suited to help effect the end of slavery; and the final phase defended the means, motives, and ends of northern antislavery societies. This is, of course, a mere glimpse at the structure of the *Appeal,* but it suggests something of the text's presentation; the *Appeal* is notably systematic, untouched, as Lerner observed, by the excesses thought to plague public controversy. That Grimké was well aware of this poise is made evident in the text itself and is made to serve its own rhetorical ends. "Be not afraid then to read my appeal," she asked her reader, "it is *not* written in the heat of passion or prejudice, but in the solemn calmness which is the result of conviction and duty."[9]

The circumstances of Grimké's world, her life, and the text itself argue against such minimal description, however. The *Appeal* was, in fact, a complex performance, a field of rhetorical action stressed at both ends by the competing forces of opportunity and constraint, and our understanding of that performance can only be enriched by accounting for the complexity. The interpretation offered here seeks to extend upon available readings by asking persistently after the rhetorical work embedded in the text. We know that the *Appeal* was prompted by, designed for, and offered to the public: but which public? To what end? And how does this work proceed within the fairly disciplined economy of the public letter?

All of these questions in one sense or another help us get at what I take to be the fundamental action of the *Appeal*. The public letter, moreover, provided Grimké the opportunity to set on display a way of reading that countered any claims against women's capacity for reasoned deliberation. It is conspicuously well reasoned, empirically grounded in textual specifics, and absent any appeals that might be stigmatized as "typically" feminine. It is, in short, a model of rhetorical hermeneutics, in its very execution proof that women generally and her audience specifically were fully up to the task of debating significant issues "rationally" and to effect. It is about the very possibility of community, about its formation, deformation, and reformation in a world as uncertain about the future as it was damaged by the past. At the very root of that possibility, the source of its expression and moral authority, was the identity of the *Appeal*'s author, as yet unknown, still shaken by private doubts, still laboring to grasp what she had done to her family, her name, her past. Much work lay ahead.

I take as a starting point the question of to whom this *Appeal* was addressed. On reflection it does not take long to realize that, however obvious the answer might be in one respect—the Christian women of the South—in another respect that answer is wholly unsatisfactory. Excepting slaves themselves, it would be difficult indeed to find a class of Americans less empowered to act on Grimké's solicitations; excepting the slave masters, it would be difficult to find a class less inclined to so act. The anomaly can be resolved quickly, perhaps, by simply acknowledging, with Lerner, that Grimké "was already beyond practical considerations. Had not God shown her the way?" My own view is that although God may have been showing Angelina the way, much remained of a practical—hence rhetorical—nature to be done. The question of audience, with all its implications about agency and social action, needs accordingly to be shifted to a more general set of questions about exemplarity, the tenuous relationship that always obtains between self and community, and the role of rhetoric in constructing those relationships. The meaning, force, and function of the *Appeal* may thus be stated along these lines: it simultaneously asserts the identity of its author even as it exemplifies a rationale for public action; its *appeal* is not to those structures of authority that would isolate author and reader by region, denomination, or habit, but to a community at once historical, enduring, and inescapable: sisterhood. Now, the public encounter invoked by the *Appeal* takes on greater significance for the fact that this was a community that Grimké had knowingly violated. She had therefore the double challenge of recouping and repairing that community— even as she announced the principles obliging her to leave it in the first place.[10]

The key to understanding this process, I suggest, may be found by doubling the sense of community at work in the *Appeal*. At least two conceptions seem to drive the text to its public reception. One such conception can be termed "real community," by which I mean to designate the historical constraints inherited by Grimké and against which she acted—including the lived realities of family, class, religion, region, and gender. Something like this sense of community clearly shapes Grimké's discourse generally and imprints the *Appeal* specifically. Yet, there is also apparent in the text another sense of community, "imagined," as it were, from the very terms established by its competing other. By imagined community I mean to indicate Grimké's insistence that out of her past could be found a way of acting and authorizing, could be found opportunities and rewards sufficient to reconstitute community under optimal conditions. The *Appeal* does not therefore advocate turning away from a shared and powerful history; it argues instead for a researching of that history, there to find an alternative and authentic warrant for social change. The real and the imagined thus could be made to stand not in contrast, but as in a dialectical relationship, the resolution of which constitutes the rhetorical achievement of the *Appeal*.[11]

The *Appeal* was a singular contribution to the rhetorical culture of the 1830s. In both form and content, however, readers would have recognized it as a familiar mode of public expression. A hybrid of public letter, petition, declaration, and political broadside, the text partook of popular rhetorical conventions; they were, not incidentally, resources to which those otherwise disadvantaged could avail themselves. By condition of servitude or voluntary displacement, the aggrieved might through such means receive a hearing—if not on the Senate floor then from more distant realms of the public domain. Within the more immediate environs of northern abolitionism, Grimké's *Appeal* may readily be identified among a small but important set of "appeals." It is not clear whether Grimké took direct inspiration from these works, and it is not especially important that such a case be made here. Certainly she would have been familiar at least with Elizabeth Heyrick's *Immediate, Not Gradual Emancipation* (1826); David Walker's *Appeal in Four Articles* (1829); L. Maria Child's *Appeal on Behalf of that Class of American Called Africans* (1833);and the collected essays of Elizabeth Margaret Chandler, published by Benjamin Lundy in Philadelphia in the summer of 1836. Each of these works is different in important ways, but collectively they allow us to bring the text before us into greater focus.[12]

Of the abolitionist appeals that most captured the reform imagination of the decade, surely Walker's was among the most explosive. A free black from Massachusetts who was to die mysteriously in 1830, Walker wrote directly to those whom he believed willing and able to effect massive social change. "Men of colour, who are also of sense," Walker announced, "for you particularly is my appeal designed. Our more ignorant brethren are not able to penetrate its value. I call upon you therefore to cast your eyes upon the wretchedness of your brethren and to do your utmost to enlighten them—go to work and enlighten your brethren!" The presumption of human agency driving Walker's *Appeal* was clear, present, and dangerous; for white critics of slavery as well as for southern apologists, its rhetoric was an unmistakable incitement to violence. Lundy for this reason could "do no less than set the broadest seal of condemnation on it," and even Garrison at this early stage thought it an unfortunate blend of independence and "injudiciousness."[13]

Walker's *Appeal* was never anything except notorious, and so we need not generalize beyond the shared resentment and rage to which he gave voice. In its appeal to the dominant cultural codes of the time—to Scripture and to the founding texts of the republic—the *Appeal* is nevertheless consistent with what David McInerney calls the "political gospel of abolition." Walker's tract can serve both as a precedent and as a contrast to Grimké's own work: his prose is more angry, the implications more violent, but Walker, too, would throw that tradition back into the teeth of those who would utter its pieties without extending its province to all Americans.[14]

Lydia Maria Child's *Appeal* bestowed upon its author notoriety of another kind. Within the confines of Boston, at least, it would be difficult to find two abolitionists more different in background, artistic temperament, and social place. Before its publication three years after Walker's poisoning, Child could look forward to an already well established career as an author of children's literature, domestic advice, and fiction. The *Appeal* put an end to that particular path, but it did offer up to the public a virtually unprecedented investigation of its subject. Indeed, Carolyn Karcher notes, "so comprehensive was its scope that no other antislavery writer ever attempted to duplicate" its achievement. "Even today," Karcher concludes, "the book's wide-ranging scholarship, consummate rhetoric, and signal prescience command attention." Composed of eight chapters and running to more than two hundred pages, the *Appeal* is an elaborate and systematic study of the historical, economic, political, institutional, intellectual, and moral dimensions of the slave system.[15]

As a public tract with specific rhetorical purposes, the *Appeal* is especially interesting as a statement on the nature of collective action. The very comprehensiveness to which Karcher alludes, the sheer accretion of barbarities and of complicities exposed, may seem to dampen the hopes of even the most optimistic reader. Child was insistent, however, that given even these realities, given even the unclear way from commitment to action, the wellsprings of reform could be located in public sentiment. "Perhaps it may seem of little use for individuals to maintain any particular *principle*," Child explained, " while they do not attempt to prescribe the ways and means by which it can be carried into operation." Still, Child argued, "the voice of the public is mighty, either for good or for evil; and that far-sounding echo is composed of single voices."[16]

Child's *Appeal* and that of Walker's differ dramatically in scope, tone, and aim. Both, however, were written under the presumption that citizens could be called into action, that silence ought not to be read as a sign of incapacity, and that through such appeals might be unleashed enormous moral forces now laying dormant in the body politic. If Walker was willing to see these forces expressed in violent upheaval, Child was still sanguine enough to envision the end of slavery through moral suasion. In the early years of the decade that was not a naive conviction, but it did demand a rapid transformation from latent energy to kinetic action. Child's tract sought to effect this change by tapping into apparently hidden sources of community. "The union of individual influences produces a vast amount of moral force," Child reasoned, "which is not the less powerful because it is unperceived. A mere change in the *direction* of our efforts, without any increased exertion, would in the course of a few years, produce an entire revolution of public feeling."[17]

Whether through insurrection or suasion, the work of abolition was to be carried out through communities called into being for that purpose. But while both Walker and Child presumed that possibility and addressed their tracts to appropriately broad audiences, neither constructed particularly intimate relationships with their readers. Cast rather to a very general sense of the public, they sought to reach the broadest possible spectrum of readership. By contrast, Grimké's *Appeal* works in the opposite direction; directing her argument ostensibly to the "Christian women of the South," she designated her audience by region, gender, and religion—even as she confronted the historical limitations posed by such categories. Although this remains one of Grimké's distinctions, she was not entirely alone. In Elizabeth Margaret Chandler could be found a writer much closer to Grimké's style and sensibilities than either Walker or Child. Like Grimké, Chandler saw very early on that women had a special and complicated role to play in the antislavery cause, and like Grimké she sought to address them in terms specified by gender, region, and religion.

Chandler remains an unaccountably obscure figure. That is unfortunate, for in Chandler we have an important voice among Quaker abolitionists and a highly regarded contributor to Lundy's *Genius of Universal Emancipation*. In her role as editor of the paper's "Ladies' Repository," Chandler pushed for immediate abolition, promoted the free-produce movement, and beckoned women specifically to organize on behalf of these causes. Lundy, an enthusiastic supporter of Chandler throughout her brief public life, thought her to be "the first American female author that ever made the subject the principle theme of her active exertions." As for the character of Chandler's writings, Lundy effusively concluded that "It is not enough to say, that her productions were chaste, eloquent, and classical." In addition, he wrote, Chandler's "language was appropriate, her reasoning clear, her deductions logical, and her conclusions impressive and convincing. Her appeals were tender, persuasive, and heart-reaching; while the strength and cogency of her arguments rendered them incontrovertible."[18]

Young, female, orphaned, a birthright Quaker with strong convictions and a ready command of the language, Chandler was able to bring to her rhetorical craft a perspective that others, especially women, found compelling. From 1826 until her death in 1834 at age twenty-seven, Chandler published a series of poems, essays, and epistles on slavery; among these her "Letters on Slavery" were directed specifically "to the Ladies of Baltimore." In general the letters are consistent with arguments advanced in numerous other short pieces in her column—the baleful effects of slavery on master and slave alike; the need to boycott plantation goods; the call of Scripture and duty to free the slave. Chandler made no claim on the novelty of these arguments, indeed frankly acknowledged their wide currency. She was rather concerned with bringing author, reader, and subject into a certain proximity, as if through such intimacy questions might be asked with a candor not otherwise possible. There is in any case a sense of direct address not evident in Walker or Child, a quality particularly clear throughout the "Letters on Slavery." "Can the female sex," asked Chandler, "who form so large a part of her [America's] population, be free from the pollution of this sin? Had they all used properly their influence as Christian women, in opposition to this crime, would it till this day have darkened the volumes of our country's history? We have no hesitation," Chandler answered, "in saying that they have yet a duty to perform for the advancement of abolition."[19]

As the above lines suggest, such direct address to slave-state women entailed no concession on the author's part: slavery's evil she thought absolute and not to be accommodated for rhetorical gain. Hence, like Grimké, Chandler had to negotiate certain dilemmas, wherein she was required to ask those complicitous in a system of oppression to voluntarily act to overthrow that very system. The key for Chandler was to remind her readers of their capacity for comprehending the suffering of others—a faculty she referred to as "mental metempsychosis"—and so appeal to those "who look with anxiety and regret on the broad cloud that flings its deep shadow over their country—and reflect with pain and humiliation on the depredation which she continues to heap upon so many of her children."[20]

Together, Chandler's essays demonstrate her conviction that women had a distinctive ability and opportunity to comprehend the full enormity of the slave system. At the same time, she recognized that such a capacity required for its realization an instrument, a means to act itself out in the divine drama of abolitionism. Here, then, is the second key, and it is one that Grimké would use with great facility in her own rhetorical work. The instrument was collective action: "Let an association be formed among you," Chandler wrote, "having for its object the support of the free system and the diffusion of your principles. Union will give you activity and strength—it will enable you to devise and carry into effect plans, which you would find it otherwise impossible to execute; and while it imparts authority to the sentiments you inculcate, will give a wider extent to the sphere of your usefulness."[21]

Grimké's *Appeal* may be seen as an elaboration upon many of the themes, arguments, and images embedded in the foregoing works. Together, Walker, Child, and Chandler provided a set of rhetorical antecedents which might at least be said to inform its general design and to suggest certain points of comparison and contrast. Like Walker, Grimké found in Scripture and the Declaration of Independence an unavoidable logic with which to combat the proslavery host; like Child, Grimké was confident in the existence and possibilities of public opinion, even as that opinion had first to be awakened and then given leadership; and like Chandler, Grimké looked to women specifically to provide that leadership through organized advocacy. Each represented different positions and voiced diverse approaches to the abolition of slavery, but together they testified to a faith in collective action as a means to that end. This faith ultimately underscored the aims and achievement of Grimké's *Appeal*: in it, she sought to recuperate the possibilities of community from a past at once hostile to and productive of that possibility.

The challenge before Grimké was as great as the stakes were high: to create a future from a damaging past; to rebuild a community she had herself violated; to address those not yet ready to hear. The first step had already been taken in Angelina's decision to make her *Appeal* a public one. In this way, she was able to open up at least the possibility of change by placing ideas, people, and events into broader contexts of meaning, to exhibit the need for community and the very process through which it might come about. Hence the inaugural lines from the book of Esther do not so much announce the subject of the *Appeal* as they capture the text's interplay of constraint and freedom: "And Esther bade them return Mordecai this answer:—and so will I go unto the King, which is not according to law, and *if I perish, I perish*." To thus begin with Esther's words is to begin by announcing the triumph of duty over danger, of will over authority, of speech, finally, over silence itself.[22]

The risk inherent in encounters such as that staged by the *Appeal* is the risk of publicity itself. This risk Grimké sought to justify and celebrate; her willingness to engage in such encounters, indeed the confidence that such engagements would be worth it all, was then to be made exemplary to her readers. The task therefore was to establish in these early pages evidence of strong if unseen attachments: "It is because I feel a deep and tender interest in your present and eternal welfare," Grimké began, "that I am willing thus publicly to address you." Within this dynamic of identity and difference, of bonds that unite and those that oppress, Grimké generated the basic terms structuring the author-reader relationship. "Some of you have loved me as a relative, and some have felt bound to me in Christian sympathy, and Gospel friendship," Grimké acknowledged, "and even when compelled by a strong sense of duty, to break those outward bonds of union which bound us together as members of the same community, and members of the same religious denomination, you were generous enough to give me credit, for sincerity as a Christian, though you believed I had been most strongly deceived."

The ties of kinship and faith could be presumed strong enough to sustain at least a hearing, and if a degree of respect might be exchanged in the process, then that, too, was proof of what a shared past made possible. These terms of endearment served the rhetorical purpose of recovering intimacies once thought lost; they could not, however, remain limited to the author's immediate circle and still advance the aims of the *Appeal* in general. The more expansive conception of community required that she move beyond such intimacies, and Grimké was well aware that "there are other Christian women scattered over the Southern States, a very large number of whom have never seen me, and never heard my name, and who feel *no* interest whatever in *me*."

The rhetorical problem was acute. Unlike Child, for example, Grimké could not afford to cast her *Appeal* to a wide and vaguely defined "public"; she needed under the circumstances to literally summon relationships known to be possible but not yet called into being as an audience. Whatever hope she professed must then lay in neither gender nor faith alone, but in the power generated through both. "Sisters in Christ I feel an interest in you, and often has the secret prayer risen on your behalf, Lord 'open thou their eyes that they may see wondrous things out of thy Law.' It is then, because I *do feel* and *do pray* for you, that I thus address you upon a subject about which of all others, perhaps you would rather not hear anything."

To the degree that Grimké's opening appeals are effective, they help to mitigate what is perhaps the greatest risk inherent to the rhetorical encounter: the failure to command a hearing. If Grimké was to be successful in calling forth her desired audience, it would be because she was able to make good on certain implicit promises. Having asked her readers to attend her words and act upon her counsel, Grimké now had to show herself as acting from conviction and good will. It was this mutually arrived at exchange of commitments that would make communication possible; indeed, the community to which Grimké aspired presumed this rhetorical feat. "It is true," Grimké assured her reader, "I am going to tell you unwelcome truths, but I meant to speak those *truths in love*, and remember Solomon says, 'faithful are the wounds of a friend.' I do not believe the time has yet come when *Christian women* 'will not endure sound doctrine,' even on the subject of slavery, if it is spoken to them in tenderness and love, therefore I now address *you.*"

These, then, are the terms through which Grimké would undertake her *Appeal*: "interest"; friendship"; "duty"; "love." They are more than logical premises: they act rhetorically by cementing a tentative pact between reader and author, by steadying, if only for a moment, a relationship already damaged by time and transgression. The final paragraph of the introduction builds on this pact even as it initiates the argument proper; even at this early point it is clear that Grimké was interested in departures, not returns, a restoration of sentiment from which new community could be imagined. That community, that imagining, could only come about if her readers were willing to countenance a truth greater than themselves.

There were those, Grimké knew, who would resist such truths by building "a wall of adamant around the Southern States whose top might reach unto heaven, in order to shut out the light which is bounding from mountain to mountain and from the hills to the plains and valleys beneath, through the vast extent of our Northern States." The light of abolition, Grimké warned, would surely overwhelm these modern "builders of Babel"—this, "Because moral like natural light, is so extremely subtle in its nature as to overleap all human barriers, and laugh at the puny efforts of man to control it." Such imagery would become a prominent feature of Grimké's rhetorical expression; through it, she helped create an invincible logic that must find its ends in social revolution and the obliteration of evil. God's truth sheds its light, and discriminates authentic from false community and hence righteous from specious speech. In this case, the battle of words over slavery, "All the excuses and palliation of this system must inevitably be swept away . . . by the irresistible torrent of a rectified public opinion." Grimké's trust in public opinion recalled Child's, who three years earlier had written that "In a community so enlightened as our own, [prejudices] must gradually melt away under the influence of public discussion." With Walker and Child, Grimké saw in the republican inheritance a structure of commitments and a cultural logic that could effect God's will on earth. Inasmuch as the South shared in that order, felt itself entailed by that logic, it was thus obliged to assent to the principles here being given voice. "[If] it is a self-evident truth," she wrote, "that *all* men, every where and of every color are born equal, and have an *inalienable right to liberty*, then it is equally true that *no* man can be born a slave, and no man can ever *rightfully* be reduced to *involuntary* bondage and held as a slave, however fair may be the claim of his master or mistress through will and title-deeds."[23]

As important tactically and ideologically as was the republican principle, Grimké's appeal to it represents a relatively brief phase of the text. Given her audience, argument, and identity, she had available to her a cultural vocabulary of massive symbolic weight; and if in the Declaration of Independence she found textual resources of real power, how much more the Bible might offer a means to subvert the slaveholders' claim to moral authority. These secular and scriptural traditions did not in any sense compete as rationales for public action: in the words of Daniel McInerney, the republican code, "animated religious zeal, channeled the energy of their beliefs, and identified a transcendent imperative to complete secular obligations." In Grimké's case, nevertheless, we might need to reverse the current to better see how Scripture animated secular precepts.[24]

Roughly one-third of the *Appeal* is devoted to a series of arguments aligning the claims of Scripture and slavery. Angelina's case takes the form of seven propositions, each one of which refutes standard defenses of the system: Slavery is contrary to the Declaration of Independence and to the Adamic charter; "that the fact of slavery having been the subject of prophesy, furnishes no excuse whatever to slave holders; that slavery did not exist under the patriarchical dispensationor the Jewish dispensation; that "slavery in America reduces a man to a thing, a 'chattel personal' robs him of all rights as a human being, fetters both his mind and body, and protects the master in the most unnatural and unreasonable power, whilst it throws out the protection of the law"; and finally, Grimké argued, "slavery is contrary to the example and precepts of our holy and merciful Redeemer, and of his Apostles."

With each, Grimké was able to counter with brief but pointed exegeses of Scripture or historical event, the Bible being, in her words, "my ultimate appeal in all matters of faith and practice, and it is to this text that I am anxious to bring the subject before us." The tone throughout is authoritative, the method systematic and textually evident. The effect sought through such rhetorical means is equally explicit, for the *Appeal* is a staged critique of scriptural (mis)appropriation. Thus Grimké's own performance works by deconstructing the South's unwarranted deployment of Scriptures; by preserving the primal authority of that code, moreover, she was able to retain the conditions of prior community— a sisterhood of faith to which she could appeal in the second and final stages of the text.

The rigor, efficiency, and command of detail marking these refutations remind us that Grimké was already well prepared for the arts of public debate. Certainly she seems to have developed a sophisticated assemblage of arguments well before the trip to New York and ostensible tutelage to Weld. In addition to her own research and reflections, Grimké could look to a number of other abolitionist assaults on the proslavery stance, including those which would go point for point on questions of biblical authority. Amos Phelps's *Lectures on Slavery* (1835), Lury Sunderland's *Testimony of God Against Slavery* (1835), and Francis Wayland's

Elements of Moral Authority (1835), among other such treatises, offered some-times elaborate and always detailed and spirited arguments on behalf of the Bible as an antislavery text. Grimké's own brief is clearly recognizable within this tra-dition, and indeed she borrowed directly from Child's *Appeal* to better describe the realities of the slave system.[25]

The rhetorical force of the *Appeal,* however, resides neither in its novelty nor in its shared propositions. It depends, rather, on the author's ability to foreground her argument as an act of conspicuous interpretation: here Grimké critically engaged a set of cultural commonplaces, disputed them in a stylized clash of arguments, and confidently proclaimed the ultimate victory of truth over error. This phase of the *Appeal* thus serves not only to rehearse what would soon become a set of stock arguments against biblically sanctioned slavery; in the very rehearsal Grimké made public the work of female abolitionism and so made dra-matic by example the principles embodied in the text.

If there was little new in Grimké's arguments or surprising about their scrip-tural warrants, there were unmistakable signs that she saw in them a means to advance a critique of slavery beyond its usual terms. In the aggregate these refu-tations take on a weight of their own and the sum becomes greater than the mass of its accumulated parts. Embedded within the many citations and quotes, his-torical examples and logical entailments, we find a persistent concern for the pos-sibilities of enlightened and collective agency. Put another way, the work of this argument is designed to free its reader from a debased tradition, a counter-rhetoric of scriptural justification, and, having done so, to restore the reader within an exalted and empowering discourse of human freedom. Far more than an exercise in scriptural exegesis, then, Grimké's refutation locates the reader within two contested discourses. That location cannot be made placid, for to be in it is to be confronted with a realization and therefore a choice. The effect is to heat that place beyond tolerance, to compel rightful choice by appealing simulta-neously to the reason and emotions. It was within this crucible that Grimké intro-duced the vexed relationship between slavery and sex. Nowhere else was Grimké's own voice as present as when she inserted the matter into a given interpretation. In addressing the Hebrew legacy, for example, she explained that daughters were never sold into bondage: "But do the fathers of this Christian land often sell their daughters? My heart beats, and my hand trembles, as I write the awful affirma-tive, Yes! The fathers of this Christian land often sell their daughters, not as Jewish parents did . . . but to be the abject slaves of petty tyrants and irresponsible mas-ters. Is it not so, my friends?"

By obliging her readers to reckon with such questions, Grimké kept her case grounded in the lived realities of the system. This gendering of the institution accordingly operated as a force against the abstract pull of religion and history, and writes the "Christian women of the south" into a logic heretofore denied. "I appeal to you, my friends, as mothers; Are you willing to enslave your children? You start back with horror and indignation at such a question. But why, if slavery is no wrong to those upon whom it is imposed? . . . Why not place your children in the way of being supported without your having the trouble to provide for them, or they for themselves?"[26]

The question hints pointedly at what is to follow. Seven propositions posed, seven arguments countered, the movement of the text comes momentarily to rest. Working together to systematically rebut the proslavery argument, individually the propositions keep open the question not only of what can be done but more specifically by whom. The cumulative effect was to sharpen Grimké's focus on women—southern Christian women—as subject to the *Appeal*'s terms, to unburden these citizens from the weight of false community and the past it represents. In this, the destructive phase of the text, the author refused to her audience its own appeal to history, religion, gender, or class, the consequence of which was to give guilt no place to hide—not even in faith itself. "For unto whomsoever much is given," Grimké concluded, "of him shall much be required; and to whom men have committed much, of him they will ask the more. Oh! Then that the Christian women of the south would ponder these things in their hearts, and awake to the vast responsibilities which rest upon them at this important crisis."

The *Appeal* thus far suggests that Grimké understood change—radical, sweeping change—to require first the dismantling of one language and its replacement with another. The odds of success in any immediate sense were not, to say the least, great. As Weld recalled years later, Grimké's tract was greeted in Charleston with something less than enthusiasm: copies of the *Appeal* were seized and officials warned against the author's return to the city at the risk of her personal freedom. Yet the drama enacted in and through the text reduced these problems to elements of the script itself; indeed, far from checking its success or dispiriting the author's voice, such material consequences were anticipated and written into the general rationale of abolitionism. Grimké here resisted regionalizing guilt or differentiating responsibility along a North-South axis. All but the slave were in some way complicitous in the system: all therefore shared in the duty to effect its overthrow.

The *Appeal* has so far shown Grimké to have great faith in the capacity of public opinion to recognize this claim; it has illustrated as well the assumption that certain classes of Americans—ostensibly among the most invested in the system—will act upon that recognition. This faith—it could be no more—is borne out in the second major phase of the *Appeal*. Directed specifically to her southern sisters, the argument can claim some novelty, if not in its propositions then surely in the audience being summoned on their behalf. Of more significance here is

Grimké's appreciation for the historical and cultural distinctiveness of that audience, even as she worked to free it from the weight imposed by such bonds. The key to the slaves' freedom, in other words, was to be the emancipation of women themselves, by themselves. The rhetoric of the *Appeal* was, in effect, designed to turn that key and to find in the past an alternative language and a more powerful argument for moral action. This much, at least, represents the constructive phase of the *Appeal*, to which we now turn.[27]

What are the possibilities for action—especially action against social order—in a world where authority for such action is inconceivable? In one way or another Grimké had been struggling with this question since early childhood; having led her out of the South, this struggle now seemed to lead her back, symbolically at least, to confront those left behind with the answer. Whatever the vicissitudes of her own journey, Grimké had come to realize fully that the absence of authority—at least publicly recognized and state-sponsored authority—could not itself excuse moral quiescence. Given what surely must have seemed to many the outrageous stance and ends of the *Appeal*, the point may serve as a reminder that its argument is as much about the conditions of reform as it is about specific proposals. Near its heart is the insistence that ultimately there can be no such excuse, that the state can impose no lasting silence upon its citizens. In this sense the *Appeal* is actually a call to speech as much as to action—indeed, it collapses the false distinction between speaking and doing and refashions from it both means and end to the work of reform.

To answer the question, then, is to see and employ resources of power not beholden to the authority of the state. These are the resources of rhetoric, mined outside the surveillance of the laws, removed from the province of legislative politics; they are accordingly the weapons of those written out of such politics who nonetheless must share in their consequences. Grimké's didactic purpose was thus to specify and make compelling a range of discursive opportunities available to her audience. The *Appeal* itself was to be evidence at once of such resources and the power to which they might be put.

It was easy enough for Grimké to anticipate the questions that would follow: "why appeal to women on this subject? We do not make the laws which perpetuate slavery. No legislative power is vested in us; we can do nothing to overthrow the system, even if we wished to." Northern readers would not have been surprised by Grimké's response, and many would have found it as simplistic, perhaps, as the questions here contrived. The larger implication, however, is that we have at this moment in the *Appeal* an important extension on the antislavery position. The argument is directed to a specific class of southern women, a class whose power, however circumscribed by the realities of political culture, could nevertheless be retrieved and exercised from within that condition. "I know you do not make the law," Grimké answered, "but I also know that you are the wives and mothers, the sisters and daughters of those who do; and if you really suppose you can do nothing to overthrow slavery, you are greatly mistaken." At least four such opportunities could be seized upon: reading, prayer, persuasion, and action. Together, they represented a kind of counterpolitics through which abolition might be secured; that this politics was per force domestic, noncoercive, and mediated largely through intimacies of speech was not, in Grimké's eyes at least, a shortcoming as much as a way of redefining the terms of shared moral commitment. "It is through the tongue, the pen, and the press," Grimké insisted, "that truth is principally propagated. Speak then to your relatives, your friends, your acquaintances on the subject of slavery; be not afraid if you are conscientiously convinced it is sinful, to say so openly, but calmly, and to let your sentiments be known."

If Grimké knew that such a politics was possible, however, she knew better than most that it was also uncertain and dangerous. She had only to reflect on Garrison's recent troubles to see what might befall those who would practice even a less subversive—because more distant—form of insurgency. The *Appeal* is mindful of what it asks, and Grimké acknowledged to her readers that the reconstituted community she sought would come at a cost; that risk was both necessary and inevitable. In the familiar constellation of duty, suffering, and redemption, however, Grimké sought to make that risk explicable, indeed, to underwrite a new world through its terms. "Consequences," she assured the reader, "belong no more to you than they did to these apostles. Duty is ours and events are God's. If you think slavery is sinful, all you have to do is set your slaves at liberty, do all you can to protect them, and in humble faith and fervent prayer, commend them to your common Father."

These are precisely the kind of words that helped make antislavery in the South the dangerous business it was, and it would not be unreasonable to criticize Grimké for appearing less than sensitive to that fact. But this is a radical text: in it Grimké was seeking the wholesale removal of one moral order for another, and to that end she had to invoke a language unrestricted by the cultural and economic logic of the current system. Furthermore, if the quality of cunning could ever be ascribed to Grimké's argument, it resided in her ability to cement that language, radical as it is, within the shared legacies of religion and politics. "If a law command me to sin I will break it," she explained, "if it calls me to suffer, I will let it take its course unresistingly. The doctrine of blind obedience and unqualified submission to any human power, whether civil or ecclesiastical, is the doctrine of despotism, and ought to have no place among Republicans and Christians."

The politics being modeled here and to which Grimké would have her audience aspire is as complex as it is demanding. It is grounded domestically but realized publicly; privileges in its moral geography neither North nor South; and seeks radical ends through culturally recognized vocabularies. By thus rejecting the false simplicity imposed by church and state, Grimké gave to her argument its broadest possible purview, even as she continued to specify it with reference to the Christian women of the South. This specificity, so important to the general economy of the *Appeal*, was further achieved not only by movement from premise to conclusion but by invoking a lineage of powerful women, exemplars of individual courage who stand at once as examples and as guides for work ahead. In this, too, Grimké was working within a tradition dating to Margaret Fell's *Womens Speaking* (1666), the first in a distinguished tradition of Quaker testimonials on the subject. This very familiarity, indeed, strengthened Grimké's pointed reminder: "Have not women stood up in all the dignity and strength of moral courage to be the leaders of the people, and to bear a faithful testimony for the truth whenever the providence of God has called them to do so?" To the objection that as women southern Christians were not up to the trials of persecution, then, Grimké asked: "Are there no women in that noble army of martyrs who are now singing the song of Moses and the Lamb?"[28]

Grimké's account of "that noble army of martyrs" represents the most compressed and rhetorically dramatic phase of the *Appeal*. The names were certainly familiar—Miriam, Deborah, Jael, and Esther; Elizabeth, Anna, and Mary Magdalen; more recently Elizabeth Heyrick and Maria Chapman—and the story of faith, suffering, and redemption in which they are embedded was readily identifiable within narratives across cultures. But more than the often-told martyrology, Grimké's narrative may be seen as reconstructing community across time as well, to make available a different and more exalted tradition into which the audience might write itself. Hence the cadence of her prose, the persistent "who?"— "woman!" refrain, the graphic examples of courage and violence, give to that possibility the status of a moral imperative.

This was not to say, of course, that the terms of entry into such community might easily be met; Grimké was alive to the authentic and pressing distinctions between author and reader, present and future, North and South. This diversity, indeed, forms part of the *Appeal*'s rationale, and there is no evidence in the text of a wish to gloss it over in the hopes of achieving a sudden harmony. As we might expect, rather, Grimké sought to resolve discordance through the mutual exercise of duty, and thus to preserve moral agency even as she insisted upon persuasion and its instrumentalities. The women of the North, Grimké explained, "feel no hostility toward you, no bitterness or wrath; they rather sympathize in your trials and difficulties; but they well know that the first thing to be done to help you, is to pour in the light of truth on your minds, to urge you to reflect on, and pray over the subject." The work of persuasion ultimately was to stop where her audience assumed the duty to act: "you must work out your own deliverance," Grimké stressed, "with fear and trembling, and with the direction and blessing of God, you can do it. Northern women may labor to produce a correct public opinion in the North, but if Southern women sit down in listless indifference and criminal idleness, public opinion cannot be rectified and purified at the South."

If northern appeals could reach only so far into southern consciousness, Grimké's martyrology might nevertheless be seen as serving other rhetorical purposes. It was not, for one, a hagiography, nor was it designed as an epideictic exercise. On this Grimké was insistent: "Have I been seeking to magnify the sufferings, and exalt the character of women, that she 'might have praise of men?' No!" Whatever scriptural and historical power this lineage might possess was designed rather as a call to action, but more specifically it was a call to women, "to arouse you, as the wives and mothers, the daughters and sisters, of the South, to a sense of your duty as women, and as Christian women, on that great subject, which has already shaken our country, from the St. Lawrence and the lakes, to the Gulf of Mexico, and from the Mississippi to the shores of the Atlantic; and will continue mightily to shake it, until the polluted temple of slavery fall and crumble into ruin." Among the martyrs, too, could be found the voices of prophecy, and thus a means to embody in female form a privileged capacity for reading the events of the world. This capacity Grimké addressed recurrently, as if in appealing to it she might remind her audience of powers forgotten. "Perceive you not that dark cloud of vengeance which hangs over our boasting Republic? Saw you not the lightenings of Heaven's wrath. . . . Heard you not the thunders of Divine anger. . . . Can you not, my friends, understand the signs of the time; do you not see the sword of retributive justice hanging over the South?"

Grimké's appeal to the faculties of apprehension is suggestive, but not because it locates some moral organ unique to women. The logic of the text requires no such principle, nor indeed do we find anything in Grimké's writings that indicates much interest in exclusive attributes. What the summons to scriptural and historical women does signify, however, is that she recognized in this shared capacity a basis for authority; that in activating it the author might recall for her audience a rationale for action not subject to the false authority of the state. So much, at least, would be consistent with the terms of the *Appeal* thus far: if the Christian women of the South were to transform their culture, they had first to transform themselves, through themselves. Grimké's rhetoric was justified accordingly as a means to reactivate a shared faculty for moral action. While women shared both guilt for and a duty to end slavery, they just as certainly felt the onus of the system in distinctive ways. It was therefore incumbent, Grimké argued, that women arise "in the majesty of moral power . . . embody themselves in societies, and send petitions up to their different legislatures, entreating their husbands, fathers, brothers, sons, to abolish the institution of slavery; no longer to subject woman to the scourge and the chain, to mental darkness and moral degradation." Grimké's call to action was thus a call to action of a certain type by Americans of a certain class. The rhetorical force of the essay depends now on extending beyond agency to its instruments. This process of specification has already been hinted at with reference to "societies" and petitions; it will eventually require that she defend such agencies as productive of good and not of ruinous discord. Whatever confidence could be accorded these means, they had to presume one belief: ultimately, Grimké proclaimed, "there is something in the heart of man which will bend under moral suasion." This claim, this faith, may be understood as fundamental to the rhetoric of the *Appeal,* and although stated explicitly in the middle of the text, directs its implicit logic throughout. Certainly it helps us grasp what might otherwise seem to be Grimké's unfathomable expectations of her audience. Grimké's Christianity required faith in God *and* in people's capacity to change, to convert, to turn toward. It was, in more ways than one, a religion of the word, whereby transformations were wrought through the effect of language on soul and of soul on language. Thus when Grimké pressed her audience to see that the "women of the South can overthrow this horrible system of oppression and cruelty, licentiousness and wrong," when she assured them that "such appeals to the legislatures would be irresistible," when she said of man that "there is a swift witness for truth in his bosom, which will respond to truth when it is uttered with calmness and dignity," then she was, in a sense, merely stating the obvious in unlikely circumstances.

In this logic, the challenge rested not only in the apparently insuperable barriers of class, race, ideology, and tradition, but in the conduct of persuasion itself. Grimké's advice was pointed and telling: "If you could obtain but six signatures to such a petition in only one state, I would say, send up that petition, and be not in the least discouraged by the scoffs and jeers of the heartless, or the resolution of the house to lay it on the table." The higher aim, the greater exercise of duty, was to act together in a spirit free from hardened conventions and false community. Regardless of resistance, Grimké wrote, "It will be a great thing if the subject can be introduced into your legislatures in any way, even by women, and they will be most likely to introduce it there in the best possible manner, as a matter of morals and religion, not of expediency or politics."[29]

The third and final phase of the *Appeal* elaborates upon the prospects of collective action. Largely a defense of northern antislavery work, Grimké's argument is most obviously an advertisement for the American Antislavery Society and its satellite operations. We will have missed its more subtle functions, however, by reading the text at this level alone. The opening series of refutations, we recall, deconstruct biblical arguments in support of slavery; the intended effect is thus to deauthorize one system of reading slavery and supplant it with another. To the degree that it was Grimké conducting the attack, and given the audience to whom it was addressed, it burdened the author-reader relationship in specific ways. The superintending presence of the author gives way in the text's second phase to a revitalized sense of audience, invested by Grimké now with the force of moral agency and the means to act on that realization. The concluding passages may be seen not only as defending northern reform practices, but as reuniting author and reader within possibilities generated from the previous two phases. The formal achievement of the *Appeal*—its reconstruction of opposing forces—may then be viewed as an iconic representation of its substantive ends. Rhetorically this process works by renegotiating the competing claims of identity and community. Our key to understanding it is to read Grimké as she reintroduces herself as an exemplary southern woman, simultaneously asserting herself as a free moral being *and* as a member of a radically conceived sisterhood.

The prophets were clear: the way to the millennium must be cleared of slavery. But how? Not through miraculous power, Grimké explained, but through regenerate moral power. "God designs to confer this holy privilege upon *man;* it is through *his* instrumentality that the great and glorious work of reforming the world is to be done." The northern reform societies were thus human means to divine ends, ideal communities effecting massive social change even as they functioned independently of the machinery of profane politics. "And see you not," Grimké asked, "how the mighty engine of *moral power* is dragging in its rear the Bible and peace societies, anti-slavery and temperance, Sabbath schools, moral reform, and missions?" Could her readers not see that such societies composed "the beautiful tints in that bow of promise which spans the arch of our moral heaven?" The societies, moreover, held out the promise of community even to those seemingly at greatest remove: Grimké's southern readers could always find in their company "the spirits of other Christians, who will mingle their voices with ours, as the morning or evening sacrifice ascends to God." The antislavery societies in particular, Grimké emphasized, offered a means to act together in a spirit of duty, to "take away the stone which has covered up the dead body of our brother, to expose the putrid carcass . . . and having done all it was in our duty to do, to stand by the negro's grave, in humble faith and holy hope, waiting to hear the life-giving command of 'Lazarus, come forth.'"

Grimké, of course, knew that whatever the virtues of northern reform, and however ecstatically she waxed over the antislavery societies in particular, her readers required more. They required a reason to believe, a voice powerful enough to carry over the chasm of North-South suspicions. It was at this point, then, that Grimké reasserted herself as a theme in her own argument, at once a source, subject, and vehicle of conviction. It was a crucial moment. Raising again the question of her authority—moral and rhetorical—Grimké addressed her readers directly: "You know that I am a Southerner; you know that my dearest relatives are now in a slave State. Can you for a moment believe that I would prove so recreant to the feelings of a daughter and a sister, as to join a society which was seeking to overthrow slavery by falsehood, bloodshed, and murder? I appeal to you who have known and loved me in days that are passed, can you believe it?" Her readers ought not to believe it, Grimké suggested, because they ought to see that she was acting on the basis of a distinctive perspective—as a Southern woman who had "lived too long in the midst of slavery, not to know what slavery is." It is this perspective, this capacity for moral insight, that binds author and reader within a community of purpose. Grimké's presence here is exemplary, but to different ends than in the first phase of the *Appeal.* There it was to open an interpretive space; now that space is closed through a kind of mutual acknowledgment of interests and identities. Grimké is not, in this reading, as much a prodigal as a pilgrim, her text a beckoning to those yet unwilling to exercise powers rightfully their own.

It is worth noting at this point that, for an appeal to Christian women, relatively very little space is devoted explicitly to gendered conceptions of community. In part, we may say, this is because the principle is implicit throughout the text; from its title to its conclusion, the reader is summoned by a vision of gendered morality and collective action based on that morality. The argument, moreover, does not require for its ends a more elaborate appeal to women *as women;* Grimké seeks rather to constitute her audience as a specific means to the related end of social transformation. The full import of these lines can be appreciated only when we note their placement in the unfolding economy of the text. Coming as it does after the critique of slavery and before the defense of northern reform societies, Grimké's appeal to women serves to mediate two potentially damaging arguments. The positive image of an enlightened community of women thus mitigates the negative indictment and strengthens the basis from which she can defend abolitionism. The way has been cleared, in short, for Grimké to complete her *Appeal,* confident that however volatile such issues may be, she can nevertheless assume a vested readership.

The final moments of the *Appeal* are thus devoted to the work and prospects of the antislavery societies. These societies in turn represent in real terms instruments of moral agency to which Grimké had alluded earlier. Her characterization of these societies as "wielding a two-edged sword, which even here, cuts through the cords of caste, on the one side, and the bonds of interest on the other," indicate that Grimké had no interest in blunting their claim on her readers' conscience. At the same time, Grimké was at pains to feature such work as manifestly rhetorical, as committed to the possibilities of persuasion in spite of the violence turned against it. Abolitionists "had studied this subject," "had told the story of the negro's wrongs," they unveiled, unmasked, exposed, testify, prayed, preached, wrote, printed, and prophesied. When they spoke, like George Thompson, it was "with the smooth stones of oratory taken from the pure waters of the river of Truth" and with "commanding eloquence." As agents of change, then, the abolitionists were defined by a collective commitment to the power of language—a power not only to transform slavery out of existence, but to transform slaveholders back into genuine community.

In this respect, the abolitionists exemplify in the aggregate what Grimké sought to exemplify individually in the *Appeal:* a reconstitution of community through language and hence to the greater good. The final lines of the *Appeal* reaffirm this essentially rhetorical vision; in effect, they serve to underscore the communicative intentions of the text and to unite author and reader within those intentions.

> Sisters in Christ, I have done. As a Southerner, I have felt it was my duty to address you. I have endeavored to set before you the exceeding sinfulness of slavery, and to point you to the example of those noble women who have raised up in the church to effect great revolutions, and to suffer for the truth's sake. I have appealed to your sympathies as women, to your sense of duty as Christian women. I have attempted to vindicate the Abolitionists, to prove the entire safety of immediate Emancipation, and to plead the cause of the poor and oppressed.

Every act of communication implicitly reaffirms the possibility of communication. On this truism we can see that Grimké's *Appeal* is designed to act on that possibility, indeed to dramatize it by addressing those least likely to grant the point. For those unable or unwilling to grant women the capacity for rational argument, moreover, the *Appeal* is evidence to the contrary: both its composition and its reception would henceforth stand as proof that author and reader were each equipped to dispute in public in a reasoned, responsible, and compelling manner. We thus have reason to believe that the *Appeal* was in fact addressed specifically to the announced audience, and that Grimké's motives were not thereby naive or indirect. We might see the *Appeal* instead as an act of resistance, an orchestrated refusal to let die the conditions of communication. The key to this perspective is to recognize in the *Appeal* its sustained interplay between self and community, past and future, real and imagined, speech and silence, constraint and agency, destruction and reconstruction, author and reader. These are the tensions directing the moral and rhetorical energy of the text; the message is carried neither by eliminating any one term nor by resolving the dialectic into stasis. Rather, the *Appeal* functions by negotiating the cultural and symbolic power of those terms to optimal effect. The result is a revitalized conception of human agency. In this reconception, agency is made possible through, rather than defeated by, the lived realities of gender, region, class, and religion. It is a stunning rhetorical performance: an appeal that works by addressing the least empowered and transforms its audience by investing it with resources of agency it already possessed.

Grimké's completion of the *Appeal* in the late summer of 1836 marked a turning point in her career as public reformer. The letter to Garrison had been written explosively, the hurried and passionate production of one glimpsing for the first time the possibilities of going public. It was brief, declarative, an improvised effort to throw down a gauntlet as much at her own feet as before others. Picking it up as quickly as it had been delivered, Grimké sought now to extend and elaborate upon her vision and to address not just Garrison, not just anyone, but a specific and formidable audience, known to her much more intimately, more poignantly, than any other. And she knew it. "I have just finished my Appeal to Southern Women," Angelina wrote Sarah, noting, too, that it had taken two weeks to compose and wound up longer than she had expected. "How much I wish I could have thee here, if it were only for 3–4 hours that we might read it over together before I send it to Elizur Wright." Without the benefit of Sarah's keen eye, Angelina nevertheless sent her manuscript off to the New York offices of the American Anti-Slavery Society. Wright was ecstatic. Noting, as had Garrison a year previously, that the author was the sister of Thomas Grimké, Wright announced in the pages of the *Quarterly Anti-Slavery Magazine* that "Among Anti-slavery writings there are two classes—one specially adapted to make new converts, the other to strengthen the old. We can hardly exclude Miss Grimké's *Appeal* from either class. It belongs pre-eminently to the former," Wright reasoned, confident that the "converts that will be made by it will be, we have no doubt, not only numerous but thorough-going."[30]

Wright was optimistic, as befits a magazine editor. Well received by northern abolitionists, the *Appeal* met with rather less enthusiasm from Grimké's own Quaker community, and with downright hostility from the good citizens of Charleston, who upon receiving copies heaped them upon the pyre along with other tracts sent by incendiary northern reformers. Yet the *Appeal* had in one sense at least met its ends, for in its inception, composition, and publication, the text had catalyzed Grimké's will to public action. If the letter to Garrison had opened the door to public life, the *Appeal* announced that she had crossed and entered. Whatever else may have resulted as a consequence, it is certain that Grimké herself would never be the same. "I sometimes feel frightened," she wrote Sarah that fall, "to think of how long I was standing idle in the marketplace and I cannot help attributing it in a great measure to the doctrine of nothingness so constantly preached in our society." The *Appeal* gave notice that this "doctrine of nothingness" would not go unchallenged, and that in its place was to be found a commanding rationale for change.[31]

CHAPTER 4

"An Entirely New Contest": Grimké, Beecher, and the Language of Reform

Saturday, 12 August 1837. Groton, Massachusetts. In the midst of her speaking tour and with a twelve-mile ride to Roxboro scheduled for the Sabbath, Angelina relaxed in the way she knew best: by writing letters. In Theodore Weld she could count on a reader at once sympathetic and challenging, and on this day she had much to communicate. After months of travel throughout New England and endless hours spent in speaking and debate, the sisters had accumulated enough notoriety to last a lifetime. For Angelina, the experience was a learning one indeed. However anxious she may have been about such exposure, Grimké could not escape a rare moment of delight in the scenes she had helped create. "My auditors literally sit some times with 'mouths agape and eyes astare,'" she recalled, "so that I cannot help smiling in the midst of 'rhetorical flourishes' to witness their perfect amazement at hearing a woman speak in the churches."[1]

Although it is difficult to picture her with mouth agape and eyes astare, Catharine Beecher was surely among those watching closely the scene before her. As a prominent if not altogether successful advocate for educational reform, and as the eldest daughter of the famed Beecher clan, Catharine had a certain claim on public consciousness. The Grimké tour thus represented to her something more than a curiosity. Beecher herself had undertaken the ardors of an Eastern tour throughout the spring, summer, and fall of 1836 to promote, not antislavery, but various and vague schemes for new schools and schooling. During that tour, as Kathryn Kish Sklar observes, Beecher "had counted Angelina Grimké among her chief competitors for the allegiance of a newly self-conscious generation of American women." In their respective ways, Beecher and Grimké understood the stakes in this competition to be very high, higher, indeed, than the personal fortunes of either; and they knew, too, that the world in which it was to be played out contained in it much that was unprecedented. In the words of Grimké, "we are placed very unexpectedly in a very trying situation, in the forefront of an entirely new contest—a contest for the *rights* of woman as a moral, intelligent and responsible being."[2]

How Beecher and Grimké chose to contest the province of woman can tell us much about the province of rhetoric itself. Their public exchange, represented here by the 1837 publication of Catharine's *An Essay on Slavery and Abolition with Reference to the Duty of American Females* and Angelina's response in *Letters to Catharine E. Beecher,* is an outstanding example of the art as a form of public moral argument. Together, Beecher and Grimké managed to display, defend, and challenge the basic commonplaces through which the reform imagination of antebellum America was exercised.[3]

More specifically, this chapter is designed to illustrate that the encounter between Beecher and Grimké was not only a public argument of an extraordinary kind, but that its extraordinariness is due in no small part to the fact that the contest is itself about public argument. It represents a serious and systematic discussion of the language of reform, the province of public action, and the role of women in the work of the early republic. I suggest further that in the end Grimké triumphs because her arguments are entailed consistently from the very structure of the commitments that brought the two disputants into contact; as a public, political, and rhetorical performance, Grimké's encounter with Beecher enacts the promises of public life even as it pushes open spaces for greater participation in the work of public moral reform.

The exchange put on exhibit, moreover, the image of two women radically different in background and belief, yet similar in their commitment to reform, their command of the symbolic resources of public debate, and their ability to contest a principle without diminishing the humanity of its advocate. There is also, of course, an unmistakable irony in Catharine Beecher, the learned, articulate, tireless campaigner for the reform and advancement of female education, who, seemingly unable to shed the mantle of family and culture, must defend the home as the privileged site of woman's life. In this, Catherine Birney wrote, "she presented the singular anomaly of a strong-minded woman, already successful in taking care of herself, advocating woman's subordination to man, and prescribing for her efforts at self-help limits so narrow that only the few favored as she was could venture within them."[4]

The *Essay* and *Letters* take on their life and meaning as they encounter each other. They perhaps can stand alone, but to read either in the absence of the addressed is to rob them of this identity. In turn, our need to broaden the unit of analysis to embrace the exchange carries with it certain responsibilities. It burdens the interpretation, surely, to account for how the other is anticipated, how echoed and answered, how engaged through the encounter. My reading seeks to provide such an account in two interrelated ways: *first*, through a thematic emphasis on moral relationships and how they are established and rent; here the focus is on appeals to identity and difference, on false and authentic conceptions of community, and on what it means to make commitments to principle and to each other. These themes sound against each other in identifiable and important ways, and thus occupy a good deal of our attention. Still, we know that such themes cannot be extrapolated without damage to context, and that any given account of principle must in some sense be an account of its place and function within the dynamics of the speech act. I hope to prevent such damage by stressing, *second,* the intertextual process through which the interlocutors open up space for debate, and suggest how Beecher and Grimké create for themselves the conditions under which public argument is possible and productive. My focus is accordingly on the formal moves, on the generic appropriation and displays of self-reflexivity that coach the reader in the ways of the rhetorical imagination. I begin by inquiring into the formidable repertoire that Catharine brought to the encounter; then proceed to read the *Essay* closely and with special attention to its thematic and formal sense of engagement; and move finally to the *Letters.*

Beecher and the Protocols of Moral Action

Fanny Wright's days as a public speaker were over, but she had burned an image into Catharine Beecher's mind that smoldered still. The dress, the robust self-confidence, the dreams of a New Harmony, the sheer effrontery that was Fanny Wright galled this preacher's daughter then and it galled her still a decade later. "There she stands," Beecher wrote in 1836, "with her brazen front and brawny arms, attacking the safeguards of all that is venerable and sacred in religion, all that is safe and wise in law, all that is pure and lovely in domestic virtue." Wright's personal qualities were not at issue here, Beecher reasoned; indeed, "Her talents only make her the more conspicuous and offensive, her amiable disposition and sincerity only make her folly and want of common sense the more pitiable, her freedom from private vices, if she is free, only indicates that without delicacy, and without principles, she has so thrown off all feminine attractions, that freedom from temptation is her only, and shameful palladium." In all, Beecher wrote, "I cannot conceive anything in the shape of a woman, more intolerably offensive and disgusting."[5]

At a minimum, Beecher's attack on Wright reminds us of just how volatile was the issue of women speaking in public. As if to underscore and contrast her own standards, Catharine offered up her views in the form of a public letter, for that reason constrained by the protocols of epistolary discourse. The passage quoted helps us further to position Beecher as a public advocate prior to her encounter with Grimké. In it we detect in compressed form the commonplaces of propriety, virtue, the province of reform, and the boundaries thought to naturally separate the public from the private and the ways in which either realm becomes, in our language, gendered in the process. In it, too, can be found a prevailing tone of voice, a characteristic style that polishes disdain to a high gloss. Beecher carried her disgust well, but she carried it everywhere. At her best, she was able to direct such energy into a sustained critique of social issues, including educational policy, women in the professions, woman's sphere, and antislavery. Often, though not always, Beecher integrated these pressing questions into a unified analysis; we may well read her life's work as one very long text, a comprehensive argument that took into its sweep nearly every important contest of the century.[6]

Catharine's voice in the cultural work of her time has never, accordingly, been seriously questioned. What that voice signifies, however, and in precisely what ways she contributed to the status and prospects of women in the nineteenth century remain unsettled questions. Like so many members of that extraordinary family, Catharine seldom enjoyed the pleasure of a stable reputation: even her cherished work for the reform of female education was more planting than harvest. Her historical reputation has been similarly uncertain, as she has, in turn, been celebrated as a patron saint of domestic virtue, resented as a siren of woman's subordination, and, more recently, reincarnated as a major voice in the very complex process through which women claimed a space of their own. If my reading of the Beecher-Grimké encounter is sympathetic to any one of these interpretations, it is with the latter. My aim, however, is not so much to fix Beecher's reputation as it is to let her be heard in ways not yet appreciated. For this, let us turn first to her address to the American Lyceum (1835) and her *Letters on the Difficulties of Religion* (1836). On the basis of these texts, we can learn, in effect, how to read Beecher as Beecher came to read Grimké.

The American Lyceum, so ran its advertisement for Beecher's published address, "particularly desired to enlist female influence in favor of the diffusion of knowledge and the improvement of education." In Catharine the women of New York had not only the support of a Beecher, but an indefatigable fund-raiser, advocate, and visionary. Beecher's speech, though an early effort, bears the unmistakable marks of her public address: it is ambitious, morally strident, absolutely without ambiguity or nuance. This much, at least, was wholly in keeping with Beecher's immediate needs: this was to be no epideictic exercise, but a call to arms, and through the media of oratory and the printed essay Beecher sought to present, in the words of Sklar, "a detailed plan for shaping a national morality."[7]

At its most explicit, Beecher's address is an appeal for the moral and financial reform of American education. Such broad-scale reform was necessary, Beecher reasoned, because the stakes were high and, in the face of immigration, demographic shifts, and cultural change, getting higher. The resulting need for teachers generally and female teachers in particular was thus unprecedented and urgent. This was a refrain that Catharine was to sound for decades to come, and if it was met with varying degrees of enthusiasm, she never altered its basic chords. At another level of analysis we can detect the pattern on which these arguments were based: a persistent regard for the ends, means, and duties of social action. What Beecher had to say about education thus bears directly on our study of Grimké, for in Grimké's response can be heard precisely the same concerns.[8]

Of the need for reform Beecher was adamant and clear. She knew from personal experience that schools—especially female schools in America—lacked the stability of genuine institutions. Catharine understood, in her own way, that this problem was attributable to the asymmetries of power that plagued her society: "The character, the conduct, and the continuance of those who are so extensively to mould the character of the future wives and mothers of this nation," she pointed out, "are almost entirely removed from the control of those most deeply interested." Beecher's diagnosis of the problem was sharply observed, and it entailed a telling set of remedies. These solutions are offered up as a way of rationalizing, of ordering and making fit what was previously incoherent and mismatched. Beecher saw the means to reform as, literally, a process of re-formation; her task was to convince others of what fit properly with what. Hence Catharine's frustration with the arbitrary nature of most female curricula: "Their course of study is varied to suit the notions of parents, or the whims of children, or the convenience of teachers; and if a young lady secures a regular and thorough course of education, it is owing either to the uncommonly good sense and efforts of parents, or to the rare occurrence of finding teachers sufficiently stationary and persevering to effect it."[9]

More than this, however, Beecher told her audience, was required. The way to get education to where it should be was to realize the distinctive obligations and capacities of women. This was the heart of Beecher's analysis: by matching what she took to be a unique quality of her gender to the work of social reform, she willfully ignored whatever was left of the boundary between private and public modes of action. This is not to say that Beecher left one sphere and entered another; it is, rather, to suggest that in this context, at least, such assignations were irrelevant. The rhetorical action of the *Essay* is its reordering, its recognition of the relationship between virtue and action. Here that relationship is conceived in the terms of duty, a principle that governed for Beecher the optimal ordering of self and community. What, she asked, "is the most important and peculiar duty of the female sex? It is the physical, intellectual, and moral education of children. It is the care of the health, and the formation of the character, of the future citizens of this great nation." The proper exercise of duty, then, presumed that talent be given its object: "It is for such varied duties," Beecher continued, "that woman is to be trained. For this her warm sympathies, her lively imagination, her ready invention, her quick perceptions, all need to be cherished and improved."[10]

Beecher's rhetorical strategy here is characteristic, never transgressing conventional categories but always interlocking them into a tightly sealed case for prudential conduct. Virtue could only find its object and fulfillment as it was put in service; and as it was made serviceable, virtue extended its reach from home to classroom to culture itself. The timing, Beecher felt, was perfect for the collective commitment involved in such an undertaking as she voiced: "the taste of the age is altered; and, instead of the fainting, weeping, vapid, pretty play-thing, once the model of female loveliness," Beecher found now that "those qualities of the head and heart that best qualify a woman for her duties, are demanded and admired." These were demanded, she argued, because in America citizens were not ruled by physical violence, and had therefore to be checked in other ways. Virtue was for Beecher, then, a type of power—not power as it was practiced by males in politics and government, but as a restraint on that practice. "For a nation to be virtuous and religious," Catharine declared, "the females of that nation must be deeply imbued with these principles; for just as the wives and mothers sink or rise in the scale of virtue, intelligence, and piety, the husbands and sons will rise or fall."[11]

Beecher's address before the American Lyceum may thus be taken as a double-gestured statement on human agency. As with much of her work, Beecher here sought to discern the optimal conditions under which a higher good might be met. These conditions included a cultural commitment to education, and, not at all incidentally, to those best equipped to meet the challenges of education. It is an argument at once empowering and delimiting, an appeal to social change and to age-old verities about female character.

Another version of this argument can be found in Beecher's *Letters on the Difficulties of Religion,* published a year later as a compilation of responses to friends and disputants.[12] Conceived amidst the strife of local religion and politics, family turmoil, and Catharine's own flagging efforts at public acceptance, the text is overtly constrained, its patently rationalistic and conciliatory tone underscoring its author's sense of order. Beecher was in part seeking to legitimate the evangelism that her father had thrust upon a wary Cincinnati select; more generally, the text may be read as a guide for civil debate. As if to enact the domestic virtues proclaimed in her Lyceum address, Beecher here projected onto the scenes of public argument not just standards of right reason, but the protocols of discussion appropriate to her avowed sphere. The *Religion* letters can, like the Lyceum address, help us anticipate the Grimké encounter because they so clearly mark what their author took to be the possibilities and limits of public discourse.[13]

As we might expect, Beecher insisted early on that she was no stranger to the ways of dissent, public or private. This was a persona that served her well, if paradoxically, in her effort to circumscribe the spheres of social reform. No innocent, the author could claim a certain perspective on these matters, and she exercised that perspective through her adroit capacity for rhetorical depiction. "The writer has had opportunities of mingling, on social and familiar terms, with persons of great variety of moral and religious sentiments," including, we learn, supporters and critics of temperance, abolition, and colonization. "Indeed," Beecher recalled, "there are few discussions which have agitated the public mind, in which she has not heard the advocates of both sides. The result of this has been, the anxious and oft-repeated inquiry, 'what is the best method of promoting right intellectual views of truth and duty, and that right state of heart which will lead men to practice what they know to be right?'"[14]

Beecher's *Religion* letters are a response to that question. They are important for our purposes because of the manifest stress they place on the protocols of dispute. For if the Lyceum speech was about the placement of power, this text is about how power ought to communicate itself. It thus represents a significant moment in the process through which Beecher came to Grimké, and must then inform our reading of their encounter. What, then, are we to understand these protocols to be? Above all, Beecher argued, we are to remember that "it is the truth and not the combatants in which the public has an interest." Taking this as a given, Beecher reasoned that "As the prejudices, feelings, and bad passions of men are the greatest obstacle to correct intellectual views of the truth and duty, make it a point as much as possible, to avoid all that shocks the prejudices, wounds the feelings, or excites the passions of men." We are, rather, to "Let the discussion be confined to principles, avoiding all personalities, especially in public discussion."[15]

The disjunction between principle and personality, passion and reason, truth and rhetoric: these binarisms drive her argument forward, and if she failed at times to abide by the path they cleared, she certainly never ceased to be convinced of their essential worth as working principles of debate. The rules they sponsored had the merit, in any case, of being clear: "Never use satire, sneers, severe rebukes, or invidious epithets, toward any man or body of men, whose intellectual views you are aiming to correct," Beecher warned, "lest a sense of injury, anger, and personal ill will, blind the intellect and warp the judgment." Disputants were obliged on this basis, Beecher continued, to "Always be fair in stating the opinions and arguments that are to be controverted, and never allow a triumphant, self-sufficient and overbearing manner, to mar the efficacy of the arguments and facts that may be opposed."[16]

All this is not to understate Beecher's own stress on what such civility was for. Virtue remained here, as in the Lyceum address, the object of her argument; but it is equally clear that for Beecher the question was how to best provide for virtue's voice. Ultimately, her answer to this question devolved upon the attending issues of context, role, and protocols. Within this logic, virtue was a function of place; one could only act virtuously, indeed, as one occupied a status proper to one's identity. Beecher thus could say with perfect equanimity that when a woman stepped out of her assigned role, "a thousand things that in their appropriate sphere would be admired, become disgusting and offensive. The appropriate character of woman," Beecher insisted, "demands delicacy of appearance and manners, refinement of sentiment, gentleness of speech, modesty in feeling and action, a shrinking from notoriety and public gaze, a love of dependence, and protection, aversion to all that is coarse and rude, and an instinctive abhorrence of all that tends to indelicacy and impurity, either in principles or actions."[17]

Together, Beecher's Lyceum address and *Letters* may be read as rhetorical antecedents to the *Essay on Slavery*. While concerned with different issues, they collectively treat the same problems of human agency, power, and virtue that eventually are inscribed into and shape the later work. They share a preoccupation with the proper language of reform: what it should look like, where it should be heard, who owns it. Thus Beecher's anxiety about power and its place is ironically expressed as a rhetoric of reform—not so much of public commitments, but of the language through which those commitments are communicated and challenged.

This implicit critique becomes fully articulated in the *Essay on Slavery*. Beecher represents her position first as an attack on the methods of abolitionists and then, only then, as a defense of woman's sphere. At more than one hundred and fifty pages, the *Essay* offers a substantial analysis of issues hinted at a year or two earlier, but gives the author's arguments a new clarity and strength. Surely Beecher's choice to go public with a response to Grimké was itself a strategy designed to construct for those arguments a likely but formidable audience. By going public, moreover, Beecher helped set an encounter between two of the most compelling female advocates of the antebellum era; here was an act of courage and imagination, the inherent drama of which could pay off nicely for Beecher. By challenging Grimké directly and the abolitionists generally, she was calling out commitments across the spectrum, from antislavery to women's rights, and obliging her disputants to respond accordingly. Here was public debate worthy of a Beecher.[18]

The argument here was about language: its power, ends, and the protocols by which it was controlled. It was crucial, therefore, that Beecher make clear the reasons she was addressing Grimké as she was, and why such a mode of dispute was consistent with the following prescriptions. Beecher was careful to create with Grimké a relationship that would make her *Essay* at once compelling and reputable. At a minimum, this relationship was structured with reference to tradition, to virtue, and to the world of public letters. "The honoured and beloved name" that Grimké commands,

> so associated as it is at the South, North, and West, with all that is elegant in a scholar, refined in a gentleman, and elevated in a Christian,—the respectable sect with which she is connected,—the interesting effusions of her pen,—and her own intellectual and moral worth, must secure respect for her opinions and much personal influence. This seems to be a sufficient apology for presenting to the public some considerations in connexion with her name; considerations which may exhibit in another aspect the cause she advocates, and which it may be appropriate to consider.[19]

Much the same could be said of Beecher herself, of course. By positioning Grimké as she did, as a woman speaking outside her assigned sphere and in violation of her preordained role, Beecher constructed for herself and the general reader a radical other. She was careful, however, not to let this relationship remain as a static binarism—to do so, indeed, would be to fail her own duty. For Beecher was to Grimké as domestic virtue is to public action; the author must, on her own terms, reach to retrieve her reader, to constrain and thereby to rehabilitate Grimké and all other women who would presume upon the world of politics.[20]

Beecher's critique of the abolitionist program takes the form, appropriately, of a corrective. Its tone is didactic, never hostile; tempered, never excessive; patient but always pointed. Although of necessity a public text, the *Essay* is an exemplar of private virtue, its end to be realized as it virtually domesticates the discourse of its ostensible reader. Beecher's bill of particulars against the abolitionists is only in a limited sense an indictment of the movement; within the larger profile of the *Essay*, it provides an opportunity to point out honest mistakes of judgment and to offer specific remedies. Grimké, Beecher noted, was simply misinformed: "Your remarks seem to assume, that the principles held by Abolitionists on the subject of slavery, are peculiar to them, and are not generally adopted by those at the North who oppose their measures." In truth, she argued, there was no difference of opinion at the level of principle, and Grimké's harsh condemnation of fellow reformers was thus all the more unfortunate for its being unfounded. There was, accordingly, "no necessity for using any influence with northern ladies, in order that they may adopt your principles on the subject of slavery; for they hold them in common with yourself, and it would be unwise, and might prove irritating, to approach them as if they held opposite sentiments."[21]

Within the logic of Beecher's analysis, Grimké was not a bad person but rather a poor interpreter. She had misread northern sentiment, and on the basis of that misreading had allowed herself to be pulled into the unseemly world of public reform. On top of this mistake, Beecher pointed out, Grimké was now complicitous with an organization patently offensive to standards of cultural civility. The American Antislavery Society, Beecher stressed, was committed to methods of reform that "are not either peaceful or Christian in tendency, but they rather are those which tend to generate party spirit, denunciation, recrimination, and angry passions."[22]

More than any other feature of the organization, this lack of restraint and violation of protocol fired Beecher's indignation. It was not that its members, as individuals, were necessarily evil—indeed she conceded that they were "men of pure morals, of great honesty of purpose, of real benevolence and piety"—but as a group its discourse was unacceptable on its face. We have already seen in the Lyceum address and especially in the *Religion* letters Catharine's sensitivity to the protocols of reform ("Never use satires, sneers, severe rebukes, or invidious epithets, toward any body of men, whose intellectual views you are aiming to correct"). In language that reasserts this desire, this will to reform the language of reform, she cited as evidence the gross mistreatment of the American Colonization Society. "And the style in which the thing was done," Beecher wrote, "was at once offensive, inflammatory, and exasperating. Denunciation, sneers, and public rebuke, were bestowed indiscriminately upon the conductors of the enterprise, and of course they fell upon many sincere, upright, and conscious men, whose feelings were harrowed by a sense of the injustice, the indecorum, and unchristian treatment, they received."[23]

What was Beecher saying? At a very basic level Beecher was calling into question the ways in which communities went about persuading each other. As she interrogated one instance of this process, Beecher let surface those pieties with which she is usually identified and for which she has predictably taken heat ever since. These pieties, to be sure, remain vulnerable on many fronts. At a certain level of analysis, however, Beecher's argument is neither trivial nor wholly inaccurate: Garrison and his acolytes had savaged the ACS, and the radical arm of the movement was quickly cutting out the middle ground where collaboration and compromise was possible. The most conspicuous feature of the movement was the language it deployed. Beecher understood, perhaps more than the abolitionists themselves, that such a rhetoric carried with it grave moral implications. The closer Catharine examined this rhetoric, the more she found it wanting, and the closer she came to the heart of her complaint with Angelina Grimké.

On the principles of abolitionism all Christians could agree. Beecher rather objected to abolitionist methods, and thus shifted the basis of her critique from ends to means. These means, to the degree that they relied upon the capacity of language to incite and destabilize collective commitment, presumed a certain if implicit theory of language. This presumption, in turn, required a kind of criticism we might call rhetorical. Among its other aims, the abolitionist movement threatened to abolish linguistic convention; and that, Beecher understood, was incompatible with the conditions of community itself. For this reason Beecher strained to spell out the consequences of the abolitionists' "indiscreet and incorrect use of terms." Words, she explained,

> . . . have no inherent meaning, but always signify that which they are commonly *understood* to mean. The question never should be asked, what ought a word to mean, but simply, what is the meaning generally attached to this word by those who use it? Vocabularies and standard writers are the proper umpires to decide this question. Now if men take words and give them a new and peculiar use, and are consequently misunderstood, they are guilty of a species of deception, and are accountable for all the evils that may ensue as a consequence.

This passage, which I suggest is central to the meaning and function of Beecher's *Essay*, is worth some reflection. We note, to start, that this particular strain of linguistic conservatism relies nonetheless on a theory of meaning located in human community. Beecher does not contend that meaning is immutable or transcendent—indeed it is because meaning is so contingent on its collective construction that it needs to be controlled. Second, Beecher may be said to consider more frankly than most the moral consequences of using language reckless of convention. In this sense, Garrison was wrong, and morally wrong, to use language as he did because he believed himself not accountable for its results. There is, we must even now confess, a disturbing silence amongst many abolitionists on this issue of consequences, including the plight of "Free Blacks," who routinely bore the brunt of antiabolitionist mobs. Finally, we recognize that in many ways Angelina Grimké might be said to hold these same principles—at least as descriptions of the nature of language. Where she differed, of course, was in her willingness to radically disrupt the conventions that bound people to their words, and from that disruption to create new associations and new commitments; to create, ultimately, new communities of meaning.

Over and against the abolitionist discourse of reform Beecher imposed a counterdiscourse, a language respectful of tradition and building on it to accomplish the work of the world. The abolitionists used a rhetoric ungrounded in convention, beholden to public display, unjustified by nature or history; Beecher believed she could offer a superior alternative, a language grounded in community, enriched through private expression, made sensible through the laws of mind and experience. "Christianity," Beecher explained, was such a "system of persuasion, tending, by kind and gentle influences, to make men willing to leave off their sins—and it comes, not to convince those who are not sinners, but to sinners themselves." This "system of *persuasion*" was categorically opposed to the rhetoric of abolitionism, and relied on "a system of *coercion* by public opinion," the absurdity of which was evident by the fact that, "in its present operation, its influence is not to convince the erring, but to convince those who are not guilty, of the sins of those who are."[25]

Beecher's preferred "system of persuasion" was on its own terms subversive. It repudiated in principle and practice dominant modes of public rhetoric. This critique of antislavery discourse needs to be kept in mind as Beecher undertakes her analysis of women's role in moral reform. It is predominantly a statement on the rhetoric available to women reformers, and should not be considered independent of her foregoing argument. As that argument bears on "the woman question," it may best be summarized with this claim: "Let a man's enemies, or those who have no interest in his welfare, join to rebuke and rail at his offenses, and no sign of penitence will be seen. But let the clergyman whom he respects and loves, or his bosom friend approach him, with kindness, forbearance, and true sincerity, and all that is possible to human agency will be effected." Here is the clearest possible indication that Beecher did not see antislavery as any less pressing than Grimké did, nor as any less the province of female agency, but as an end to be effected through a categorically different language of reform.[26]

It is perfectly consistent, then, that Beecher should embed her description of female roles within a critique of public debate. Women reformers were, by this reasoning, to function as a kind of pressure group, extrapolitical but not for that reason any less influential. True, Beecher noted, "woman holds a subordinate relation in society to the other sex," but that relation was itself designed so that "the mode of gaining influence and of exercising power should be altogether different and peculiar." Beecher, in effect, sought not to displace female agency, but relocate it where it could, by her utilitarian standards, do the most good. In this way, her argument responds to and directly anticipates Grimké's claim to public life. Man, Catharine argued, "may act on society by the collision of intellect, in public debate; he may urge his measures by a sense of shame, by fear and by personal interest; he may coerce by the combination of public sentiment; he may drive by physical force, and he does not out step the boundaries of his sphere." Women, conversely, were to make their influence felt by exercising a power based in "kindly, generous, peaceful and benevolent principles." In this way—and only in this way—"fathers, the husband, and the sons, will find an influence thrown around them, to which they will yield not only willingly but proudly."[27]

In the light of her world it is difficult to understand Beecher's confidence. She had a venerable set of pieties upon which to draw, and she could not predict the intensity with which antifeminists would, in the decades to come, fight even the most modest claims to public power. Yet there were more immediate pressures at work that help make the *Essay* explicable and which bridge it with Grimké's *Letters*. Catharine's text was not a philosophical meditation on the nature of human agency: it was an attack on public debate and a defense of women's sphere as a superior site of moral reform. It was, in brief, a rhetorical document, pointed ostensibly at a particular reader but appealing to a curious public. Because it was rhetorical, Beecher's *Essay* was at once self-serving and principled: she was deeply invested in her own alteration of the status quo, and in promoting her aims she had to contest alternative voices. She needed women in the classroom, not on the platform; she needed to expand the space and scale of her leadership, not allow others to crowd it. It is, I think, too much to say that Beecher could not tolerate Angelina Grimké; but she could not let pass uncontested a figure of such commanding force and one who seemed, in spite of Catharine's strictures, to be treading where she herself feared to go.[28]

Grimké's Letters and the Rhetoric of Moral Agency

In Grimké the reader beheld the spectacle of a woman who, while professing pacifist sentiment, could speak so forcefully, so *publicly*, of donning the armor of God and laying waste the system of slavery. True, as Grimké worried in private, her speaking had introduced the volatile issue of women's rights into an already formidable reform agenda; what was done was done, however, and she could make no apologies for upsetting the waters. "I cannot help feeling some regret," she confided to Weld, "that this sh'ld have come up *before* the Anti Slavery question was settled, so fearful am I that it may injure that blessed cause, and then again I think this must be the Lord's time and therefore the *best* time, for it seems to have been brought about by a concatenation of circumstances over which we had no control."[29]

Grimké, of course, had done a good deal to bring about that "concatenation of circumstances," and through the media of argument she sought vigorously to control its terms. This much was essential, if only because Grimké was rapidly positioning herself as a representative of her sex—a process, as Catharine Beecher well knew, that heavily pressured the arts of public appeal. "What we claim for ourselves," Angelina now declared, "we claim for every woman whom God has called and qualified with gifts and graces." Thus in Beecher's *Essay* and Grimké's *Letters* we find a critical encounter on just this question of what kinds of claims could be made on behalf of all women, as well as a mutual recognition that the issue was somehow bound up deeply with the cause of abolitionism. Among the first of their kind, these texts are not alone antislavery tracts or women's rights manifestos: they are competing statements on the conditions under which freedom is possible.[30]

The fact that Grimké's response was made publicly and in the form of an argument, that her letters are rhetorical in motive, form, and effect, is not incidental but definitive of their status as cultural texts. That Grimké chose, moreover, to respond at all suggests that she was aware that here was an opportunity not to be missed. Beecher was by anyone's reckoning a formidable disputant, and Grimké was not in a particularly strong position to engage her opponent fully. Nonetheless, she chose from among the means of persuasion available to her the public letter, and hence to respond in kind to Beecher's epistolary arguments. In doing so, in establishing a dramatically public relationship with her reader, Grimké was able not only to put on display a series of counterarguments, but to make an event out of that display.

Grimké's thirteen letters are about power—about its place, its ends, and the way in which it is communicated. This much is anticipated in Beecher's *Essay*. But by engaging Beecher as she did, Grimké made clearer and more compelling than Beecher could that the discussion of these issues presumed a structure of commitments, a relationship born of the critical encounter that provided the very conditions for their consideration. This is why the encounter is itself an expression of power: it required choice, valuable resources, public risk. As we proceed to read the *Letters* and to chart their points of contact with Beecher's *Essay*, we will need to keep in mind this structure of commitments. It not only makes the debate possible, but presents the debate as a symbolically charged statement on the power of women to transform moral culture.

If Catharine's *Essay* was circumstantial and motivated, she nevertheless presented it as the product of enlightened reflection. Grimké chose rather to make a virtue of her necessity: her *Letters* were to be offered up from the moment's heat, composed hastily, without artifice or the luxury of revision. The posture is of course familiar in public debate, and Grimké was quickly becoming adept in exploiting it. Harried by more important issues, the author must improvise, and for that reason is to be taken as more authentic, less calculated. If successful, the strategy obscures its art and paradoxically achieves what more guileless postures cannot: the erasure of its own rhetoric. This, of course, is not to suggest that Grimké's stance was in some way deceptive; it is to draw attention to her means of persuasion. More specifically, it leads us to ask how Grimké established for herself a mode of address, a way of speaking that would establish the terms of her critical encounter with Catharine Beecher.

There is nothing particularly restrained, certainly nothing very domestic, about Grimké's salutation. It is in fact no salutation at all, but a salve, a none-too-subtle message that the niceties of epistolary form are secondary to the more important needs of public argument.

My Dear Friend: Thy book has appeared just at a time, when, from the nature of my engagements, it will be impossible for me to give it that attention which so weighty a subject demands. Incessantly occupied in prosecuting a mission, the responsibilities of which task all my powers, I can reply to it only by desultory letters, thrown from the pen as I travel from place to place. I prefer this mode to that of taking as long a time to answer it as thou didst to determine upon the best method by which to counteract the effect of my testimony at the north—which, as the preface of thy book informs me, was thy main design.[31]

The passage is designed at once to bring Catharine into proximity *and* to make clear the ground that yet separates them. On this ground, Grimké displayed her willingness to respond—and respond publicly—but she would do so on her own terms. All that follows was to bear the marks of this stylized engagement: Grimké's arguments would be, because "thrown from the pen," forthright, without contrivance, brief, authentic. We need not read very far into the passage, however, to detect a more aggressive tactic at work. As Grimké turned for the moment from the tour and toward her reader, she presented to the public an unmistakable contrast. Thus close together, how different seem their aspects: Grimké labored to resolve a pressing moral crisis, Beecher appeared bent on creating another; Grimké wrote from the outposts of a Godly mission; Beecher from moral complacency. Grimké wrote only when she could not speak, while Beecher ccould only write, and that only from the safety of her study.

All is not, however, simply contrast. As if to anticipate and preempt criticism of the abolitionists' style of public speech, Angelina's prose is noticeably restrained, her reasoning overtly rational and systematic. Letter One was to be a statement on the "Fundamental Principles of Abolitionists," and for now, at least, it worked by doing Beecher one better. Beecher had in orderly fashion sought to expose the confusions which beset abolitionist discourse. Grimké in turn could not be more clear about its logic:

The great fundamental principle of Abolitionists is, that man cannot rightfully hold his fellow man as property. Therefore, we affirm that *every slave holder is a man-stealer*. We do so, for the following reasons: to steal a man is to rob him of himself. It matters not whether this be done in Guinea, or Carolina; a man is a *man*, and *as* man he has *inalienable* rights, which is the right to personal liberty. Now if every man has an *inalienable* right to personal liberty, it follows, that he cannot rightfully be reduced to slavery.

This is a far cry from the excesses condemned by Beecher, and Grimké would lean heavily on such language throughout the *Letters*. Pressured as it was by time, events, and duty, Grimké's argument was nevertheless strong in the sense that a syllogism is strong—the premises granted, as surely they must be, her conclusions were inescapable. Thus while mirroring Beecher's prose style, the *Letters* at the same time work to interrogate and displace her arguments through a superior mode of reasoning.

In this way Letter I announces what will be a defining pattern: the author is to engage her disputant issue for issue, for this much is a matter of respect and rigor. Furthermore, Grimké, like Beecher, will not only challenge the issue at hand, but scrutinize the language in which those issues are articulated. Yet the rhetorical aim of the *Letters* cannot be scaled down to the immediate give and take of this particular debate, no matter how important it is. Grimké was seeking here to rationalize a language of power appropriate to mass moral reform. As she envisioned it, such a language was incommensurate with Beecher's; she needed as a result to effect a wholesale displacement of her rival's position. Because the fortunes of this language of power rested on the power of language, Grimké had to perform in the *Letters* a double function: she had to meet Beecher's arguments head on, and in so doing set in place a rationale that would ultimately make such debate unnecessary.

On 23 June Grimké wrote from Lynn to make clear what it was that justified such a new conception of power. She took as her point of departure Beecher's claim that her southern friend "hast not been sufficinetly informed" as to the state of opinion in the North, and must therefore be confused as to its own "animating principles." Grimké, manifestly annoyed at the imputation and the didactic strain in Beecher's voice, resolved to do a little informing of her own. Letter Three accordingly signals an important moment in the unfolding economy of this composite text. Here, and now, Grimké was compelled to dismantle Beecher's argument and reorder her terms, rhetorically to reconfigure its principles and so create possibilities of meaning. In the process, Grimké provided what might be termed a call to speech, a rationale for the very language in which those principles were to be expressed and understood.

Grimké pursued her ends in several ways. The Lynn letter functioned first to set in place a superintending principle of duty. On the basis of this principle, she was then able to contravene Beecher's argument that the abolitionists were acting without regard to the laws of history or reason. Grimké was then positioned to confront directly her interlocutor's pretensions to the realm of moral reform. Together, these lines of argument, while not exhaustive of the letter, constitute a prominent first step in the process through which power was to find its proper voice. We must remind ourselves again how deeply Grimké and her fellow abolitionists identified with that tradition: it offered up a bounteous resource for the rhetorical work of the movement, and it helped Grimké to understand how pointedly it could be used to subvert antiabolitionist arguments. Above all, its patented call to duty meant that for individual and community alike, redemption could be had only through the active abolition of sin. Far from laboring in igno-rance, then, the abolitionists were acting out of an enlightened sense of "our duty as Americans to 'cry aloud and spare not, to lift up our voices as a trumpet, and to show our people their transgressions, and the house of Jacob their sins.'" Their task was necessarily "to rouse a slumbering nation to a sense of the retributions which must soon descend upon her guilty head." Duty so understood combined principle with action, and in this context the only knowledge relevant was of the existence of slavery.

Duty thus gave to Grimké not only a moral imperative, but a rationale for public action. It functioned rhetorically as an instrument with which to expose the opposition, to counteract its appeals and arguments. This destructive work accomplished, the abolitionist might then create from the ruins of the opposition a new community of belief and commitment. Duty thus figured prominently in Grimké's letter because it was, among its other virtues, so useful. With such a principle, Grimké was able to subvert Beecher's claim to superior insight, to reassert the abolitionist program, and, most poignantly, to lament Beecher's com-plicity in a system of flagrant oppression.

It was not, Grimké argued, the abolitionists who were misinformed, but rather Beecher herself. The problem ran deeper than simply assessing the state of opin-ion in the North; it rather had to do with the premises with which culture and its problems were to be evaluated. Beecher's real error lay in her insistence that abo-litionists be judged according to standards appropriate to other, less fundamen-tal, movements for reform. She had failed, in short, to grasp the magnitude of the problem and its solutions, and without this basic insight all others were doomed to utterly miss the point. By way of pointed example, Grimké drew attention to the claim that no historical precedent justified abolitionist tracts. Exactly, Grimké argued: "we are resting on *no* experience at all; for no class of men in the world ever have maintained the principles which we now advocate."

The abolitionists could not, by this reasoning, be circumscribed by history because in a sense they did not belong to it—at least to its secular articulations. Abolitionism rather offered a way to intervene in history's development, to redi-rect it and so to purify the world. The rhetoric of abolitionism discourse was nec-essarily subversive and interrogatory: it had to effect a relocation of power from its site in tradition in order to subvert that tradition. This counterdiscourse has the unsettling effect of continuously inverting terms: what to Beecher appeared as a paradox was to the abolitionist wholly consistent with the universal demands of duty. Beecher thought it anomalous, for instance, that abolitionists should spend so much energy trying to persuade Northerners of southern sins. "Not at all," Grimké reasoned. "It is because we are politically, commercially, and socially connected with our southern brethren, that we urge our doctrines upon those of the free States." Beecher thought such criticism a violation of common sense; Grimké thought it necessary as a phase in the transformation of her world. As one who saw herself assisting in this process, Grimké was intensely sensitive to the relationships it presumed, destroyed, and empowered. Her own life was in a sense proof-positive of this fact, and she, more than most, understood what was at stake when commitments were realigned, roles confused and clarified, responsibilities questioned and ultimately answered. What made it all possible was duty, the specific force of which was to integrate individual choice with collective commitment. Within the contexts of the abolitionist movement, duty not only pressured this relationship, but made it public and dramatized its symbolic implications.

In all, duty was to place an especially heavy burden of consciousness on female reformers, whom Grimké now believed were called equally to action. This conception of duty was at the root of her encounter with Beecher, for in the *Essay* could be found a kind of false call to power, particularly damaging because it issued from so prominent, so dramatic, a voice. The pain in Grimké's words is evident; it is the pain of relationships formed and rent, of commitments once thought strong but now exposed in their falsity. It is, too, a pain that will surface repeatedly in the *Letters,* and one that functions as a statement on the problematic of commitment and feminist community. For now, Grimké could only lament that "northern women are writing books to paralyze the efforts of southern women, who have come up from the South, to entreat their northern sisters to exert their influence in behalf of the slave, and in behalf of the slave holder, who is as deeply corrupted, though not equally degraded, with the slave. No! No! the taunts of a New England woman will induce no abolitionist to cease his rebuke of *northern slaveholders* and apologists for slavery."

Grimké was in little danger of being "paralyzed" by Beecher's "taunts." Indeed, the *Essay* served the contrary purpose of provoking Grimké to greater efforts on behalf of abolitionism and its principles of public reform. As we have seen thus far, Grimké's argument required for its coherence and force a particular sense of duty, and while duty understood in this way was hardly novel, it did have the distinctive advantage of carrying with it a rationale for public dispute. Grimké's argument was therefore as much a call to language as a call to action: indeed, the one was incomplete without the other. In the Grimké-Beecher encounter, this insight takes the specific form of a preoccupation with language as such—its nature, province, and limits. If Grimké and Beecher agreed on nothing else, they did share the sense that how slavery was talked about was somehow crucial to its resolution.

Letters V through IX represent Grimké's countercharge. Beecher's provocation had given her a reason to speak, and through the relationship thus established

Grimké was able to focus her critique and advance its claims in an identifiable direction. This critique in turn may be taken as the argumentative heart of the *Letters:* in it, she presented her case for a counterdiscourse, a language of moral reform that was to radically shift the ground from beneath Beecher's argument. The process through which Grimké created this possibility may be read in different ways, but here we shall examine how Grimké defined her counterdiscourse, justified it, and established its scope and function.

Like many before and after her, Beecher was deeply disturbed by the rhetorical violence that seemed to define the abolition movement. Her argument against that violence, we recall, was based on a concern for the passions it incited and the havoc it wreaked on community. For this reason, Beecher contended, the abolition societies were in effect, if not in motive, un-Christian. To advance this claim against the diverse but uniformly devout community of abolitionists was to call into question its very spirit of action. Yet it also indicated a basic error in perception, a failure to discern not that its rhetoric was violent, for indeed it was, but that such violence was itself necessary and definitive of the Christian language of reform. Grimké's contact with Beecher on this major point could not be more direct: "Why, then," she asked, "protest against our measures as *unchristian,* because they do not smooth the pillow of the poor sinner, and lull his conscience into fatal security? The truth is, the efforts of abolitionists have stirred up the *very same spirit* which the efforts of *all thorough-going reformers* have ever done; we consider it a certain proof that the truths we utter are sharper than any two edged sword, and that they are doing the work of conviction in the hearts of our enemies." When, two years before, Grimké had read of the Boston riots, she had interpreted the violence surrounding her as something to be celebrated. Now Grimké could sharpen her defense of the obvious fact that the abolitionists meant trouble, plain and sure. Far from pretending they did not, she rather seized Beecher's point and made of it an unabashed declaration: "The character of Christianity" she reckoned to be "pre eminently aggressive; it waits not to be assaulted, but moves on in all the majesty of Truth to *attack* the strong holds of the kingdom of darkness, carries the war into the enemy's camp, and throws its fiery darts into the midst of its embattled hosts."

For all of Grimké's appeal to Scripture for evidence and support, this statement functions ultimately as a premise. As such, it works—if it is to work at all—not by arguing down Beecher's position but by utterly displacing it. Historians have been quick to note how such reasoning cuts out the middle ground of compromise and reconciliation. Indeed it does, and indeed, within the terms of Grimké's analysis, it must. Authentic and hence immediate reform could not be effected in two languages at once. The liberal and forbearing language of gradualism, whatever its good intentions and self-congratulations, had to be, in effect, shouted down. This was why, Grimké wrote, "The *aggressive* spirit of Anti-Slavery papers and pamphlets, of which thou dost complain, so far from being a repulsive one to me, is very attractive. I see in it that uncompromising integrity and fearless rebuke of sin, which will bear the *enterprize* of emancipation through to its consummation." Thus Christianity itself redefines the discourse of reform from a version of domestic benevolence to an instrument of mass redemption.

Both Grimké and Beecher comprehended what was at stake here. The fortunes of community itself—familial, regional, national, Christian—seemed to hang on the question of how the already explosive issue of slavery was to be resolved. This question, necessarily, turned on how the disputants understood the conditions of community, the sources of power by which communities were held in perpetuity, and how language provided for or violated those conditions. In taking the family as the basic unit of community, and by inscribing within its terms a set of values hostile to abolitionist rhetoric, Beecher placed herself in a defensive posture. Hers was a rhetoric of fear: fear of transgression, fear of results, fear, ultimately, of a future in which the Grimkés of the world would hold sway over a Christian nation.

Grimké at once acknowledged the prospect and embraced it. This is not to say that she was any less sensitive to the turmoil she was helping to inflict on the American community. Rather, unlike Beecher, she saw real change possible only as the conditions of community were themselves radically altered. That vision, she made clear, required a specific conception of the power and role of language. "It is *not* because we wish to wield this public opinion like a rod of iron over the heads of slave holders," Grimké explained. "We are striving to purify public opinion, first, because as long as the North is so much involved in the guilt of slavery, by its political, commercial, religious, and social connexion with the South, *her own citizens* need to be converted." Moreover, Grimké wrote, "because we know that when public opinion is rectified at the North, it will throw a flood of light from its million of reflecting surfaces upon the heart and soul of the South."

Such was the motive behind the abolitionist discourse of reform. Beecher's critique had targeted its effects as destructive of community and the Christian values that community presumed. This was not, as we have suggested, a charge to be taken lightly, and Grimké's response indicates its salience. To Beecher's complaint she had only to appeal to the terms already established in the *Letters*. Duty commanded her to speak; Scripture authorized it; the world required it. In this calculus, motive and action satisfied the divine imperatives: success or failure, consequences and ends could only be secondary. Once again, then, Grimké had shifted the ground from underneath Beecher and the antiabolitionists. Not to be constrained in the exercise of their duty by standards irrelevant to that duty, abolitionists were to walk "by *faith*, not by sight." Abolitionists rather "feel called upon to preach the truth in season and out of season, to lift up their voices like a trumpet, to show the people their transgressions and the house of Jacob their sins. The *success* of this mission," Grimké stressed, "*they* have no more to do with, than had Moses and Aaron, Jeremiah or Isaiah, with that of theirs." In any case, Grimké concluded, "The *result* of our labors is hidden from our eyes; whether the preaching of Anti-slavery truth is to be a savior of life unto life, or of death unto life to this nation, we know not; and we have no more to do with it, than had the Apostle Paul, when he preached Christ to the people of his day."

The sum effect of Grimké's argument so far is to have opened a space wherein she could assert her warrant for public action. Pressing against Beecher, she pressed against the walls of domestic virtue, and when they fell, Grimké foresaw not ruin but opportunity, not virtue assaulted but virtue expressed. As I have tried to emphasize, however, Grimké required Beecher's resistance because it drew out her own strength, made her speak more forcefully about what mattered. The encounter gave to Grimké a means to defend herself, to attack Beecher's argument, to show through the encounter what public debate ought to look like. The encounter thus enacts Beecher's position ironically and Grimké's literally, for here were two female disputants, the one arguing publicly for domestic virtue, the other arguing virtuously for going public. Here was a process, then, greater than the sum of its parts, a display of values and arguments in contest, a celebration, as Grimké well knew, of a principle near to the heart of all abolitionists. What Grimké said of the public debates over slavery may then be taken as descriptive of this process and why it was so important. The "collision of mind," she wrote, "as naturally produces light, as the striking of the flint and the steel produces fire. *Free discussion is this collision*, and the results are visible in the light which is breaking forth in every city, town, and village, and spreading over the hills and valleys, through the whole length and breadth of our land."

Into this light Grimké sought to cast the question of women's sphere and moral agency. The final two letters represent this effort, and while they may perhaps stand alone for some purposes, as rhetorical statements they are tightly woven into the fabric of the previous ten. This final moment of address folds into itself the premises and arguments, appeals and images wrought since that first missive of 12 June. In the meantime, Angelina and Sarah had been praised and blamed, attacked in a Pastoral Letter by the Congressional Association of Massachusetts, defended by John Greenleaf Whittier, and had drawn the suspicions of even fellow abolitionists. The contests perhaps gave Angelina added insight and edged her prose more sharply, but they were also taking a toll. She thus confided on 27 August in a letter to Weld that "I expected to meet with trials, *personal* trials and I (vainly perhaps) *think* I could have born THEM, but all this unsettlement and complaint among the *friends* of the cause is so unexpected that I don't know how to bear it. My only consolation is the hope that it will drive us nearer to Him who alone can guide and sustain." Grimké was sustained, as it turned out, and the following day once again took up her pen and addressed Beecher's attack on women's work in public. This letter, and the final letter of 2 September, remain among the most forceful statements on moral agency written during that century.[32]

Today's readers may find in Beecher's argument a virtual manifesto of what has been too-conveniently dubbed the nineteenth century's "cult of domesticity." It registers to modern ears as a nearly incredible, because so unabashed, accommodation to prevailing conceptions of "true womanhood" and "republican motherhood," a virtual compendium of precisely those attitudes that early women's rights activists defined themselves against. Beecher is withal a difficult figure with which to sympathize, and remains for many an enigmatic combination of female authority, enlightened educational leadership, and outright complicity with the very structures of domination against which she was struggling. So explicit and vulnerable was her position, indeed, that we are inclined, perhaps, to see her as an easy target for Grimké's finely edged skills as a public disputant. Such a view, however, rather underestimates what was in fact an impressive and influential record of advocacy on Beecher's part. Her achievement was not only personal, as Grimké recognized, but evident, too, in a substantial body of writings that addressed pressing issues about women's place in a rapidly changing social order, offered compelling advice on how women might realize their greatest talents in the world as it was, and advanced searching criticisms against those who would diminish the prospects of women's work in the early republic.

Beecher's *Essay* summarized the ideological basis of this position to startling effect—a point certified by the energy and sophistication required of Grimké to combat its potential for entrenching even further the values it put on display. Certainly Angelina felt to the quick the personal insinuations contained in the *Essay;* but she also understood the stakes involved now for abolitionists and especially women workers in the antislavery cause. In this she was prescient, for in Beecher she was reckoning with someone, as Boydston, Kelley, and Margolis have written, who "presided over the birth of a gender ideology that has survived into the late twentieth century," and whose "impact on American cultural and social history extended far beyond the perhaps several thousand women who were her students."[33]

If Grimké was daunted by the rhetorical challenge before her, she did not show it. Reserving her defense of women abolitionists for the final several installments, she confronted directly and without apology Beecher's proscriptions, as if building up and toward this subject, "the most important to the women of the country." The general strategy was simplicity—to put back together what Beecher had rendered asunder—and this was consistent with the tenor of the letters as a whole. Here, of course, the problem had been doubled, obliging Grimké to undertake a vindication not only of abolitionists, but of *female* abolitionists at that. To this end, Grimké attempted to match Beecher's arguments point for point, as we have seen before, proceeding again to first dismantle and then reassemble a structure of convictions and appeals that would eventually undergird her vision for radical change. It is not too much to say that, in the process, Grimké articulated in their most developed early formulation, her views on the rights of women as women; here her emphasis was almost wholly on the "question" of women as free moral agents. That question was naturally related to the work of antislavery, as she had made clear in her earlier *Appeal to the Women of the Nominally Free States;* but in these final letters we discover a statement, expressed with striking and unprecedented precision, on the nature and province of women's rights *as such*. It is perhaps worth reminding ourselves at this point that on the complicated issue of the relationship between abolitionism and women's rights, Grimké's own experience was deeply relevant, informing as it did the effort to forge abolitionism into a powerful rationale not only for public activism, but also for the universal right of women to participate in that work. It is not at all incidental, then, that this crucial moment in the development of Grimké's thought was prompted, shaped, and realized within the domain of public debate.[34]

At the center of Letter XI, "The Sphere of Woman and Man as Moral Beings The Same," is Grimké's claim that rights are definitive of moral being. It is on the basis of this proposition that she was able to leverage a critique of Beecher's conception of men's and women's spheres; and it is this critique that ultimately clears the way for Letter 12's reconstruction of public life as a dynamic, open, and inviting site for radical change. For now, Grimké's letter of 28 August from Brookline was to be devoted to disencumbering the analysis of moral being from the weight of false distinctions and false disjunctions, and thus from what we might now call false consciousness. At the risk of extracting too neatly the ligaments of her critique, we can identify at least six closely related lines of argument; together, they may be taken as a summary case against such views of the public sphere as Beecher and others professed.

On one matter at least Beecher and Grimké were in agreement. The public sphere was about power. On another they could not have disagreed more clearly: that it was about the exercise of power peculiarly and exclusively appropriate to one gender only. We know where Beecher came down on the issue, but that is not to say she was dismissive of any and all claims to female power; it was rather a question of where and therefore who was exercising it, and in what way. The public being what it was, certain rhetorical practices were ordained, venerable, and right. "A *man* may act on Society by the collision of intellect, in public debate," Beecher explained; "*he* may coerce by the combination of public sentiment; *he* may drive by physical force, and *he* does *not* overstep the boundaries of his sphere." Women, to whom were given the more peaceful and gentle arts of female influence, were to keep their public, as it were, at home and hearth. Grimké's first retort to this conventional argument goes rather beyond simple objections to simple arguments: by her lights, the public sphere was not reducible to nor could it be defined by the practices it allowed. If it was typically a site of conflict, collision, and physical force, that was no justification either for what passed as debate or for excluding those less inclined to a politics of intimidation. The example of Christ made that much obvious, and in any case the point was that the public sphere did not in itself predetermine its own conduct or content. By the same token, as Grimké next argued, women's sphere was not to be reduced to a kind of faux version of public life, where instead of robust public debate women were, in Beecher's language, "to win every thing by peace and love; by making *herself* so much respected, etc., that to yield to *her* opinions, and to gratify *her* wishes, will be the free-will offering of the heart." For Grimké, who had presumably had quite enough of this activity as a youth in Charleston, such principles "may do as the rule of action to the fashionable belle, whose idol is *herself*"; the self-respecting were to reject them, however, "with holy indignation."

A second set of arguments treated Beecher's venerable appeal to the impermeability of the two spheres. Tightly related to her emphasis on the conduct said to be taking place within each domain, Beecher had further stressed the perils of transgression. On this point Grimké was, of course, well prepared, and even if Beecher had not read the *Appeal to the Christian Women of the South* (she had, and indeed attributed her response to that earlier text), she could find here a handy precis of the argument contained therein. Miriam, Deborah, and Huldah, prophets male and female, gave ample scriptural testimony to the fact that women had always been "called to fill public stations in Church and State." Thus Grimké contended that there were not now nor had there ever been sealed boundaries between the public and private domains of moral action; by implication, any argument for restricting access to public life would have to assume an unsupportable burden of scriptural and historical proof.

How and to what effect the question of rights fits into the argument at this point becomes evident. To the extent that the relationship between the spheres of moral action and human rights was not self-evident, Grimké had to ground her argument in truths that were. For this, she turned to establish in the starkest language of the first premise of her general argument, indeed the premise which drives the entirety of the *Letters*. The question to which it represents an answer is rudimentary but exceptionally important to the overall movement of the argument: "From whom does woman receive her *rights?*" From God, not man, Grimké stressed, but—and here is the key to her argument—such rights are not to be understood as a gift, as something given to woman as a kind of supplement to her being. "Now, if I understand the real state of the case," Grimké wrote, "woman's rights are not the gifts of man—no! nor the *gifts* of God. His gifts to her may be recalled at his good pleasure—but her *rights* are an integral part of her moral being; they cannot be withdrawn; they must live with her forever." Far from being a supplement to one's humanity, rights in this sense are constitutive of it; they "lie at the foundation of all her duties; and, so long as the divine commands are binding upon her, so long must her rights continue."

If we step back a moment from Grimké's argument, we can readily discern precisely what is being reconstructed from her critique of Beecher. In effect, Catharine had expressed the common sense of her time, which is to say that whatever the material realities and conspicuous exceptions to the rule, the rule itself was clear: man's domain was public, woman's private. Any question of rights had necessarily to be remanded to their appropriate sphere; to presume or exercise a right in one domain that belonged to another was, in this reasoning, perverse. What is lost in this logic, among other things, is a unified conception of moral being, understood by Grimké to be a universal attribute of all humans. Grimké's task, then, was not so much to open one sphere to another, to make them traversable, although certainly that was an important implication of her argument; it was primarily to uncouple the principle of rights—constitutive as they are of one's moral being—from the notion of spheres altogether. Rights, in short, cannot be reduced to their space of operation. They are universal, the property neither of spheres, of lawgivers, nor even of God; they are held exclusively by one's self and are inexplicable except as a condition of one's very identity. No act could therefore be authorized by virtue—by "right"—of the sphere in which it was undertaken. Grimké thus found incoherent Beecher's insistence on the separate spheres of moral action, not because it was inappropriate for women to behave as men did in public, but because it was inappropriate for anyone to so behave. "All such influences are repudiated by the precepts and examples of Christ, and his apostles," Grimké noted, "so that, after all, this appropriate sphere of woman is *just as appropriate to man.*" Thus Grimké recovered from Beecher's attack the means to reestablish the essential unity of moral being, and hence moral action, conceived now not as subject to the transient categories of social division but as superintending the work required of all citizens.

The penultimate letter, "Human Rights Not Founded on Sex," elaborates upon and concludes the thesis advanced thus far. Writing from East Boylston on 2 October, Grimké offered a more sustained and explicit analysis of human rights, rendered here in the form of six propositions. These principles, as clearly and forcefully stated as we are likely to find them in antebellum discussions of the subject, may be summarized thus:

1. All human beings possess rights because they are moral beings;
2. All human rights are essentially the same because moral nature is essentially the same;
3. No human being can be alienated from her/himself; the title to oneself is perfect;
4. Sex, being incidental, is subordinate to the primary and essential rights of moral being;
5. Whatever is morally right (wrong) for a man, is morally right (wrong) for a woman;
6. The public discussion of certain rights leads inevitably to the discussion of all rights.

Even so abstracted, the premises grounding Grimké's argument may be seen as closely interwoven and textured by the encounter with Beecher. They represent, in effect, the beginning and end of her letters, applying equally to the issues of slavery, abolitionism, and women's rights. Together, they cohere into a compelling account of the possibilities for collective moral action, where rights and responsibility are compressed into each other so tightly that they explode outward, ever further, ever deeper, into the arenas of reform and radical change. As a result, the reader is made witness to a startling transformation of the scene before him or her, the encrustation of history and convention blown aside to reveal the full scope of emancipated human endeavor. For Beecher and others not yet ready to countenance such visions, passages like the following must have startled. Still, they could not have missed the rhetorical and logical consistency of purpose underwriting them:

> Now, I believe it is woman's right to have a voice in all the laws and regulations by which she is to be *governed,* whether in Church or State; and that the present arrangements of society, on these points, are a *violation of human rights, a rank usurpation of power,* a violent seizure and confiscation of what is sacredly and inalienably hers—thus inflicting upon woman outrageous wrongs, working mischief incalculable in the social circle, and in its influence on the world producing only evil, and that continually. *If* Eccleastical and Civil governments are ordained of God, then I contend that woman has just as much right to sit in solemn counsel in Conventions, Conferences, Associations and General Assemblies, as man—just as much right to sit upon the throne of England, or in the Presidential chair of the United States.

The preceding passage demonstrates and enacts the author's own claim to full humanity, as well as her characteristic effort to open up scenes of the heretofore unthinkable. The *pathos* evident in Grimké's appeal thus sets in dramatic relief the seemingly cold and excessive rationalism of Beecher's own stance. This contrast in moral sensibilities is amplified in the thirteenth and final letter, written in apparent haste from Holliston on 23 October 1837. In her concluding remarks, Angelina refuted the venerable argument that women are best suited to teaching the young, least suited to professing politics on the public stage. Beecher's was a view long enshrined by what we have come to call the ideology of republican motherhood, and Grimké would have none of it—not because she saw no need for such education, but because it precluded men from exercising their own duty to those ends. Abolitionists of both genders, moreover, were to be seen as ideal educators in such contexts, precisely because "*they alone* teach fully the doctrine of human rights," and know best that the truths of a just God "should be seduously instilled into the mind of every child in our republic." If the nation's best interests were indeed driving Beecher's analysis, then, Grimké averred, women were perfectly appropriate to the work of agitation in Congress, in northern circles of reform, and in inciting the South to rethink its own complicity in the system of slavery.

The final lines of the last letter represent among the most pointed critiques in the exhange and, in fact, in Grimké's public discourse as a whole. When all was said and done, she observed, Catharine's argument was as notable for its lack of compassion as it was for the intellectual prowess with which it was delivered. Above all this was clear with respect to the slave, who seems not to have figured at all in Beecher's thinking. Grimké had labored in the letters to stretch the realm of possibilities, to open up vistas of change that heretofore seemed clothed in darkness. By contrast, Beecher appeared trapped inside a stark rationalism that aimed to calculate an efficient and painless way out of an inherently painful situation. In all the time spent writing her letters, Angelina asked Beecher, had she "once moistened" her paper "by the tear of pity? Did thy heart once swell with deep sympathy for thy sister *in bonds?* Did it once ascend to God in broken accents for the deliverance of the captive? Didst thou ever ask thyself, what the free man of color would think of it?" Obviously not, Grimké observed, and so Beecher's work amounted to a gift for proslavery forces. Missing from all the reasoning, all the logic and appeals to expediency, was genuine sympathy; her book "might have been written just as well, hadst thou not had the heart of a woman." In this fact Grimké found much that was telling. Beecher's failure was the failure to think, feel, and argue as a woman. She had shown herself rather to be "paralyzed and spell-bound by the sorcery of a worldly-minded expediency." In failing to anticipate the response of slaves and free blacks to her writing, Beecher had withdrawn herself from a community of women, a sisterhood especially well poised to redeem the nation's sins. Grimké's concluding lines bespeak therefore a powerful sense of regret that in Beecher all women, all slaves, the nation itself, had lost a voice of singular force: "Farewell," Angelina wrote,

> Perhaps on a dying bed thou mayest vainly wish with that "Miss Beecher on the Slave Question" might perish with the mouldering hand which penned its cold and heartless pages. But I forebear, and in deep sadness of heart, but in tender love though I thus speak, I bid thee again, Farewell. Forgive me, if I have wronged thee, and pray for her who still feels like
>
> Thy sister in the bonds of a common sisterhood.
A. E. Grimké

Pressured as it was by the demands of time, her own work, and the resilience of Beecher's position, the set of letters will not be mistaken for a theoretical exposition on the nature of human rights. They are, to be sure, replete with principle, maxims, and declarations, and there can be no missing the strain outward even as she strove to anchor her argument in the exigencies of the moment. Writing to her friend Jane Smith as she was contemplating her response to Beecher, Grimké had despaired of her abilities, observing that, "I do not know how I shall find language strong enough to express my indignation at the view she takes of woman's character and duty." We may conclude that Grimké's worries were unfounded, for in the process of debate she discovered not only a language strong enough to register disapproval, but a means to reconstruct what Beecher had sought to destroy. At the ground of her reasoning was a view of human rights that carried with it imperatives of duty and collective action; but beneath even that level of analysis, she found and gave public expression to principles that remained unshaken for the rest of her life—that human rights knew no boundaries, no sex, no domain. They were the very substance of her being, her identity as a free moral agent.[35]

"To Open Our Mouths for the Dumb": Grimké, Weld, and the Debate over Women's Speech

.

After the slow and arduous spiritual journey that took her from private doubt to public conviction, Grimké had learned to act quickly and to certain effect: the encounter with Garrison in the summer of 1835; the writing and publication of the *Appeal* soon thereafter; the exchanges with Beecher: each point of contact is marked by a ready grasp of public expectations and of the words required to meet them. This much is not to say, of course, that Angelina was either especially sensitive to popular appetites or that she pandered to their interests; it is to stress that she recognized an opportunity when she saw it, and the chance to speak to audiences in the very crucible of moral reform was just such an opportunity.

The New England tour, during which, according to Lerner's estimate, the speaker addressed almost ninety audiences in sixty-seven towns to more than forty thousand people, all told, in many ways represents the apex of Grimké's public career. For all its notoriety, its scandalized clerics and anxious reform leaders, the tour was in fact a masterpiece of rhetorical timing, introducing as it did this singular voice to a culture so avowedly committed to the spoken word. This was, after all, the Golden Age of American oratory, and Boston was its very center, home to Daniel Webster, Edward Everett, Ralph Waldo Emerson, Fanueil Hall, and the Lyceum. Americans everywhere appreciated the powers of oratory, were known to "possess peculiar advantages for the cultivation of these powers," and no surprise there, for, "the native region of oratory is the land of freedom." Put another way, it would be difficult to imagine any people so prepared for the prospect of being lectured to about so volatile a subject by a woman so young, so unmarried, and so terribly righteous. History, for once, seemed on Grimké's side, and she aimed to make the most of it.[1]

The problem for Grimké and her supporters, of course, was that the age proved not so golden after all, oratorically and otherwise. In truth many observers were deeply ambivalent about the function and scope of public speech in antebellum America, and for every paean to the Golden Age of Oratory could be found many more despairing accounts of this most democratic of arts. America before the war seemed to many critics a wasteland of the spoken word, peopled by ambitious politicians, noisy reformers, and indefatigable windbags. Foreign observers like Frances Trollope wondered how it was that "No people appear more anxious to excite admiration and receive applause than the Americans, yet none take so little trouble, or make so few sacrifices to obtain it." Visitors frequently professed to be startled by the rudeness that typified so much American oratory, even in its most august chambers of law and legislation, where, as Frederick Raumer exclaimed, "some go beyond all bounds: shouting, screaming, sudden changes of the voice, smiting the table with the hand, sawing the air with the arms, shaking or nodding the head, stretching out the knee and bending back the body." But more serious to the cause of politics generally than such distinctively American forms of crudeness was the tendency of speakers to seek always the least common denominator—the "people" themselves. Indeed "the war of politics" in general, as Thomas Hamilton put it, "seems not the contest of opinion supported by appeal to enlightened argument, and acknowledged principles, but the squabble of greedy and abusive partisans, appealing to the violent passions of the popular, and utterly unscrupulous as to their instruments of attack." Oratory may be most at home in the land of freedom, as Americans were given to boast, but that was no guarantee against the corruption of either. The English writer Isabella Bishop reported back that "public morality is in a very low state," in America, and that, not at all incidentally, "To obtain political favour or position a man must stoop very low; he must cultivate the good will of the ignorant and the vicious; he must excite and minister to the passions of the people; he must flatter the bad, and assail the honourable with unmerited opprobrium."[2]

Such sentiments, even so generalized here, suggest something of the complexity of the public world Grimké was about to reenter. That world was shaped decisively by a proud republican heritage, with its attendant if often uneasy values respecting public virtue and democratic institutions; it was also being dramatically transformed, at the very moment of her ascent, by powerful cultural and economical forces that would entail serious dislocations of identity and conviction. Grimké was to catapult herself into a society at once inviting and threatening, rewarding and punitive, where questions of how change was to be effected and by whom were taking on unprecedented dimensions. We have reason to wonder, then, about Grimké's general understanding of the public world she would soon occupy; indeed, the story of her personal career is in part a story of how she confronted, interpreted, and worked to reshape the contexts of speech and moral action.[3]

I hope to suggest in the following account the ways in which Grimké's encounter with Theodore Weld helped to shape her thought and sharpen its expression on just this question. The debate worked, I shall argue, to prompt, organize, and refine Grimké's most fundamental convictions about the nature of rights and of women's access to them. Her still-emerging conception of women's rights may be characterized generally in this way: all rights cohere laterally into a biblically inscribed moral order; thus no single right can legitimately take precedence over another. Moral reform in the world, accordingly, can be sanctioned only as it invokes any given right as in concert with all others. For such work, a right is never fully constituted until and unless it is claimed as such—that is, asserted publicly and acted upon as a means to discharge one's own responsibility as a free moral agent. Such an act of proclamation was rhetorical in the most overt and important sense: it was designed to effect a unity between speech and action by according to a given appeal the status of an expressed right, granting thereby to that act authority, endurance, and at least potential effect. For a given act—a speech, argument, petition—to assume such power, it must be perceived as the expression of a known right: hence the rhetorical obligation assumed by all reformers to establish public recognition of their right to say what must be said. To fail that obligation—to ignore it, merely assume it, or subordinate it to some other expedient—was thus to fail a moral duty of the first order, to diminish the public efficacy of reform work by failing to announce the rightful grounds of such work.

By December 1836, Angelina and Sarah had completed their training, prepared now as well as the others to organize at the avant-garde of the abolitionist line, fend off counterattacks, and help spread throughout the North proof of God's judgment against slavery. What Weld and his fellow organizers could not have prepared the sisters for, of course, was the storm of protest they were to draw down upon their heads; indeed, the furthest thing from Angelina's mind now was to enter her work as the object of idle curiosity, the center of controversy, or a spectacle. From the outset, rather, the more general concern for both the front offices of the American Anti-Slavery Society and Grimké was to control for the public reception, force, and meaning of the lectures. The problem of how to manage the vagaries of popular perception would accompany them throughout the summer and fall of 1837 and well into the next year, reaching its fiery consummation finally in May of 1838. Angelina, in any case, was acutely aware of the potential for problems from the very beginning. For the most part optimistic and nonplussed herself about the prospect before them, she nevertheless worried to Jane Smith about the double bind the sisters confronted when it came to dealing with public expectations. Even before the otherwise sympathetic convention of the Anti-Slavery Convention of American Women, Angelina noted that "we felt almost in despair," knowing that "some persons here were exceedingly afraid that if we addressed our sisters it would be called Quaker preaching and that the prejudice here against woman's speaking in public was so great" that the abolitionist cause would itself be imperilled. It did not help, either, that so trusting a friend as Gerrit Smith openly expressed his fear "that we would be called a Fanny Wright meeting and so on, and advised us not to make addresses except in parlors."[4]

For the time, at least, that is precisely the forum to which the Grimkés limited their rhetorical efforts, although men could periodically be spotted attending avowedly nonpromiscuous occasions. In the meantime, much larger stages were being readied. Indeed, it is not too much to say that far from bursting onto the scene, unannounced and uninvited, the sisters were entering a region that had been expecting and preparing for some such event for years. Boston was not only the hub of radical abolitionism for most of the region—and had been since the early 1830s—but it had also proven itself distinctive for the role women played in its work of reform generally and abolitionism especially. Thus while the sisters honed their skills in the close quarters of New York parlors, members of the Boston Female Antislavery Society, Garrison, and numerous supporters continued to press for women's opportunities and access to public voice. On the same day that Angelina confided to Jane Smith about the problems of public opinion, the *Liberator* featured a familiar essay on "Female Influence" that seemed to offer a most encouraging prospect. "The daughters of America will be heard," its author declared, and "wherever there is suffering, their hands will be stretched forth to save. Already do we hear the sound of many voices speaking peace and hope to the weary and oppressed children of Africa." There will be those forces of opposition, the writer explained, who, like the South, "will endeavor to convince 'the ladies' that the contest is one which delicacy and refinement should avoid; that it is a purely political contest, in which none but Amazons will engage. But great is the truth and it will prevail," concludes "Equality." It was in any case a "base libel on the intellects of northern females to suppose that southern sophistry will much longer conceal it." Garrison's paper was by this time a veritable public relations machine for women's advocacy; if it never reached a following anywhere near that of the major mainstream periodicals, it tirelessly cultivated potential and sympathetic audiences for women's speech. "What the Ladies of Massachusetts Think" ("Let her blush to be a woman who cannot sympathize with suffering humanity; who cannot in (nor out of) her sphere plead the cause of justice and human right"); "The Power of Women" ("Whatever may be the customs and laws of a country, the women of it decide the morals"); addresses and reports from local Ladies Anti-Slavery Societies ("We have had two lectures, which gained an addition to our society. We have circulated a few publications.") Antebellum America could be and usually was resistant to the very idea of women's public speech, but in Boston, at least, the way was being paved for the advent of change.[5]

Before the summer of 1837 was over, Angelina Grimké would become after Francis Wright the most notorious woman in America. Aside from several passages in her private correspondence admitting to certain trepidations over public speaking, nothing as yet suggested foreknowledge of the storm to come. If anything, Grimké appeared to enjoy the unified rhetorical resources not only of the AASS, but of the region's female organizations as well. More than a month before the sisters departed for Massachusetts, the Ladies' New York City Anti-Slavery Society enthusiastically commended them to the world, confident in the knowledge that "they have become voluntary exiles from the bloodstained soil of Carolina, tho' it be their native one, and with a holy resolution that knows no wavering, have consecrated themselves to this pilgrimage of mercy." Abby Ann Cox, writing in behalf of the society, implored her readers to help "procure for them audiences of Northern women who need so much to hear what they yearn so much to tell them, of the deep degradation, the utter and hopeless misery of two and a half millions of our brethren and sisters of a common country."[6]

Already, audiences—promiscuous or otherwise—were responding with their feet to such calls for support, and Angelina was actually warming to her task. Far from quailing in the face of growing and diverse crowds, she was fully reconciled to the unprecedented nature of her work; thus after a speech in Poughkeepsie she proudly informed Sarah Douglass that "About 300 attended" the occasion, and pronounced it all "a very satisfying meeting I believe to all partys," noting, too, that while, "for the first time in my life I spake in a promiscuous assembly," she nevertheless "found that the men were no more to me then, than the women." By the time the sisters arrived in Boston in late May, the prospects for a triumphal lecture tour seemed bright indeed. Angelina found herself "surrounded by an electric atmosphere which yield to the stroke of the wings of effort and sends up the soaring spirit still higher and swifter in its upward flight."[7]

In Maria Chapman she found "one of the noblest women I ever saw," and observed cheerfully that there was real antislavery here: "a heart to work, a tongue to speak." Chapman, who had labored every bit as tirelessly and under as pressing conditions as Garrison, worked now to cultivate the fields she knew the sisters would soon enter. Similar in tone to the missive of the New York Ladies Anti-Slavery Society of the previous March, Chapman's included brief but telling commentary on the complex message the Grimkés could be counted on to promote. Who they were, where they were from, what they had written; all this was general knowledge. But there was more: who they were as women—as Christian women—made the sisters "eminently qualified," and marked "the elevated and Christian point of view from which they behold the rights of woman; her duties and her consequent rights." Chapman's appeal was more than a routine letter of commendation: it explicitly asserted the subject of women's rights onto the public platform of antislavery, indeed, celebrated the Grimkés' arrival on the basis not of their southern origins but because of their gender. The moment was ripe, then, for elaborating on the integral relationship between slavery and women's condition. "It is of paramount importance," Chapman informed her readers, "that both men and women should understand their true positions and mighty responsibilities to this and to coming generations. In all things spiritual their functions are identical." The sisters were to be received like prophets or apostles of old, women who *as women* might "exalt the national character of our women—so inferior to that of the Maternal Ancestry who in 1620 'fled from their spheres in England, and journeyed here with their little ones,' shelterless in the wintry air, that they might pursue their christian course unimpeded by sneers or ridicule, ecclesiastical mandates or publick outrage."[8]

Such statements on public life and its expectations give us only the briefest glimpse of what Grimké confronted as she marched toward the platforms of New England in the spring and summer of 1837. They are meant only to suggest here the extent to which the domain of political action was mapped with reference to oratory and the rhetorical arts; Grimké's own expectations and performances, the reception, support, and criticism that followed her throughout the tour, must in some important ways have been shaped by such cultural norms. Certainly the ambivalence with which popular orators were treated—especially those who sought dramatic social change—is indicative of a greater set of anxieties about the pace, leadership, and direction of American cultural dynamics generally. A well-established scholarship has by now made evident that these anxieties help account for the severity with which putative distinctions between public and private life were maintained, as well as the frequency with which they were transgressed. How else to explain the shrill paranoia of ministers like Hubbard Winslow, so fearful that

> when females undertake to assume the place of public teachers, whether to both sexes or only to their own; when they form societies for the purpose of sitting in judgment and acting upon the affairs of the church and state; when they travel about from place to place as lectures, teachers, and guides to public sentiment; when they assemble in conventions to discuss questions, pass resolutions, make speeches, and vote upon civil, political, moral, and religious matters . . . it is then no longer a question whether they have stretched themselves beyond their measure and violated the inspired injunction which saith, "Let the woman learn in silence with all subjection; but I suffer not a woman to teach, nor to usurp authority over the man, but to be in silence."[9]

To view Grimké's tour in light of these sentiments is to observe virtually at first-hand the education of one of the age's great orators. In undertaking such a mission, she had first to command the facts, arguments, and appeals of the abolitionists' message: this she had prepared for in the several years since her total conversion to antislavery and, more intensely, during the fall of 1836 at the headquarters of the American Anti-Slavery Society in New York. The speaker needed to learn, too, of the extent and depth of resistance to that message in the North and to adapt accordingly, if at all. To whom should she respond? To Beecher but not Hubbard? Why? What was the difference between counterattack and simply falling into the hands of the opposition? How were her energies, in short, best directed to optimal effect? All these questions and more asserted themselves with varying degrees of urgency before and during the tour, and helped shape her mission in decisive ways. Perhaps her most lasting lesson, however, came with the realization that her greatest challenge came not from outside abolitionist circles but from within, not from the effusions of Hubbard but from the more intimate, more subtle and mortifying objections of one Theodore Weld. Here, in her exchange of letters over the question of Grimké's espousal of women's rights in the course of a tour designed specifically for abolitionist ends, can be seen the most dramatic and arguably the most important moment in Grimké's education as an orator.

Angelina's exchange with Weld was but a phase in a much more general and protracted debate over the province of women's reform activity. Knowing this, both correspondents were able to situate their arguments in a realm between fleeting detail and airy abstractions; indeed, what strikes the modern reader about these impassioned appeals is their simultaneous grasp of theory and practice, principle and expedience, the general and the particular. To an important degree the tone, terms, and direction of the debate were initiated by Angelina's letter of 12 August. In it, she extended and elaborated upon the issues so frequently addressed in her more public debate with Catharine Beecher, inflected now with evident affection and mild good humor. Written from Groton and pressured by her speaking schedule, the text is nevertheless notable for its concentrated seriousness, and there can be no doubting that its author meant to establish the scope and depth of the subject addressed. Grimké was now at the very height of her rhetorical powers, and although nothing indicates that she deliberately set out to provoke Weld—or anyone—it is equally clear that after the Beecher controversy she was willing and prepared to engage even so formidable a disputant as Theodore Weld. Neither was it the first time Angelina had conducted arguments over women's rights with males: in early March, she and Sarah had responded publicly in print to defend their doctrines in the New Haven *Religious Intelligencer,* and on 17 and 18 July Angelina routed two men in Amesbury during

a staged debate that must have left audiences wondering who was more coura-
geous (or foolhardy)— the men, for provoking an expert on biblical arguments
against slavery, or Grimké, for not only enthusiastically stepping beyond the
bounds of private life, but actually battling over such issues on the public stage.[10]

Grimké's letter of 12 August, though recognizable within such unfolding contexts of public debate, was nevertheless unlike anything issuing from her pen
before or after. In addition to the interpersonal dynamics it set in play, and the
record it provides of the correspondents' positions on moral reform, the letter
fixed a specific structure of convictions, strengthened rather than debased by the
insistence that each argument be addressed directly, honestly, and rigorously.

In general, the letter organizes an account of her beliefs prior to Weld's explicit
objections, and establishes a rationale for giving to rights their rhetorical imperative. In this and in the following letters, the case is advanced through four
roughly discrete phases, in which Grimké first identifies prevailing situational
determinants; then underscores the need for women to assert their rights as free
moral agents; then applies that injunction directly to the work of abolition and
all moral reform; and finally drives her analysis to the conclusion that all truly
moral reform coheres into a unified rationale for acting in the world on behalf of
the world. The first phase thus bears on questions of situation; the second on
agency; the third on purpose; and the fourth on what it is that can be ultimately
said to justify women's public action.[11]

Whatever trepidation Grimké may have experienced thus far about public
speaking appears to have dissipated into the August heat. There is, if anything,
mild bemusement in her opening lines to Weld, expressing her confidence that he
had no doubt "heard by this time of all the fuss that is now making in this region
about our stepping so far out of the bounds of female propriety as to lecture to
promiscuous assemblies." Here is relish, of a kind, a newcomer's delight in witnessing the power of one's convictions forcibly expressed. It is still no small measure of the distance between Grimké and Weld at this time that she could jokingly
claim to be "waiting in some anxiety to see what the Executive Committee mean
to do in these troublous times, whether to renounce us or not." In time, of course,
the Executive Committee would feel itself forced to "caution their fellow citizens
not to confound their doctrines with such as individual members may occasion-
ally advance."[12]

The reasons for the leadership's nervous reaction were made abundantly clear
by the words immediately following Grimké's good-natured tweaking: "But seriously speaking," she announced to Weld, "we are placed very unexpectedly in a
very trying situation, in the forefront of an entirely new contest—a contest for the
rights of *woman* as a moral, intelligent and responsible being." This view, it turns
out, proved to be the actual provocation to the New York circle, concerned as it

was not with the sisters' speaking in public, nor before promiscuous audiences, but with what appeared to be a rapidly surfacing preoccupation over women's rights as such. Grimké's acute and complex understanding of situational forces, her belief in manifest signs to act now in history, did little to alleviate Weld's misgivings; nor could they possibly, for such a "contest for the rights of woman" was not the will of humans but of God, and it seemed, Grimké wrote, that the time "had come now and that the exigency must be met with the firmness and faith of woman in by gone ages."[13]

By thus announcing both the exigency and its means of resolution, Grimké effectively cemented a situation-agent relationship that would be very difficult for Weld to loosen. Couched in terms of the primitive Christianity to which they both ascribed, Grimké's appeal demanded of Weld that he make way for this "new contest" because, simply, he must, and for the same reason that Grimké must. To be sure, Angelina wrote, "I cannot help feeling some regret that this sh'ld have come up *before* the Anti-Slavery question was settled, so fearful am I that it may injure that blessed cause." On further reflection, however, the issue did not allow gradations, and the imperative to act immediately was unmistakable. "I think this must be the Lord's time," Grimké explained, "and therefore *the best time*, for it seems to have been brought about by a concatenation of circumstances over which we had no control." In thus determining the source and scope of the situation, Grimké established at this early point what might be considered the debate's uncontestable terms: a moral challenge, divinely ordered, that called for action of a specific and immediate kind.[14]

Having labored with Herculean zeal to instill abolition at the forefront of American reform, Weld could not have found much comfort in Grimké's "regret." Angelina, he knew, was incapable of being blithe about anything, but here was something close. Not only did she abjure responsibility for bringing about the circumstances that allegedly demanded discussion of women's rights; she now claimed unabashedly that women, in taking up the call, would no doubt rupture the very religious and familial vitals of society. In the notoriously crowded reform arena of the 1830s, here was a cause espoused by a credentialed "agent" of the American Anti-Slavery Society promising to disrupt "the interests of every minister in our land," and to ultimately "divide in Jacob and scatter in Israel." As if taking on the ministry was not enough, Grimké further declared that the issue of women's rights would "touch every man's interests at home, in the tenderest relation of life," penetrating finally "into the very depth of his soul and cause great searchings of heart." Such confidence in women's power to reach so deeply and so universally contrasted sharply with the animadversions of all the Hubbard Winslows of the period, with all their despair over the "sad wreck of female loveliness" that women in public must become. What Winslow said publicly, in any case, most men secretly believed, Grimké reasoned, and in the end, "There is not one man in 500 who really understands what kind of attention is alone acceptable to a woman of pure and exalted moral and intellectual worth."[15]

The rhetorical work of the letter so far is evident in these few sentences. Grimké has inaugurated a case for asserting women's rights as a viable, indeed absolutely necessary, component of moral reform; she has identified the source and moral authority behind a situation demanding change; and has written into that situation the imperative for women to act immediately on behalf not only of slaves but of all women. It remains to delimit the nature of that authority by which women's rights, including the right to speak in public, are claimed. Again, the key rhetorical move here is to link as tightly as possible such rights-based appeals to the universally recognized obligation to act on duty. Because Weld would be the first to grant that no woman has the right to surrender her moral responsibility, he must be expected to concede that they, like all free moral agents, have an obligation to act on their rights. To claim a right is in this sense simultaneously a claim to act on it as the means to realize one's duty. Public speech, in Grimké's analysis, could be no exception, and because it was universally grounded in one's identity as a human being, such rights were universal and essential. As to the matter of the sisters' Quaker affiliation, which Weld had considered useful for tactical purposes, Grimké was insistent: "we do *not* stand on this ground at all," she informed Weld, "we ask no favors for ourselves, but *claim* rights for *our sex*." For the moment, Grimké held out some hope that in the course of their communication Weld might come to see "how delightful, ennobling and dignified" was the Pauline view that "in Christ Jesus there is neither male nor female." However that might be, Grimké concluded, "*this* reformation *must begin with ourselves*."[16]

Master orator; renowned lecturer; key strategist for the AASS: Theodore Weld, it is safe to say, was not used to being instructed on the fine points of reform and human rights. Here was, after all, the awesome figure to whom Angelina had referred when she had exclaimed to Jane Smith that "I had never heard so grand and beautiful an exposition of the dignity and nobility of man in my life." But Weld was as restrained in private as he was eloquent in public, and if he was at all surprised by Angelina's increasingly vocal sentiments about the "woman question," he was disciplined enough to respond through a cautious and systematic exposition of his own views. Weld's initial reaction represents the first of three important statements on the complex question of women's rights and the nature of social reformation. As with Grimké's, it gives evidence that behind his various appeals lay a well-developed and fully coherent set of theoretical principles.[17] Weld had for years relied on these principles as guides to his own efforts and those of others, from Lane Seminary in Ohio to the AASS offices in New York City. The point is perhaps worth stressing again, in light of Weld's reputation as an impassioned orator and tactician: he was a thinker of considerable depth, and we have in this exchange a rich illustration of his mind at work. At the basis of his ideas about human rights, social change, and rhetorical strategy was a severe instrumentalism, through which all claims on the moral consciousness of the public were to be subordinated to the prior needs of the abolition movement. All questions of who should act, where, how, and when were rendered in an exacting calculus that left virtually no room for arguments like those advanced by Grimké. Her views could not be ignored, however, and in fact Weld was very quick to address them as pointedly as possible. Certainly he had good reason: from east to west across the northern states, his network of agents and supporters were working with unprecedented organization, energy, and effect. This was perhaps the single greatest concentration of reform talent in American history, and Weld had played a crucial role in its assemblage and direction. Now he was faced with the specter of his illustrious prize—two sisters from the slave-holding South—apparently seizing on the occasion of their most public appearances to introduce extraneous and distracting issues, perhaps to divide and certainly to retard the progress of the cause. It was time to put a stop to such talk before it threatened to undo his efforts altogether.[18]

Weld's first need was to clarify the grounds of debate and determine its boundaries. That meant above all not allowing their disagreement to devolve into competing claims over who spoke from higher principle. Not ordinarily defensive about his convictions, Weld now was adamant to establish his credentials as a supporter of women's rights, indeed as an activist on their behalf. "As to the rights and wrongs of women," he insisted, "it is an old theme with me. It was the *first* subject I ever discussed." Weld recalled his schoolboy days when he debated in favor of women's rights to participate in the affairs of state, bar, and pulpit. The question at issue, then, was definitely not a matter of who was or was not arguing from principle. "What I advocated in boyhood I advocate now," Weld wrote, "that woman in EVERY particular shares equally with man rights and responsibilities."[19]

If it was not to be a contest over higher ground, then in what did their difference actually consist? For Weld the issue was expediency—expediency not as opposed to principle but as an instrument for its implementation. The problem now was that the sisters were undermining the former by ignoring the latter. Typical of Weld, he saw the situation in educational terms and sought to rectify it by explaining to the Grimkés the nature of their error. What they had failed to see as yet, he explained, was that the very act of speech was itself a declaration of right, indeed, "the best possible advocacy which you can make is just what you *are* making day by day." In this respect, the right to speak was presumed and confirmed through the act of speech—quite independent of stated claims to that right. Besides, Weld argued, simply by standing up and testifying against slavery the sisters had "already converted multitudes," indeed, "Thousands hear you every week who have all their lives held that woman must not speak in public." Within this train of reasoning, the ultimate rhetorical authority behind the sisters rested not so much in their words, for there were many eloquent soldiers in the field; nor in their Quaker relation, for there were other Friends similarly engaged; nor was it even the fact that they were women: Child, Chapman, and others could claim that much. No, Weld argued, the sisters could be more effective than all the others for the simple but all-important reason that they were Southerners; they were useful precisely because of this peculiarity and no other. "Now *you two* are the ONLY FEMALES in the free states," wrote Weld, "who combine all these facilities for anti slavery effort: 1. Are *southerners*. 2. Have been slaveholders. 3. For a long time most widely known by the eminence of friends. 4. Speaking and writing power and practice. 5. Ultra Abolitionists. 6. Acquaintance with the whole subject, argumentative, historian, legal, and biblical."[20]

Behind Weld's didacticism lay a theory of social reform that was to guide virtually all of his thinking, writing, and speaking on abolitionism. At its center was the conviction that the "public mind" responded most actively to the principles in their purest and simplest form; once absorbed, such truths would drive themselves forward, eventually taking into their sweep any collateral or secondary principles as might be appropriate to circumstances. The sisters, Weld believed, were in an ideal position to give dramatic testimony to this single principle, if only they would see that "the abolition question is most powerfully preparative and introductory to the other questions." The point was not to be taken as a warrant for ignoring or displacing the issue of women's rights. Far from it: if Sarah and Angelina would continue to focus on the primary cause, they could in time expect a revolution in public consciousness on the subject. "Mind gravitates from a general principle to its *collaterals*," Weld explained, and "begins with a case self evidently clear and strong, and then takes up its ramifications." So much was exactly the course taken in England, where the Reform Bill and numerous other measures had recently been pushed through Parliament. For this reason, Weld concluded, American abolitionists ought "*first* wake up the nation to lift millions of slaves of both sexes from the dust, and turn them into MEN and then when we all have our hand in, it will be an easy matter to take millions of females from their knees and set them on their feet, or in other words transform them from *babies* into *women*."[21]

Behind these words was, more than a theory of rights, a theory of influence. Weld was at some pains to point out, accordingly, that the question at hand was not about women's rights in general or as they applied specifically to the sisters' speaking in public. Weld departed simply on tactical grounds, and disagreed vehemently that some "concatenation of circumstances" justified agitating an essentially derivative issue. All of which is to stress again the basis of Weld's argument as he expressed it: certain rights might legitimately, indeed sometimes must, be held in abeyance if such restraint would assist the cause of primary concern. This check on rights talk did nothing to diminish the right as such; it only subordinated any given right to the exigencies of time, place, and the proclivities of the public mind. A right in this logic was most fully realized as it was made expedient. To demand that the secondary issue of women's rights be introduced now would only make the sisters "so obnoxious as to cripple your influence on the subject of slavery."[22]

By the time Angelina found time again to pick up her pen, the sisters had resettled in nearby Brookline at the home of Samuel Philbrick. Philbrick, who had earlier hosted the sisters during their address to the Brookline abolitionists, at the time pronounced Angelina's performance "thrilling, eloquent and powerful." All in all, Philbrick then noted in his diary, "I have rarely seen or heard an orator that could equal Angelina."[23] The speaking engagements, the public debate with Catharine Beecher, the local skirmishes, and of course the *Pastoral Letter* were rapidly securing the sisters' claim on the public and reform conscience of New England; in truth, no female, reformer or otherwise, had ever reached such visible heights in the early republic, and Angelina was frequently called upon to offer her views on nonabolition matters precisely because she was Angelina Grimké. The response to one such request, written on the very day of her riposte to Weld and Whittier, illustrates sharply how comprehensive her vision of moral agency and the work of reform had become.[24]

In hopes of buttressing his efforts at temperance organization, George M. Chase had recently inquired after Grimké's own views about such work and the role women might play in it. Angelina was by now skeptical, it seems, of most men's capacity to consider seriously her convictions, so "ultra" were they that she doubted "whether thou wouldst assent to them, much less be willing to make any use of them." Wary she might have been, but Grimké did not hesitate to state in full the basis of her position in regard to all reform activity. Women were bound to work for all such movements, she explained to Chase, just "because she is a moral, intellectual and responsible being, standing on the same platform of human rights and human responsibilities with man, created like him only a little lower than the Angels," not, she insisted, "as our brethren suppose, created a little lower than Man."[25]

Like Weld, with whom she shared a powerfully didactic impulse, Grimké could expound readily as much on her reasoning as on her reasons. It was, she declared to Chase, important to argue first from fixed principles, and to draw inferences from these premises to determine the appropriate course of action. And if it was true that women were placed equally before the "Angels," then it must equally be true that the duties befalling men befell women alike. Any other conclusion was the result of a fundamental confusion, a point she was to advance against Weld in greater detail and with greater nuance. To Chase, Angelina confided in the most direct terms the "fixed principle" from which she derived all her inferences: "Our duties are governed by circumstances not by sex. Woman has not particular duties as a woman though she has as a mother, a wife, a daughter or a sister." As a result, she concluded, "Man will try in vain to drive us up to the performance of our moral duties, until he concedes to us our moral rights. Whilst we are kept down upon the lower platform our vision cannot extend over the whole field of our responsibilities and duties." This was more, no doubt, than Mr. Chase had asked for, but Grimké's private letter gives us certain evidence of the scope and intensity that her view had now reached, and helps account for the more fully developed and intimate response to her brethren in the fields of abolition.[26]

Writing for both Sarah and herself, Angelina wrote on 20 August her most elaborate private account of women's rationale for public action. There is in the letter very little of the mild jesting that characterized many of their exchanges, and a tone more formal than usual pervades the argument. The letter presents a systematic and unflinching refutation of a position held, it bears recalling, by one of the period's greatest polemical thinkers; but more than the sheer nerve that the letter evinces—that much had been demonstrated in a variety of rhetorical contexts—it represents a pivotal moment in the author's development as a public actor. In it, she is able to expound to both Weld and Whittier in private correspondence a fully realized theory of public moral action, the result of months, indeed years, of working and reflecting on the subject. In its general outline, the letter of 20 August is designed to explain the circumstances of the controversy over their public speaking; attacks clerical schemes to undermine the labors of abolitionists; and extends her position that all rightful reforms cohere into a unified rationale for public action. To get a better sense of the force of these arguments, however, we need to look at them more closely and examine how they work together to form what is in effect a private text about public life.

In her correspondence of 12 August, we recall, Grimké had declared openly and proudly that the sisters were entering a new contest for women's rights. Not expecting then how unsympathetic Weld would be about her discovery, Grimké portrayed the situation in New England as ripe not only for antislavery work, but for pushing ahead strongly on "the woman question." Events, she explained, were coming together in such a way that they had to act now, in concert and publicly. The rhetorical function of the letter, then, was to dramatize an imperative to act by virtue of situational exigencies. Whittier's and especially Weld's response to that argument did nothing to refute Angelina's position, but rather prompted her to a fuller and more forceful account of her reasoning, the summation of which is exhibited in the letter of 20 August. What remained for Angelina was to build on these earlier arguments—essentially historical and religious justifications for situated agency—and to establish a case for the declaration of women's rights as complementing rather than subverting the antislavery cause. If the first letter thus identified the context and responsibility for the assertion of women's rights, this one grounded that assertion by giving it purpose and by integrating it into a unified field of moral action.

The first order of business was to straighten out certain misperceptions. Weld and Whittier seemed to be under the impression that the sisters had in fact been the immediate cause of the controversy. Not true, Angelina insisted: in fact it was the *Pastoral Letter* "which did the mischief," composed as it was by panic-stricken ministers "who had commenced a most violent attack upon us." The notorious product of the June meeting of the Congregational Association of Massachusetts, the *Pastoral Letter* had managed to squeeze within its few pages a virtual compendium of clerical anxieties over the state of society, church, and the future of both. It is, in its own way, a polemical masterpiece, voicing in the most efficient manner possible the whole confused, complicated, and deeply conflicted case against the deployment of clerical resources for the purposes of social agitation. The source of exasperation that may be read in every line in truth had less to do with the sisters' activities than they were pleased to believe and more to do with the relentless assaults of Garrison and his supporters. At once traduced and exploited, dispossessed and occupied, the churches had grown exceedingly tired of what appeared to be the blithe expropriation of their very moral center by those who had least claim to it.[27]

It was the *Pastoral Letter,* Angelina informed Weld and Whittier, that "roused the attention of the whole country to enquire what *right* we had to open our mouths for the dumb." At first glance, perhaps, Grimké may be said to have overstated the case. The brief text is broken into four sections, each one addressing what the leadership determined to be issues "bearing upon the cause of Christ." The first concerned the discussion of "perplexed and agitating subjects," and recommended with notable restraint only that such discussion *"not be forced upon any church as matters for debate, at the hazard of alienation and division."* It would be difficult to imagine any organized religion, before, then, or since, in principle objecting to such sentiments; for the members of the Association, at least, it was perfectly obvious why the proper exercise of the pastoral office ought not to be interfered with, and they asked merely that those who were inclined to zealotry not "disturb the influence of those ministers who think that the promotion of personal religion among their people, and the establishment of Christians in the faith and comfort of the Gospel, is the proper object of their ministry." Surely this was a request that even the Grimké's could grant.[28]

The second topic of concern must appear, in context, as only slightly more provocative. The pastoral office was authorized, all would agree, by Scripture, and ought be exercised freely and with all due respect and deference. Again, the position assumed here was neither novel nor incendiary, at least on its own terms, and certainly would have been recognized in even the relatively liberal environment of New England as a virtual commonplace. Thus the *Pastoral Letter* noted with some alarm the fact that "this respect has been in some cases violated," especially by forces "encouraging lecturers or preachers on certain topics of reform to present their subjects within the parochial limits of settled pastors without their consent." In view of these intrusions upon the accepted grounds of the ministerial office, and "because we desire the highest influence of the ministry upon you and your children," the Congregational leaders exhorted the faithful "to reverence that office which the ascending Redeemer selected from all his gifts as the highest token of his love and care for his people." Again, for all its stress on deference to the pastoral office, there is nothing so far that would suggest, as Sarah was later to put it, that the *Pastoral Letter* would "be recurred to with as much astonishment as the opinions of Cotton Mather and other distinguished men of his day, on the subject of witchcraft."[29]

What was it, then, that so provoked Angelina to renounce to Weld and Whittier "that Clerical Domination which now rules the world under the various names of Gen'l Assemblies, Congregational Associations, etc.?" Section three of the *Pastoral Letter* comprised only four paragraphs and expressed little that the sisters had not heard before; nevertheless, it so effectively wove together the various objections to women's work in public life that it simply could not be ignored. Certainly the attention the Grimkés and others accorded to these brief passages indicate that they grasped fully how important it was to refute the arguments decisively. Angelina would leave to Sarah the task of systematic and public rebuttal, the bulk of which would appear later in *Letters on the Equality of the Sexes*. For now, Weld and Whittier were to be kept from falling into the same insidious logic as that espoused by the equally well meaning but much more dangerous General Association.[30]

The authors of the *Pastoral Letter*, chief among them Hezekiah Niles, professed to have no problem with female influence or, for that matter, influential women. The church had, in fact, a remarkable record of support for and by women. Neither was the objection against the strength, scope, or source of that influence; church leaders expressly declared that there were "social influences which females use in promoting piety and the great objects of christian benevolence, which we cannot too highly commend," and wanted to make very clear their hope that women "may abound more and more in these labours of piety and love." The issue was rather the startling aspect of women so ambitious of public acclaim as to yield "the power which God has given for her protection." In lines so similar to those of Winslow's that Grimké must have suspected collusion of some kind, the *Letter* intoned the familiar reminder that the "appropriate duties and influence of women, are clearly stated in the New Testament," and known there to be "unobtrusive and private, but the sources of mighty power." The authors of the *Pastoral Letter,* like those before and those of the several Clerical Appeals that were to follow, knew full well how important were women abolitionists to Garrison, and they no doubt imagined the terrifying prospect of the Grimkés becoming mouthpieces for his especially odious brand of anticleri-cal doctrine. Conversely, the sisters could scarcely have been surprised to read of the congregation's dismay over "the mistaken conduct of those who encourage females to bear an obtrusive and ostentatious part in measures of reform, and countenance any of that sex who so far forget themselves as to itinerant in the character of public lecturers and teachers."[31]

No, the problem was not female influence in and of itself. For the clerical lead-ers of New England, the real issue was the province wherein that influence was exercised, and to what ultimate end. The fourth and final section of the *Pastoral Letter* thus urged readers to forebear public works and to undertake instead "*the cultivation of private christian character, and private efforts for the spiritual good of individuals.*" It is worth noting, moreover, as Angelina did not, that the proscrip-tion against public agitation extended to male reformers as well. Like the Grimkés, these reformers sought to usurp the proper ground of ministerial action, forgetting in the process that if only "Christians will labor *privately* to form individual minds, especially those of the young, to virtue and religion, they will hasten the universal prevalence of religion by the most effectual means." If moral reformers truly wished to effect good in the world, the authors concluded, then "We commend the Sabbath School, and Bible Class to the members of our churches as opportunities of extensive and enduring influence."[32]

For all its animus against women speakers and reformers generally, the *Pastoral Letter* pretends to no discussion of rights. The word "right" itself is invoked but once, and indeed is not, within the rhetorical economy of the text, required for driving the argument forward. To the extent that the text may be said to express moral authority, it is almost exclusively grounded in an argument from Christian duty. And while the content of that duty is obviously different from Weld's conception, both parties would seem preoccupied with mapping the domains of responsible action. In Grimké's view, the clerical habit of imposing duties and forgetting rights was altogether to be expected; the world was grown crowded with these "priests and levites," and there could be little wonder in their reaction to the news of these "prophetesses" called from the plough. The real per-plexity was Weld's stance. Did he not recognize that the clerical objection to women's ministry was precisely the kind of resistance he and other abolitionists had experienced quite recently? "Now my dear brothers," Grimké stressed, "*this invasion of our rights* was just such an attack upon *us,* as that made upon Abolitionists generally when they were told a few years ago that *they had no right* to discuss the subject of Slavery." The congregational leadership was, rhetorically speaking, beyond hope of persuasion, but for support, Weld, Whittier, and others of the brethren had only to be reminded of their own struggle for the right to speak. They knew from experience, Grimké argued, that "*The time* to assert a right is *the* time when that right is denied," and for this reason alone the sisters "*must establish this right* for if we do not, it will be impossible for us to go *on with the work of Emancipation.*"[33]

Here was the very cornerstone of Grimké's argument. By reasserting the priority of rights before duty, and by then coupling tightly the two appeals into a rationale for effective action, Grimké not only refuted Weld but obliged him to recognize their comity of interests. In one respect, of course, Grimké's position could hardly have been otherwise: it would have made no sense for this evangelical to declare or exercise rights sheerly for the sake of doing so. The more pressing and coherent problem was to make her case compelling in the context of moral reform, and to this end she had to give meaning, purpose, and effect—an end—to such work as would be enabled by the public recognition of women's speech. Rights were a means to a greater end, and Weld's highly charged argument from expedience would have to buckle under the weight of Grimké's insight. As to his claim that the great audience turning out to see her was evidence of her effectiveness sans rights talk, Grimké was unimpressed: they were curious only, it being "a new thing under the sun to see a *woman* occupy the place of a lecturer," and not yet engaged enough to counteract "the leaven which the ministers are so assiduously working into the minds of the people." Most people in New England, Grimké found, were oblivious to women's rights, and those that did dare to declare for them were likely to have "their opponents throw perverted Scripture in their faces and call O yea, clamor for *proof,* proof, PROOF! And this *they cannot* give and are beaten off the field in disgrace." There was for all this a real appetite and need for the message, for stockpiling arguments on behalf of women's rights and educating the public accordingly. Surely, Grimké asked, was it now "wrong to give those views in a series of letters in a paper NOT devoted to Abolition?"[34]

Weld was fixed in a difficult position, and he was to respond with frustration and bewilderment to that fact. As Grimké's letter unfolded, it increasingly appeared that his resistance to Angelina's rights talk was of a piece with the very forces of opposition he was himself battling. By the midpoint of the letter he found himself made vaguely complicitous in the logic driving the *Pastoral Letter,* where "we are gravely told that we are out of our sphere even when we circulate petitions; out of our "appropriate sphere" when we speak to women only and out of them when we *sing* in the churches. Silence is *our* province," Grimké recounts, "submission *our* duty." These were, of course, sentiments very distant from Weld's own, but the reductio is not without a basis: Weld, whether he knew it or not, was counseling to the same effect a policy of silence—if not altogether, then under certain circumstances, and that much was not so very far from the ministerial view. This being the case, Grimké wrote, "If we 'give *no reason* for the hope that is in us,' that we have *equal rights* with our brethren, how can we expect to be permitted *much longer to exercise those rights?*"[35]

That Grimké should feel obliged to explain the nature of human rights to her readers thus must have struck Weld with no little surprise. Still it seemed to Grimké that he had much to learn, and on more than one front at that. For one thing, the issue of their Quaker affiliation was irrelevant; they did not stand on that ground, if only because according to Friends' doctrine, "Women are regardless equal to men on the ground of *spiritual gifts,* not on the broad ground of *humanity.* Woman may *preach,*" she conceded, for "this is a *gift;* but woman must *not* make the discipline by which *she herself* is to be governed." Their ground was rather humanity itself, the assumption of which was blocked by an organized and enormously powerful clergy, fearful of losing its claim on the people and determined to keep women off the stage of public life. Could Weld and Whittier "not see the deep laid scheme of the clergy against us as lecturers?" In their campaign to silence the sisters, the ministers threatened to eliminate a prime force in the transformation of public opinion. "They are springing a deep mine beneath our feet," Grimké warned, "and we shall *very* soon be compelled to retreat for we shall have no ground to stand on." Without that ground, threatened now too by the brethrens' objection to the discussion of rights, the sisters would virtually cease to be agents of the antislavery vanguard. "If we surrender the right to *speak* to the public this year," she reasoned, "we must surrender the right to petition next year and the right to *write* the year after and so on. What *then* can *woman* do for the slave when she is herself under the feet of man and shamed into *silence?*"[36]

Among its other effects, Grimké's argument systematically eliminated her critics' appeal to either principle or expedience. Weld's position was not without merit, but to the extent that he banked his position on the inexpedience of women's rights talk, he overlooked what was becoming obvious: women were most useful when they were free to speak publicly against slavery. For Grimké, the failure of her friends to apprehend the essential truth of this claim was symptomatic not so much of moral shortcoming or ill will, but of a certain habit of mind. The effort to so distinguish between principle and expedience was but an instance of a more general tendency among the abolitionist leadership, Grimké observed, and she was anxious to remedy the cause. Like Weld and Whittier, she claimed, "Anti Slavery men are trying very hard to separate what God hath joined together." Once joined, it would be impossible to drive a wedge between women's rights and those of the slave, and hence the movements for the restoration of those rights must be recognized as harmonious expressions toward the same end. Moral reformations, Angelina explained, "are bound together in a circle like the sciences; they blend with each other like the colors of the rainbow; they are the parts only of our glorious whole and that whole is Christianity, pure, practical christianity." Here, finally, was the fundamental principle upon which Grimké stood, posed as a criticism of the antislavery leadership but so close to their own sentiments that it would prove ultimately unresolvable.[37]

"Pure, practical christianity": an ideal to which Weld could scarcely object, in pursuit of which Grimké was willing to lay waste the false temples and all other barriers to genuine moral reform. Weld had imagined that slavery might be overturned by training a host of agents, holy warriors who would spread over the land and declare the message to the hearing and deaf alike. Grimké sought now to remind Weld of that vision, and of the responsibilities entailed by it, where "Men and Women will have to go out on their own responsibility, just like the prophets of old and declare the *whole* counsel of God to the people." Weld, whose own inclinations were similarly "primitive," read not for the first time that "The whole Church Government must come down," that "the clergy stand right in the way of reform," and that therefore "this stumbling block too must be removed *before* Slavery can be abolished, for the system is supported by *them*."[38]

Grimké's vision was thus not only sweeping, but swept aside any and all barriers to its fulfillment; if it is useful at all to speak of her radicalism, surely it rested in this demand for the unfettered exercise of human moral agency. That will to action was embodied not in the institutions of the visible church or its priests, but in the prophets and apostles to which Grimké now turned. Once this principle was in place and recognized, she explained to Weld and Whittier, three inferences were inescapable: first, true ministers were called from the plough, orchard, customs, and sea; second, ministers ought no more to be paid than prophets; and third, "As there were prophetesses as well as prophets, so there ought to be now female as well as male ministers."[39]

Weld could not but agree. He had spent a good deal of his adult life operating under just such an assumption, and he was again quick to protest any imputation against his record of support for women's ministry. Yet here again Grimké clearly showed herself willing to go where Weld could not, if only because his understanding of social influence prevented him from seeing beyond the tactical requirements of the antislavery cause. Grimké proved similarly steadfast, and neither was to yield the argumentative ground they had been called by the other to protect. Weld elaborated on his views in a heated letter of 26 August, in which he underscored his major claims and again pressed the essence of his theory of moral reform—or, more precisely, his theory of how the rhetoric of such reform was to be given optimal effect. "Since the world began," Weld reasoned,

> Moral Reform has been successfully advanced only in *one* way, and that has been by uplifting a great *self evident central* principle before all eyes. Then after keeping the principle in full blaze till it is *admitted* and *accredited* and the surrounding mass of mind is brought over and *committed* to it, *then* the *derivative* principles which radiate in all directions from this main central principle have been held up in the light of it and the mind having already embraced the central principle, moves *spontaneously outward* over all its *relations*.[40]

Weld proceeded, as was his habit, to amplify on the claim through example, inference, and entailment, but there was little new he could introduce into the exchange at this point. Given the premise that drove all his reform work, he could not help but simply conclude once again by asking, rhetorically, "what is plainer than that the grand primitive principle for which we struggle is HUMAN rights," and that, therefore, "the rights of *woman* is a principle purely *derivative* from the other?"[41]

Grimké had already answered to her satisfaction that question, and while she and Sarah continued an active correspondence with Weld, the crux of their respective positions had already been established. That Angelina was in the end unmoved by Weld's objections and principles of reform psychology is evident from a letter written to Henry C. Wright—on the same day as her 27 August response to Weld. Even as she confided to Weld that she was surprised at being thought the "ostensible cause of the Clerical movement," and professed her doubts about being able to bear "all this unsettlement and complaint among the *friends* of the cause," Angelina persisted in her original views. Wright, who was to incur the full brunt of Weld's jealousy by being removed from New England altogether, was for now close enough to the action that Grimké asked what thought about Garrison's *Liberator* "abandoning Abolitionism as a primary object and becoming the vehicle of all these grand principles?" The radicals' radical, Wright's eyes had been opened to the knowledge that "the Lord is preparing the minds of the people for the great and sublime principle" of total moral reform. The time for such a change in the *Liberator*'s mission was coming soon, Grimké urged Wright, and trusted that "brother G—may be divinely directed."[42]

Theodore Weld, disputant extraordinaire, had lost the argument. But of course this remarkable exchange of views in the harried summer of 1837 was not about scoring debaters' points. Neither could it be reduced to yet another example of feminist action-antifeminist reaction in the already well-stocked annals of early women's rights. Bearing so much in common, Grimké and Weld spoke to their differences; sharing so much of the weight of moral reform, they wondered together where their labors ought best to be directed. And finding themselves at once such private and yet such public figures, Grimké and Weld found in their correspondence a ready but ultimately frustrating medium for airing their respective views. The exchange of August 1837 illustrates several dimensions of Grimké's rhetorical imagination, and they are suggested in the following, but they hint, too, at Weld's slowly developing, conflicted, and perhaps unwitting affection for his interlocutor. Weld, who knew as well as anyone how to turn a negative into a positive, reckoned in the end that their mutual struggle to make sense of each other argued all the more for immediate contact. Letters would not do for such serious concerns, Weld noted guilelessly: "Now in conversation, there is opportunity to ascertain on the spot exactly what is meant, and to be sure of understanding a position before we attack it. In a word," Weld wrote, "if God ever permits us to meet, we will then take up the whole subject and find with Divine help the beginning, middle, and end."[43]

That time would come soon enough, but for now Grimké had still to confront the unfolding drama in which she played such a willing part. The prospect was daunting, no doubt, but Grimké ranked foremost among that kind of moral reformer who, so driven by duty to act, could yet seem so heedless, indeed uncaring, about the consequences of her action. To the unsympathetic or hostile, this moral stance was evidence of a paradoxical complacency that marked antebellum activists, where the self-congratulatory "we have done what we could" left unacknowledged the damage wrought by righteous zeal. Some reformers might profess surprise when little if anything changed as a result of their efforts; some, like Grimké, were genuinely surprised when they succeeded in provoking such reactions as those sounded during the New England tour. In retrospect, we can see that even if paradoxical, the moral and rhetorical position from which the reformers advanced their cause was not thereby inexplicable; it was coded deeply into the spiritual logic from which immediatism developed and from which they drew strength and inspiration. It further gave to them a complex mixture of courage and naivete that was productive of much of the pathos—and bathos—of the reform period generally. More specifically, this imperative to act on behalf of another formed in the most profound ways the education of Grimké as a public figure, and as an orator, precisely because it made her confront the question of her role as a "free moral agent" in ways she had not heretofore considered.

We have no truly sustained set of reflections, much less an explicit theory of public life from Angelina's writings. We do possess, however, a rich store of commentary on her experiences during the New England tour, the substance and argumentative force of which ground the interpretive work of this chapter. At this point, it will be productive to establish a more general set of premises about Grimké's conception of the public, if only as a way of making sense of her specific claims and of directing the analysis that follows. What we have seen of Grimké's rhetorical performances thus far allows us to speculate along three planes; together, these premises help to construct an implicit theory of the public that undergirds her thought.

In the first place, Grimké fully grasped that the public represented a space of power, where authority expressed itself and frequently did so in the form of political compromise and sometimes corruption. At certain points in her life, Grimké made this perception the basis for a vague kind of "comeouterism," the result perhaps of intimate and intense conversations with Sarah, but also with Henry Wright, Garrison, and other Boston radicals who oversaw the Grimkés throughout the tour. Yet whatever aversions she may have felt about the business of politics and public affairs, Angelina seldom gave any indication that she felt personally victimized by them or, indeed, excluded from access to public opinion. I do not mean to suggest that Grimké was obtuse about the class-stratified, gendered, and racially exclusive structures of authority that defined public life in antebellum America. Quite the contrary, as her life and work amply testify. I do mean to highlight the quite extraordinary degree of self-confidence with which she leveraged herself into public consciousness. The public, however vaguely defined, seemed not in and of itself either source or object of complaint. Grimké's attacks on clerical acquiescence or censorious abolitionists, for example, did not derive from a conviction that these failings were somehow inevitable, given their contexts of public utterance. Indeed, when Angelina resolved to combat these views, she did so in and through explicitly public media. In this sense, at least, her self-confidence was corollary to a kind of political confidence in Americans to ultimately act on their own consciences and deploy their own resources to transform the world they had helped make.

In the second place, Grimké saw the public as a realm of possibilities, where things could be made to happen by virtue of argument, appeal, and image. Entering that world, indeed, reshaping it in the very process, Grimké never indicated that she was thereby compromising her principles or in any way being co-opted by it. It is no small part of Grimké's legacy that this diminutive, so conspicuously plain Quaker, self-denying and severe, could with such clear-eyed calculation lay claim to the moral capital of New England, indeed to the world. She was not and never claimed to be a pariah; Angelina considered herself part of what she called the "moral elite," whose duty it was neither to secede from public life nor to accept what was therein unacceptable. At least during this stage of her career, Grimké had no reservations about acting publicly to get what the public could give—the means for change—and if those means were rooted in public opinion, she would take herself to the very chambers of the Massachusetts Legislature to strike at its root.

In the third place, Grimké's working conception of public life, so clearly informed by the drama of commitments at risk and so infused by the religious imagination, owed nothing to such figures of resistance as theater or carnival. This point is obvious, perhaps, but it may be worth recalling just how "rational" rhetorical ambitions actually were. There was mention of "turning the world upside down," and certainly Grimké grasped the dramaturgical potential in all social reform, but for all that there remained steady before Grimké's eyes a very clear image of what kind of activity was best suited to achieve the desired ends. Since that activity was rhetorical, and since rhetoric in this context meant presenting one's case in sites of public deliberation, Grimké would adapt her argument to norms of civic action and seek the assent of her audience through reasoned appeals. By temperament, training, and talent, Grimké was ideally prepared for that most orthodox requirement of all such deliberation in actually existing democratic settings: to present the argument as clearly and forcefully as possible; to synthesize appeals to reason, passion, and character; and on this basis to effect a transformation in the judgment of the audience, confident that the best arguments surely prevail.

Grimké's encounter with Weld on the subject of rights was significant for additional reasons. This was not the only time Grimké would be called to justify herself, but it was the first time she was so ably challenged, taken so seriously as an independent thinker and voice of change. Grimké's response to that challenge, in one sense private and personal, in fact constitutes a major event in the development of one of the century's most important public figures. What then did the exchange between Grimké and Weld accomplish? What did it do?

The most obvious upshot was personal. As Grimké's biographers have amply demonstrated, her attraction to Weld dated back to the fall of 1836, when she came very quickly to appreciate the "moral and intellectual feast" Weld was then serving up at the New York training sessions. If the attraction was more than moral and intellectual at that point, neither party was willing or able to show it; more importantly, these two personalities, among the most forceful, articulate, and independent of their age, were to come into real contact for the first time through an argument over human rights. This was hardly the first such instance of romantic love following a dispute over ideals, but we ought not to lose sight of how this very singular and very public relationship originated: within the medium of language, through pointed differences and sharply edged arguments over what mattered to both. Although many reform relationships were to follow which derived energy from similar sources, few, if any, in nineteenth-century

America could be said to precede the Grimké-Weld encounter as a model of public intimacy.

In addition to drawing tighter the personal ties that were to bind the two, the exchange revealed fully the theoretical structure and content of their thought. It is a frequent lament that neither Grimké nor Weld, especially, left much in the way of formal writing and speech transcripts. The frustrations entailed are real enough, but we have in the August dispute a highly compressed and rhetorically charged text of their respective views and characteristic modes of argument. To put those arguments under scrutiny is to see at least two major implications for our understanding of Grimké's reform rhetoric. First, she complicated a conventional disjunction between principle and expedience well beyond what historians and even Weld sufficiently recognized. From a certain perspective, as we have seen, Grimké's position can be attacked for confusing the accepted means-ends calculus for getting the job of abolition done; subordinating human rights to women's rights, she threatened to undo the prodigious labors of the Anglo-American antislavery movement by selfishly exploiting her gender's claim to equality. Leaving aside the fact that to those outside the abolitionist community, any talk of expedience from such immediatists as these was bound in any case to be laughable, we can see that Grimké demolished such binary oppositions as that between principle and expedience as logically, rhetorically, and morally incoherent. Weld, in this sense, was fated to "lose" the argument, not because he was either unprincipled or inexpedient, but because he—master strategist though he was—had not yet followed through the entailments of his own thinking. Grimké had seized Weld's lynchpin argument from expediency, removed it, and built her own defense of women's rights on its strength. In thus establishing the position that women could not act as free moral agents in the cause of human rights when their own rights were systematically subordinated, Grimké in effect collapsed any such disjunction between principle and expedience and reunified them into a superior rationale for public action.

The structure and content of Grimkés thought is revealed through the exchange with Weld in a second way. Together and by virtue perhaps of the very differences that defined the argument, Grimké and Weld helped create a middle ground that at least held the promise of broad appeal and collective effort. One way of suggesting the point is to briefly note what the two actually *agreed* on, at least in principle: human rights; immediate abolition of slavery; women's rights; equality of the sexes; a certain anticlericism and antisectarianism; the importance of public testimony and focused rhetorical effort. In holding such shared preoccupations, the two could speak to their differences confidant that the center of their shared moral universe would hold. In view of the disintegration of organized American abolition a few years later, it is perhaps glib to stress the rhetorical achievement implied here; still, it is important to note that Grimké's position was not, for all its controversial possibilities, an especially radical one within the abolitionist host. In spite of her professions of "ultra" principles, she was, after all, insisting on women's right to act in the world, for the world, and by means of the world. Theodore Weld, on the other hand, was no more an Amos Phelps or Hubbard Winslow than Grimké was a Nathaniel Rogers or Frances Wright. He was, as we have seen, genuinely proud of his credentials as a supporter of women's rights, and could appeal to a nearly unrivaled record of acting on those convictions. At no point did he, nor would he ever, discourage women's work of moral reform, public or otherwise. He was in truth an avid supporter of women's right to public speech and the power it might entail, and was contemptuous of those who, like Hubbard, would remove such agents from the field by vice of their sex. Weld's objections to Grimké's alleged stumping for women's rights was based expressly on tactical considerations that, while ultimately dismantled, ought not to be remanded to the ranks of the decade's far more conservative and reactionary voices.

Grimké's encounter with Weld was productive of much that was positive, then, and warns us away from the view that because they were orators and activists, they were not therefore thinkers, that they were dogmatists because driven by conviction, duty, and temperament. In truth, although, as their arguments make clear, Grimké and Weld were possessed of certain theories of right and action, that did not make them thinkers. It was the fact that they were willing to put those theories to the scrutiny of formidable criticism, to risk conviction, and to recognize the probity of each other's claims that did. As a result, we are led finally not to draw invidious comparisons, but to see that the encounter helped to designate for both interlocutors the limits of their own rhetorical judgment and moral will. Theodore Weld was never again to raise systematically the issue of his friend's speaking on behalf of women's rights; and while the reason for this may be attributed to many things, surely Grimké had made clear through the exchange that it would do no good even if he did.

At the same time, we cannot help but note that Angelina Grimké, among the preeminent feminists of her time, never did assume the public platform for the sole purpose of proclaiming the rights of women. Angelina was well aware of the irony, and observed to Jane Smith latter that, "With regard to speaking on the rights of women it has really been wonderful to me that tho' I meet the prejudice against our speaking everywhere," still, when it came to speaking before audiences, "I never think of introducing anything about it." Very few people before 1848 would have done so, of course, and if this account of her argument with Weld holds, such an ambition would not have been consistent with her position that all such appeals to right needed to be integrated into one "science" of moral reform. Grimké, in any case, had grown exasperated: "What is the matter with thee," she asked Weld in September, "One would really suppose that we had actually abandoned the A. Sl'y cause and were scouring the country preaching *nothing* but *women's rights*, when in fact I can truly say that whenever I lecture I forget *every thing but the* SLAVE. HE is," Grimké assured him, "all in all for the time being." And so the slave would remain for the foreseeable future, during which time Grimké, having defended her right to speak as a free moral agent, would devote the exercise of those rights to their freedom alone. It was an uneasy truce at best, for having encountered Weld, Grimké confronted the limits of her own patience for the work of the world. For the moment, perhaps, Grimké could rest easy knowing that "the Lord orders these things so, driving out of my mind what I ought not to speak on. But if the time ever comes when this will be a part of my public work," she insisted to Jane Smith, "then I shall not be able to forget it."[44]

CHAPTER 6

Violent Inventions: Witnessing Slavery in the Pennsylvania Hall Address

And from the days of John the Baptist until now the kingdom of heaven suffereth violence, and the violent take it by force. *Matthew* 11:14.

Angelina Grimké's rhetorical career was begotten in violence, and so it ended. In the summer of 1835, she had been startled into action by reports from riotous Boston, and, by presuming to give counsel to abolition's most notorious leader, dramatically announced her entrance into public life. The letter to Garrison provided Grimké with a highly compressed, artistically complex medium through which to give form and effect to this new identity, and thus to imagine before others the possibilities of renewed community and the convictions required for such renewal. Grimké had never seen a mob before, much less Boston's distinctive brand of street politics, but she knew then that, far from destroying the will to collective action, violence might be made its catalyst. "Let it Come," she had written to Garrison, "for it is my deep, solemn, deliberate conviction, that this is a cause worth dying for." And of course the violence did come, in fact settled into a routine feature of public life in virtually all the major northern cities. From the year of Grimké's entrance into abolition work to that of her Pennsylvania Hall address, well over one hundred mobs were reported to have attacked, hassled, or otherwise declared their intentions against the abolitionist host. That reality could not be spoken away, Grimké knew, but it could be transformed from a source of despair into a rationale for collective renewal and purposeful action.[1]

Still the question persisted: how to keep the violent from bearing it away? How, that is, to resist the claim of violence on human community? The Pennsylvania Hall address may be read as one particularly evocative answer to that enduring question. Grimké's "finest, most accomplished performance as an orator," in Lerner's words, "unforgettable to all who witnessed it," displayed in the most dramatic terms possible the rhetorical work required to reinvent violence, to transform sheer physical threat into an available means of persuasion.

Certainly much has already been said of what Karlyn Campbell judges a "rhetorical masterwork," of the oratorical heights to which the speaker rose "in adapting to the terror and violence of the immediate scene and in selecting a rhetorical persona for herself that would overcome resistance to her as a woman speaker." Garrison breathlessly reported, on hearing the speech, that, "As the tumult from without increased, and the brickbats fell thick and fast, (no one, however, being injured,) her eloquence kindled, her eye flashed, and her cheeks glowed, as she devoutly thanked the Lord that the stupid repose of the City had at length been disturbed by the force of truth."[2]

The scene of Grimké's triumph soon became a fixture in narratives of the anti-slavery and women's rights movements, and by century's end historians could still discern in it the physical details Garrison himself had imagined. Almost half a century later Catherine Birney recalled that neither, "was a tremor or a change of color perceptible, and though the missiles continued to fly through the broken sashes, and the hootings and yellings increased outside, so powerfully did her words and tones hold that vast audience, that, imminent as seemed their peril, scarcely a man or a woman moved to depart." Knowing a good object lesson when they saw one, the famed editors of the *History of Woman Suffrage* pressed the point to more specific ends: "The experience of the heroines of anti-slavery show that no fine-spun sentimentalism in regard to woman's position in the clouds ever exempt her from the duties or penalties of a citizen. Neither State officers, nor mobs in the relishment of passion, tempered their violence for her safety or benefit."[3]

Yet here is more than perseverance, something more than a record of trial and survival. The speech is, we know, at once about and subject to violence; and its triumph is rightly recorded as a triumph of oratorical over physical power. "Speaking in the teeth of the mob," as Jean Fagan Yellin writes, "interrupted by shouts and breaking glass, she had made violence her subject. To the women, Grimké's presence, like her scriptural language flung in the face of the terror, created an unforgettable image of embattled heroic womanhood." Rhetorical critics in particular have noted the transformative power of the speech, especially, in Campbell's words, as "it illustrates the remarkable rhetorical skill of a woman who could exploit a terrorizing mob as evidence for her claim, and who could subtly appropriate the language of the Bible in order to assume a persona that transcended male-female roles and legitimated her rhetorical action." Together, Yellin and Campbell remind us of how exquisitely improvised can be the rhetorical act, how text and context can be made to collapse into a reordered field of meaning and action.[4]

The account following seeks not so much to supplant these insights as to extend them in two directions. By way of context, I elaborate upon the several dimensions of violence that inform Grimké's address, its delivery, and probable reception. In particular, I ask what, in addition to the hard facts of physical threat and destruction, violence might have meant to speaker and audience. How was violence itself rhetorically constructed and put to symbolic use? We know that in addition to being the perpetrators of and participants in mob action, "gentlemen of property and standing" were also vociferous critics of abolitionists as incendiary demagogues, indeed the very spark to the violence complained about. How did antiabolitionists speak of violence, and to what effect? Second, by way of text, I try to account in some detail for the rhetorical action of the speech, not in order to isolate it from its discursive environment but to see how the speech interacts decisively within and against it. Aside from attending at a different level to the interplay of text and context, my reading departs in several ways from previous accounts. I am less inclined to interpret this speech exclusively as a protofeminist tract, devoted alone to creating an "image of embattled heroic womanhood." It is, to be sure, a speech about the rights, duties, and dignity of women and all human beings, and certainly women's rights activists recognized the rhetorical gain to be had in its retelling. But it is also, and most immediately, about slavery and the moral resolve necessary to the elimination of that system.

I shall try to offer a reading that neither discounts nor exaggerates either fact. In addition, I tend not to stress, at least in the same way, what others very plausibly see as Grimké's prophetic persona, nor, in a related sense, her appropriation of Scripture for tactical ends. In the context of Grimké's life and writings, there is very little that I can discern to suggest that she saw Scripture simply as an available means of persuasion, an option among several to be used as needed in pursuit of her rhetorical end. It is perhaps putting too fine a point on the matter, but I proceed under the conviction that Grimké did not *use* Scripture but *lived it;* she saw the world through the moral order she believed it imposed, and the question of choice in this sense simply did not assert itself. Grimké did not speak like a prophet; she *was* a prophet. She did not fling scriptural language in the faces of others, terrifying or not; she spoke the truth as she knew it before others so that they might know it too. This chapter is designed to show what happens when that stance is assumed, what changes are thus wrought and what ends achieved.[5]

How to keep the violent from bearing it away? Not through violence in turn, nor in abject martyrdom, but by changing it into something other than what it was. The rhetorical action of this address, accordingly, is to transform violence into a means for inventing new worlds. This transformation was effected in and through Grimké's assumption of the role of witness, in which she was able to publicly exhibit and rehearse the revaluation of violence from a brute and silencing force into a productive and liberating agent. The key to this reading lies in observing how, by virtue of her status as witness, Grimké superintended and orchestrated the unfolding possibilities of collective action; in the process, we shall see, the speaker exposed the lineaments of false community, then turned to the work of reconstituting what was essentially a crowd into an audience, her audience into an expression of public opinion, and public opinion finally into an international movement for the liberation of the enslaved. In this sense the speech is about the renewal of covenant, the success of which depended on Grimké's ability to leverage faith on the fulcrum of violence. Hence the rhetorical resources of violence as Grimké may be said to offer: from crisis, rebirth. These resources are summarized below; in turn we examine certain patterns of witnessing familiar in contexts of abolitionist activity; and finally we move to a reading of the text as itself a witness to Grimké's art.

For all the attention paid to antiabolitionist rhetoric and violence, it is well to remember that for many the true source of violence lay in the abolitionist community itself. On reflection the eye is drawn irresistibly to Garrison under siege, Lovejoy murdered, Douglass stoned. Even moderate northern observers, however, insisted first that such reactions were anomalous, and second that they were the result of a prolonged and intolerable warfare waged by the abolitionists against the patience of civil society. The problem was not antislavery as such, commentators stressed, for that was surely a fit subject of discussion; it was rather that the wrong people in the wrong places were arguing about it wrongly. Important issues were to be properly discussed, the *Boston Quarterly Review* noted, by "wise and sober men, men of strong intellects and well-informed minds." Above all, such issues were not to be bandied about "in a crowd, where people of all ages and both sexes are brought together, and by the strong appeals of impassioned orators thrown into a state of excitement bordering on insanity." For more imaginative and paranoid critics, abolitionists threatened to bring down the very foundations of society itself, a threat against which a few mobs seemed benign indeed. James Paulding fervently denounced in 1836 their "deriding all social duties and sympathies, all feelings of patriotism; instigating an ignorant population of millions of blacks to insurrection; sowing the seeds of a servile war; and last and worst of all, converting the precepts of Holy Writ into an excuse for violating its spirit and doctrines," snatching thus, "a burning brand from the throne of God, to set fire to our institutions and consume our Union to ashes."[6]

Whatever their motives, there is no reason to suspect that such antiabolitionist sentiments were anything but sincere. From one perspective, indeed, we can almost grant to them a certain probity, paranoid as they may now appear: violence *did* seem to follow the abolitionists, and in fact their message *did* strike at the roots of society as they knew it. Immediate emancipation *was* radical, and the consequences *were* bound to be cataclysmic. And, of course, one did not have to look very far or very hard to see who was at the center of these disturbances; violence

had a face, and it was the orator's. The demagogue as social type had been a commonplace for centuries, to be sure, but the danger from such individuals could
seem unprecedented. "The demagogue," explained the *New England Magazine*
(1835), "having his aggrandizement in view, is heartlessly blind to all the mischief
his maneuvering may occasion. What cares he," the writer asked, "that inflammatory speeches guide the mob against the dwelling of a citizen, whose opinions may
not be agreeable to the sovereign people?—that the torch is applied to Protestant
or Romish church?" As the years fell by, antiabolitionists saw plainly that these
demagogues were the true cause of violence; what little that was returned upon the
offending source was as nothing in comparison. "Witness their incessant appeals
to the worst passions of the excitable, the restless, the ignorant, deluded and reckless portions of the community; their bold and unscrupulous denunciation and
ridicule of civil and ecclesiastical rulers, politicians, literary and professional men,
and . . . their incendiary attempts to excite the feelings and mould the sentiments
of their followers in opposition to the authority of every kind of government, and
of those sacred and social institutions by which licentiousness and depravity are
restrained."[7]

There was perhaps no decade as loud with the human voice as that of the
1830s, and when it came to exposing fault and arraigning instigators in the press
and pulpit, that voice proved tireless. Antiabolitionists, as might be expected,
were soon on to Garrison's ways, and pointed out that "He knows very well, that
the more numerous, violent, and powerful mobs against him became, the
stronger necessity good men will feel to join him." Yet however readily they recognized the demagogue at work, however quickly they might respond in kind,
critics remained stupefied at one sight that seemed to have no precedent and certainly no reason: women abolitionists. Here it is worth being reminded again of
Linda Kerber's admonition against taking the rhetoric of separate spheres at its
own word, and to note again how strange could be the mix of reactions to
women's presence in public affairs. For all the talk of delicate sensibilities and
domestic virtue, of the "parcel of silly women" who frequented these outings,
such women were suspected of wielding a remarkable degree of power to "excite
commotion in the city," and were rumored to be found frequently "in the midst
of the melee, and participating in the affray." Far from being an antidote to the
sickness that pervaded public dispute, women were proving "delicate adepts in
the science of brawling," and now strained belief itself; after the Garrison riots,
the *Boston Atlas* could only despair, "that respectable females should have played
a part in such a scene of violence and disorder," and found it all "hardly credible."[8]

Women's rights and antislavery leaders were quick to seize on their critics' profound confusion over the spheres and powers of women. Maria Chapman's *Right
and Wrong in Boston,* a production of the Boston Female Anti-Slavery Society,

gleefully reprinted outraged passages from the local press that unwittingly accorded to women almost supernatural powers to instigate mass disturbances. Members of the BFASS must have felt reassured to read of their role in George Thompson's ill-fated visit. "Has it come to this," asked the *Commercial Gazette,* "that the WOMEN of our country—not content with their proper sphere, the domestic fireside—must hold public meetings to encourage the efforts of a foreign emissary to destroy our peace? Are there not sufficient deluded men already engaged in the work of abolition, that the interference of females may be dispensed with?" Readers of the *Boston Courier* similarly were asked to consider the ways and means of public women and female abolitionists, for were they not on record as intending "to interrupt and eventually destroy the union of these states and to lead more directly to scenes of lawless violence, by exciting a state of feeling, which may not be so easily subdued or provoked?" If it had no other effect, such rhetoric magnified the scope and intensity of abolitionism, offering up to the public mind such visions of chaos and destruction as it scarcely dared imagine. At the very center of the maelstrom stood the female orator.[9]

The profound frustration that worked itself into antiabolitionist discourse was, in a sense, perfectly explicable. Heedless to all calls for moderation or restraint, self-righteous beyond endurance, meddlesome in business in which they had no business, fond of their own notoriety, contemptuous of complex political, social, and religious affiliations with fellow Americans to the south, the abolitionists seemed to exemplify the worst of that class of reformers, who "mounts its hobby and rides away, condemning all as children of the Past, as wedded to old abuses, as the enemies of truth and virtue, who will not do the same." To the charge that they were the real source of civil unrest, abolitionists had little to offer in the way of defense or excuse. Most maddening, perhaps, was that having provoked ordinarily peaceable citizens to violence, abolitionists proved incapable of learning from the experience, indeed seemed to relish their own bruises, to use them as badges of honor in an ongoing assault against civil society. The rhetorical art at work here, this transformation of physical victim into symbolic capital, is as ancient as humanity itself, but seldom has it been put to use more enthusiastically than by northern abolitionists.[10]

For their opponents, violence was an available means of action when speech failed; it was effected to bring matters to an end. Abolitionists conversely availed themselves of a rich martyrology, allowing, Chapman wrote, that "no opportunity to escape us, of doing and suffering the good pleasure of God. Nothing is more acceptable to him, than to see in his children, a joyful and ready agreement to profit by pain." Violence was, in this logic, not an end but a beginning: the more severe the assault, the greater the prospects of salvation. This could be, needless to say, an exasperating basis for social reform, and no one put this martyrology to work or exasperated so thoroughly as William Lloyd Garrison. He had made certain, indeed, that its logic and the resolve it demanded had been literally inscribed into the charter text of the American Anti-Slavery Society, where in its very final lines the Declaration of Sentiments promised to "wipe out the foulest stain which rests upon our national escutcheon—and to secure to the colored population of the United States all the rights and privileges which belong to them as men and as Americans—come what may to our persons, our interests, or our reputations—whether we live to witness the triumph of JUSTICE, LIBERTY and HUMANITY, or perish untimely as martyrs in this great, benevolent and holy cause."[11]

The appeal of such declarations was unmistakable. Irresistible to Garrison's followers and maddening to his opponents, the martyrology provided to abolitionists an inexhaustible fund of images and arguments, of allusions to Stephen and Christ, of calls to strength and forbearance and of wrath turned away. There was in all of it a primitive and compelling logic that was also its rhetoric. According to this logic, all opposition, all expressions of resistance in words or deeds were readily subsumed into a calculus of inverse proportions: the more negative the reaction to their message, the more certain were abolitionists in its truths. Looking back on the recent events of the summer of 1835, the BFASS accordingly made perfect sense of the riots by invoking what was by then an utterly familiar explanation: "The nature and violence of the opposition we had encountered—the grossness of the misrepresentation, the insult and outrage threatened, all convinced us that our course of action was the right way of professing those principles of truth which can never be upheld without exciting rage in those who love error." Hence the equation that held violence to be a form of proof, evidence of a particularly clear, dangerous, and dramatic type. "Violent opposition only proves the strength of existing evils," Lydia Maria Child wrote, fearing that "there are those who urge this very violence as a sufficient reason for discontinuing our exertion." Child need not have worried: abolitionists thrived on such opposition, knowing, like Francis Jackson, that "mobs and gag laws, and the other contrivances by which fraud or force would stifle enquiry," ultimately must "betray the essential rottenness of the cause they are meant to strengthen." Death itself was not to be feared, indeed could be imagined as a source of renewal and exaltation. So what if abolitionists "should fall untimely, as martyrs? The effect of their heart-stirring example, of their wisdom, energy, and christian devotedness, are beyond the reach of man."[12]

There were, of course, limits to the rhetoric of martyrdom. Falling in an untimely fashion did not in and of itself qualify anyone for the role of "heart-stirring example." And certainly those who perished with arms in hand had no claim on the figure; as Grimké was to argue in the pages of the *Liberator,* even Lovejoy fell short of the standards for martyrdom: "Place in the mouth of the dying Lovejoy the last prayer of the dying Stephen; 'Lord, lay not this sin to their charge.' How would these heavenly expressions of forgiveness and good have sounded from one," Grimké asked, "who wore a deadly weapon at his side—and was determined to resist his enemies by force of arms?"[13]

But for all the urge to suffer evident amongst the abolitionist leadership, and indeed for all the rhetorical capital that could be generated from scenes like the siege of the BFASS offices, Garrison's misadventures, and Lovejoy's murder, Grimké very seldom expressed herself according to the prevailing martyrology. She knew herself to be not slavery's martyr but its witness, whose duty it was, having seen, to speak, and in speaking thus to transform the inert into agents of radical change. To be a witness in this sense was not to assume a role or adopt a vocabulary; it was above all a way of being; it was who Grimké was, the chief expression of which was to bear herself through the word, to testify. In this way of being she collapsed what we would now call identity and agency into a single, unified rationale for social action. To better get a sense of the resources available to her and what she might have expected her audience to recognize in her act of bearing witness, a brief review of what might be called the rhetorical context may prove useful.

Abolitionists had by 1838 had frequent opportunity, as we have noted, to practice and refine the arts of martyrdom. Hence the violence to which they were subjected played a significant role in the very recruitment, composition, and work of the movement. Far from destroying its morale or structure of convictions, antiabolitionist mobs and rhetoric pushed their opponents onto ever higher ground, where appeals to scriptural truths, human rights, free speech, and patriotism could be made to sound ever clearer, ever more compelling. Yet all the martyrs and prophets, speeches, tracts, and fairs could not hide the fact that most Northerners were, willfully or otherwise, ignorant of the realities of slave life. The problem was epistemological and therefore rhetorical: how could Northerners be turned against slavery if they had no real, no palpable sense of its savagery against human life? By extension, the mobs worked greatest harm not with stones, but by tempting abolitionists into a preoccupation with *northern* violence, by so circumscribing the battle as to leave unheard the slaves' cry.[14]

It was left to Grimké, though not Grimké alone, to make that cry heard again. She had been witness to violence against the souls and bodies of the slave, and could thus testify before those who had no such knowledge. This fact of her life marked her rhetorical responsibilities; because she had seen, she must therefore tell. To do so was not only to impose a claim on the convictions of her audience, but to call that audience into being, to activate it and give it renewed purpose, by first literally reminding them of a reality to which they had no experiential access.

This much, of course, had been the basis of Weld's argument the previous summer: not her gender, nor her religious affiliations, but her distinctive identity as a southern witness against slavery gave her words the power to awaken sensibilities dulled by slavery: "You can do ten times as much on the subject of *slavery* as Mrs. Child or Mrs Chapman. Why? Not because your powers are superior to theirs, but because you are *southerners.*" The epistemological distance between North and South worked a double mischief, however, by calling into question the status of testimony itself. Who was to be heard, what was to be believed, what kind of judgment exercised as a result? Thus Grimké confronted not only violent opponents and slumbering supporters, but fellow Southerners testifying to friendly northern audiences. The kind of barrier this posed to Grimké and the abolitionists generally was unmistakable: "It is one of the worst effects of slavery," admitted one writer for the *American Quarterly Observer,*

> that it blunts the moral sensibilities. There are certain habits, growing out of the social relations of slavery, which are universally witnessed and acknowledged in a slave-holding State, which would do violence to the sensibilities of a northern man. In regard to many points, a distance from the scene itself is an advantage. . . . Besides, we are willing to rely, for the opinions which we form on the subject, wholly on the testimony of slave holders. This testimony may also be such as all parties will acknowledge to be unimpeachable-testimony collateral, cross examined, weighed, and sifted.[15]

Grimké's speech on the evening of 16 May was devoted explicitly to subverting such faith in the testimony of slaveholders—and to declaring as a former slaveholder truths of a different and starker cast. She was in this regard at once the source and product of a more general strategy, and hers was scarcely the only such voice to be heard above the Mason-Dixson line. Indeed, as Stanley Harrold insists, "the use of southern emancipationists as symbols of progress, as antislavery heroes, as proof of the effectiveness of northern abolitionist tactics, and as illustrations of the oppressiveness of slaveholders was characteristic of the entire antislavery movement." Grimké and her audience could accordingly rely upon a rich if limited body of testimonial literature, a brief review of which will help situate her address, identify common themes, and suggest points of departure.[16]

As he did in so much else having to do with strategy and implementation, Theodore Weld recognized early the rhetorical potential inherent to testimony from former slave owners. Having caught wind in May 1834 of James Birney's conversion to immediate emancipation, he assiduously worked to edit, publish, and distribute his friend's *Letter on Colonization.* The *Letter,* Weld assured Birney, would "accomplish more for the *Great Cause* than the operation of all other instrumentalities employed hitherto." Published first in the Lexington *Intelligencer* and later by the American Anti-slavery Society in New York, the *Letter* was pure gold for abolitionists, who saw in it confirmation and encouragement that, having found their mark in the South, their words might be directed to the unredeemed North. "Born in the midst of a slave holding community," Birney recalled, "accustomed to the services of slaves from my infancy—reared under an exposure to all the prejudices that slavery begets—and being myself heretofore, from early life, a slave holder—my efforts at mental liberation were commenced in the very lowest and grossest atmosphere." Folding personal experience into a public attack on colonization, the *Letter* is an effective if businesslike repudiation of false sentiment, a pilgrim's progress toward enlightenment and away from slavery's grasp. It was not a complex story, nor was it told with much eloquence or rhetorical flare, but for the time being abolitionists were deeply grateful to have it at all.[17]

Weld was in the event as ecstatic as he was ever likely to be: "On account of the peculiar relation which you have sustained to the *South*," he plumped Birney, "the system of slavery, the system of Colonization—your mature age, long observation, intimate knowledge of the subject, profound character, very extensive acquaintance and a variety of other considerations unnecessary to name . . . I have not a doubt that you will be able to accomplish more *far* more for the termination of the system of slavery and the elevation of the free colored race than any other man in the Union."

Birney's *Letter* was widely praised by northern abolitionists, among them Lewis Tappan, who confessed to reading it "with tears of joy and gratitude," and Elizur Wright, who exclaimed to Weld, "You cannot tell how I am electrified by that whole letter of Birney's. I am rejoiced beyond measure that Mr. B. is ready to devote his whole energy to this cause."[18]

In the years following, similar accounts would be seized by northern abolitionists, many of whom pined after more graphic and forceful depictions both of slavery and of the slaveholder's dramatic conversion. John G. Fee obliged as best he might, recalling in detail the spiritual anguish and final rebirth into abolitionism that readers had come to expect. "I had in the grove near the seminary," Fee wrote in his autobiography, "a place to which I went every day for prayers, between the hour of 11 and 12. I saw that to have light and peace from God, I must make the consecration. I said, 'Lord, if needs be, make me an Abolitionist.' I arose from my knees with the consciousness that I had died to the world and accepted Christ in all the fulness of his character as I thus understood him."[19]

Like Birney, David Nelson was deeply influenced by Weld, and as an agent of the American Anti-Slavery Society left behind his native Tennessee to preach the gospel of immediatism. His symbolic worth, as Weld knew, was similarly a function of his former status as a slaveholder. Nelson's story, one editor observed, provided many fine anecdotes, "of things personally known to the lectures." They offered "excellent illustrations of principles, and are highly attractive," so much so, in fact, that he "often wished that James G. Birney and Angelina E. Grimké made more use of them." The plot was in any case fittingly and familiarly cast:

> I lived for many years without having a suspicion that there was anything wrong in holding slaves. Even after I had an interest in Christ, there seemed to be nothing amiss in it; just as pious people went on making and selling rum, without troubling their consciousness. Oh, that I then could have had faithful Christian brethren, to rouse me with the voice of exhortation and rebuke! I should not have approached the table of our Lord with fingers all dripping with the blood of souls![20]

A decade before Frederick Douglass revolutionized the art of antislavery testimony, the tracts of former slaveholders like Birney, Fee, and Nelson represented some of the most promising abolitionist literature of its time. Its circulation through northern reform circles was, as Harrold and others have shown, part of a more general strategy not only to inspire northern abolitionists but to cultivate and sustain what influence could be exerted in border states. White, male, and slave-holding, they bore a distinctive kind of witness, the rhetorical force of which depended not so much on their eloquence or literary merits as on the sheer fact of their authorship. But however limited aesthetically, these works took on power by virtue of their status as testimony: to bear witness in this way was first of all to give experience formal expression; to declare and profess it in and through the speech act. It was, in addition, to do so publicly, as an act of shared recognition, as if in holding one's past before others it was thereby made manifest, present because proclaimed. Testimony in this sense was definitively an act of display and hence of disclosure. To testify was through speech and public profession to constitute the truth of that experience; to certify as proof the evidence of experience. This much, at least, Grimké could count on as she undertook to bear witness in her own right on the stage of Pennsylvania Hall.[21]

In one sense, to be sure, Grimké's entire public career had been a protracted series of testimonials against slavery. Certainly she did not need Weld to remind her of the rhetorical advantage of being the daughter of southern slave holders; from her opening letter to Garrison in 1835, Grimké professed her "deep, solemn deliberate conviction, that this is a cause worth dying for. I say so," she made clear, "from what I have seen, and heard, and known, in a land of slavery, where rests the darkness of Egypt, and where is found the Sin of Sodom." That Angelina was prepared not simply to acknowledge her experience but to use it to specific rhetorical advantage was similarly evident in her *Appeal* a year later. Having pled with her readers to "bear a faithful, open, unshirking testimony" against slavery, she deployed the facts of her own past to insist that "I have lived too long in the midst of slavery, not to know what slavery is. When I speak of this system, 'I speak that I do know,' and I am not at all afraid to assert, that Anti-Slavery publications have not overdrawn the monstrous features of slavery at all." Three months before the Pennsylvania Hall address, finally, Grimké offered to the Massachusetts legislature as precise and moving a statement on the moral province of the witness as can be found in the antislavery literature:

> I stand before you as a southerner, exiled from the land of my birth, by the sound of the lash, and the piteous cry of the slave. I stand before you as a repentant slave holder. I stand before you as a moral being, endowed with precious and inalienable rights, which are correlative with solemn duties and high responsibilities; and as a moral being I feel that I owe it to the suffering slave, and to the deluded master, to my country and the world, to do all I can to overturn a system of complicated crimes, [built] upon the broken hearts and prostrate bodies of my countrymen in chains, and cemented by the blood and sweat and tears of my sisters in bond.[22]

For listeners familiar with the writings of Birney and other former slaveholders, or indeed with the several ex-slave testimonials of the late eighteenth and early nineteenth centuries, Grimké's words would have rang out in familiar tones. The themes of exile and deliverance, conversion and confession, resolve and redemption, were the very stuff of almost all such testimonials. There were, of course, significant differences: Angelina and Sarah were unique as southern women, distinctive as orators as well as writers, and, of course, they had been neither slaves nor slaveholders as such. They could not, as a result, lay claim to the pathos of the fugitive bondman, or to the ethos of the enlightened slaveholder. Angelina's presence especially and her rhetorical power as a witness rested rather in her ability to take that which had been given to her and with it reconstitute the terms of collective action. She did not dwell on images of the assaulted slave because that was not the object of her witnessing; to the extent that the rhetorical aims of the Pennsylvania Hall address were met, she gave witness not to the past but to a future heretofore unspoken.

The ground of the witness is a space of privileged insight and rhetorical authority. By assuming it, Grimké supervised a collective reassignment of violence from that which silences to an available means of persuasion. To better grasp the performative and transgressive dimensions of this work, we might consider for a moment the role of violence in conventional rhetorical formulations. At its most primal and enduring level of articulation, rhetoric has been imagined as precisely that art which displaces violence; it is what violence is not, finds its chief rationale over and against the forces that brutalize and so make us less or other than human. Just because "there has been implanted in us the power to persuade each other and to make clear to each other whatever we desire," Isocrates wrote in the *Antidosis*, "not only have we escaped the life of wild beasts, but we have come together and founded cities and made laws and invented arts." Brought thus together into conditions of polity and commerce, humans were thought to be most human not when fighting but when speaking; so, too, Aristotle perceived the capacity for rational speech to be more definitively human than that of physical prowess. Cicero's reflections on speech and community likewise echoed and anticipated a commonplace in the rhetorical lore. As Crassus is made to say in *De oratore*, "the one point in which we have our very greatest advantage over the brute creation is that we hold converse one with another, and can reproduce our thought in word. . . . What other power [than eloquence]," Crassus asks, "could have been strong enough either to gather scattered humanity into one place, or to lead it out of its brutish existence in the wilderness up to our present condition of civilization as men and as citizens, or after the establishment of social communities, to give shape to laws, tribunals, and civic rights?" Later efforts to theorize rhetoric required God's hand and voice, but the classical exporting of violence into the wilderness remained consistent. "God called theim together by utteraunce of speache," Thomas Wilson explained in his *Arte of Rhetorique*, "and perswaded with them what was good, what was badde, and what was gainefull for mankynde . . . yet being somewhat drawen and delighted with the pleasauntnes of reason, and the swetenes of utteraunce: after a certain space, thei became through nurture and good advisement, of wilde, sober: of cruel, gentle: of foles, wise: and of beastes, men."[23]

Traditionally understood, violence was antithetical to speech; it kept beasts from becoming men. While rhetoric could itself be violent, might displace violence, be destroyed by it, or give rise to it, there is little in classical thinking on the subject to suggest how violence might be incorporated into the art as an inventional resource. Grimké's speech gives us an exceptional opportunity to examine in some detail what it might mean to reinvent violence as a means of persuasion, resistance, and cultural transformation. As we approach our reading of the text, I will underscore again the key to its internal action and hence to our interpretation: violence—both as a theme and as a pressing contextual force—is made in the speech to effect a series of transformations; these transformations thus represent the unfolding rhetorical action of the text. Such a perspective commits us to asking persistently what violence *does* in this speech—not simply in what ways it is addressed or managed, but what, specifically, changes *by virtue of violence?* Thus posed, the question drives the following analysis and positions us finally to see how Grimké reinvented violence as a means to greater rhetorical and moral ends.

When, on the evening of 16 May 1838, Angelina Grimké stood to address an informal but large gathering of the reform community, she was perhaps the most outrageous woman in American public life. She knew as much, indeed had delighted in "turning the world upside down" during her New England tour only months before, and had apparently conquered recurrent bouts of anxiety over her abilities as an orator. At the same time, she had become increasingly apprehensive over the motives that drew such large crowds to her lectures. In all, Grimké had found her hosts friendly and receptive, and was especially impressed by Friends in the region, of whom she noted slyly that "The slave is dearer to them than Quakerism." Nevertheless, she professed herself uncertain as to the actual effects of these talks, and there was, she wrote to Sarah Douglass, "No doubt [that] great numbers who have attended them come out of mere curiosity; some to make fun of such a strange anomaly as a *Woman's* addressing a Committee of Legislature." Months of speaking before promiscuous audiences had inured Grimké to criticism, but she could not ignore the fact that she had become what we might now call a celebrity, a figure who, working to expose the spectacle of slavery, had herself become a spectacle. This development, together with the week's formalities and public displays, must have quickened Angelina's sensitivity to the question of her relationship to the cause or, more precisely, of the cause's relationship to her. This much is evident at the very beginning of the address.[24]

"Men, brethren, and fathers—mothers, daughters and sisters, what came ye out for to see? A reed shaken with the wind?" Interrogating the motives of those who had gathered to hear would not seem the better part of rhetorical judgment; at best, the opening might appear to be a kind of inverted version of the classical *ingratio,* where, instead of speaker obsequies, the audience is roundly scolded for assembling under false pretenses. In truth, however, the opening allusion to Christ's dialogism in Matthew 11:7 is altogether familiar in the Jeremiadic tradition, and far from violating expectations, almost certainly was understood as an altogether appropriate means to introduce the evening's subject. Samuel Danforth's classic "Errand into the Wilderness" (1670) takes the passage as its text and offers a virtual commentary on the proem, explaining in some detail what Grimké later implied. "The phrase," Danforth then spoke, "agrees to Shows and Stage-plays; plainly arguing that many of those, who seemed well-affected to John, and flock'd after him, were Theatrical Hearers, Spectators rather than Auditors; they went not to hear; but to see, they went to gaze upon a new and strange Spectacle." As with Grimké, the second-generation Puritan was anxious to discern just what it was that signified genuine conviction. Christ's question goes to the very heart of the issue, Danforth explained, and was "to be understood negatively and ironically; q.d. Surely ye went not into the desert to behold such a ludicrous and ridiculous sight, A man like unto a reed shaken with the wind."[25]

Grimké's is accordingly a question designed to call into question. It disrupts the speaker-audience relationship before it even begins, and announces from the very start that the problem is not with promiscuous audiences, but with assemblies who think themselves audiences for having gathered into vicarious spectatorship. That the object of so much curiosity should draw attention so readily to her audience's motives suggests perhaps something of Grimké's impatience with the run of reform and antislavery conventions; certainly elements of fatigue and a building skepticism about the state of abolition societies may be glimpsed in these early lines. More generally, however, she can be seen explicitly calling into question their very reason for being: "Is it curiosity merely," Grimké asked, "or a deep sympathy with the perishing slave, that has brought this large audience together?" Thus a pattern that would assert itself throughout the text became immediately evident: Grimké imposed a disjunction where none was thought to exist; set the resulting binary on display; and confronted her listeners with the choice of complicity or redemption. The effect was to take that which had been assumed—of course this was a genuine community of actors—break it into its false and real aspects—motives either from curiosity or sympathy—and demand of her listeners a renewed commitment to the cause.

In the event, Angelina's line of questioning was loudly interrupted by the mob now forming outside Pennsylvania Hall. The speaker could not have been especially surprised, given the rumors, innuendo, and provocation on both sides since early in the week. Mob unrest, as we have noted, was hardly uncommon at abolitionist meetings, and Philadelphia in 1838 was surely among the last places in America an antislavery orator would hope to find peace. Still, the very size and proximity of the crowd outside must have been daunting to the most steadfast abolitionists; indeed, many of these were inside the hall now, pondering, perhaps, how they had arrived in such a place as to be threatened without by the mob and arraigned within by a southern female of slave-holding family, so apparently certain of her own faith and skeptical of theirs. In any case, Grimké moved quickly not to distance those within from those without, but to literally write them into each other's not-so-distinctive logics. "The voices without ought to awaken and call our warmest sympathies," Grimké declared,

> Deluded beings! "They know not what they do." They know not that they are undermining their own rights and their own happiness, temporal and eternal. Do you ask, "What has the North to do with slavery?" Hear it—hear it. Those voices without tell us that the spirit of slavery is here, and has been roused to wrath by our abolition speeches and conventions: for surely liberty would not foam and tear herself with rage, because her friends are multiplied daily, and meetings are held in quick succession to set forth her virtues and extend her peaceful kingdom.

Grimké's improvised assimilation of the violence mounting out of doors represents the first of several important such moments. Again, to the question, What does violence do in this address? We have already at least several responses: it sets in dramatic relief the difference between curiosity and sympathy; it summons Grimké's listeners away from spectatorship and into being as an audience; and it testifies at once to the blindness of the mob and to the effectiveness of the abolitionists' best efforts. Figuratively this complex process is represented by the juxtaposition of voice and sight, where the shouts of the mob, though unseen and delusional, at least give certain evidence of the true state of things; by distinction, the merely curious, though seen and seeing, as yet remain, as it were, insignificant. Hence Grimké announced her faith in things unseen, her insistence on the moral force and certainty of the world as yet unbeheld by others.

If Grimké had rhetorically separated her listeners from themselves—that is, effected a break in consciousness between complacent spectatorship and authentic engagement—she reconnected identity and agency immediately thereafter. Within the terms of her address, that is in part the work violence is made to do; by moving violence indoors, by refusing to ignore or succumb to it, Grimké allowed violence to do what it does best: to make evident the stakes involved in moral choice, community, and action. Violence reveals the weakest link in the structure of convictions holding such relations together, probes and exposes complicity within the virtuous; it thus works to destroy false sentiment as preliminary to the reconstruction of genuine sympathy. "This opposition shows that slavery has done its deadliest work in the hearts of our citizens," Grimké announced. "Do you ask, then, 'what has the North to do?' I answer, cast out first the spirit of slavery from your own hearts, and then lend your aid to convert the South."

The point is sharp: Grimké was well practiced by 1838 in responding to opponents of abolitionism who, like Beecher, marveled at the arrogance of northern reformers. On this score, at least, they had a strong case, and indeed Grimké seemed prepared to grant it. The abolitionists before her now were really only three steps away from themselves being slaveholders: they were not owners of other human beings, not a mob as such, but complicitous in a system of production and consumption, of complacency and self-righteousness, that in one way or another facilitated the hated system. The violence mounting outside unmasked that reality. Having, as the allusion to Christ's admonition suggests, cast the beam out of their own eyes before going after their brothers', abolitionists could prepare themselves for renewed conviction and action. "Each one present has a work to do," Grimké urged, "be his or her situation what it may, however limited their means, or insignificant their supposed influence. The great men of this country will not do this work; the church will never do it. A desire to please the world, to keep the favor of all parties and of all conditions, makes them dumb on this and every other unpopular subject." As Grimké had observed in her letter to Garrison three years previously, mobs usually asserted themselves before law, and took on thereby an authority of their own, even as they were eventually accommodated by government and its structures of domination. Though powerful, however, such institutions were rendered mute by being enslaved, as it were, to vested interests, and so, being "worldly-wise," God, "in his wisdom, employs them not to carry on his plans of reformation and salvation. He hath chosen the foolish things of the world," Grimké reminded her listeners in reference to Paul, "to confound the wise, and the weak to overcome the mighty."

That government and institutionalized religion were complicitous in the slave system, and therefore not to be counted on for its remedy, was to be sure conventional wisdom. One did not have to be "ultra," a Sabbatarian, nonresistant, or any other brand of "radical" to appreciate how unmovable were entrenched northern interests, and abolitionists of many different stripes could happily gather under banners proclaiming the power of the weak to overcome the mighty. There is as well much here of the ritualized scouring, cleaning, and refurnishing common to the evangelical host gathered in the hall that evening. We need not make a case for the uniqueness of Grimké's arguments, appeals, or imagery, however, in order to see in the speech her distinctive management of reform commonplaces. Here, it is not the putative "content" of the address that proves singular as much as who it was giving voice and movement to that content—and to what lasting effect. As witness, the speaker oversaw the dismantling of one state of allegiance and the reconstruction of another; in speaking, she testified and in turn projected the power of testimony onto the one force that would seem to destroy speech: violence. What, in fact, violence was made to do under the circumstances was not to render the faithful dumb but to reanimate and provoke yet more speech.

Hence the power of the witness: to see, to speak, and thus to make others see and speak in ways heretofore unthought of. But while privileged by virtue of experience and unique as one who is simultaneously in community and out, the witness may be said to have presence only within the speech act. To be a witness and to witness is to assume a responsibility of a kind; it is to speak worlds unseen and so to bring together those who would live that world. The relationship that must obtain between violence and the witness is therefore complex and deeply significant to the prospects of reform; the witness bears unusual responsibility to report violence, to assign it value, and to make it productive of change. Slavery, understood as a massive and exemplary instance of violence against the bodies and souls of other human beings, imposes with unmistakable clarity this imperative to speak on those who have seen it. By virtue of its being witnessed, slavery is made thus to speak, hence to speak against itself.

We have seen this kind of semiotic transformation with respect to mob violence: in bearing witness to it, Grimké, in effect, allowed violence to testify against itself by awakening in others the capacity to see it for what it was. So now with slavery. "As a Southerner," Grimké continued, "I feel that it is my duty to stand up here to night and bear testimony against slavery. I have seen it—I have seen it. I know it has horrors that can never be described. I was brought up under its wing: I witnessed for many years its demoralizing influences, and its destructiveness to human happiness." Grimké's first explicit reference to herself as a witness positioned her tactically between an immediate present and a past that could not be forgotten. It would indeed be her purpose to reestablish community by coming together in remembrance; that much, of course, is the function of most kinds of witnessing, certainly of those which seek to strengthen conventional bonds. Violence works its most insidious ends by making people forget; it displaces remembrance, thus community, by instilling fear in those who are most able to effect radical change. The rhetorical function of testimony for this reason is to establish in the most compelling terms possible the accuracy of that which is being recollected; subject as it is to the forces of violence, it will need to be re-presented as a basis for future action. Grimké was thus adamant to clarify distortions in the picture of slavery painted by its supporters.

> It is admitted by some that the slave is not happy under the *worst* forms of slavery. But I have *never* seen a happy slave. I have seen him dance in his chains, it is true; but he was not happy. There is a wide difference between happiness and mirth. Man cannot enjoy the former while his manhood is destroyed, and that part of the being which is necessary to the making, and to the enjoyment of happiness, is completely blotted out. The slaves, however, may be, and sometimes are, mirthful. When hope is extinguished, they say, "let us eat and drink, for to-morrow we die."

The image of the dancing slave had been circulating in proslavery and antiabolitionist rhetoric for years, and it would become the object of eloquent scorn in the recollections of Frederick Douglass. Here it illustrates how wide and dangerous was the space between northern public opinion and the realities of plantation life. Positioned between both, Grimké was able to correct and regulate the interpretation of slavery as a social fact; bearing witness, she discerned, distinguished, and offered up what had been seen as the appropriate object of understanding. The ocular imagery in this passage contrasts tellingly with that of the speech's opening lines, where the act of seeing is rendered passive, an idle sense disengaged from its object and unable to discriminate between basic motives. The witness, conversely, not only knows what she sees, but makes known what she has seen; she literally creates knowledge by communicating it to others.

The audience of three thousand was then pointedly reminded of the stakes and consequences of such knowledge by a barrage of stones crashing through the hall's impressive new windows. The noise outside could not be ignored, and within, growing unrest threatened to cut Grimké's address short. Nonplussed, the speaker asked her audience to consider in the context just what a mob actually meant. "What would the breaking of every window be?" Grimké asked, "What would the leveling of this Hall be? Any evidence that we are wrong, or that slavery is a good and wholesome institution? What if the mob should now burst in upon us, break up our meeting and commit violence upon our persons—would this be anything compared with what the slaves endure?" As with the first assault, Grimké's immediate response to incursions of violence was to make it productive, to make it signify and confirm, to turn violence itself into a form of speech.

Even at this early stage in the address, the accumulative effect is apparent: the first lines of the oration introduce thematically the distinction between transient curiosity and abiding sympathy; embodied as it is in the person of Grimké, the speech retains a constancy of purpose and meaning even as it is rocked by the spectacular events outside. The performance thus may be said to instantiate the message, embracing and transforming meaningless violence into the unfolding economy of the text. Having assisted in the transformation of curious onlookers into a real audience, violence works now to specify the task and content of that audience. Thus in answer to the question—"would this be anything compared with what the slaves endure?" Grimké insisted "No, no: and we do not remember them 'as bound with them,' if we shrink in the time of peril, or feel unwilling to sacrifice ourselves, if need be, for their sake. [Great noise.] I thank the Lord that there is yet life enough to feel the truth, even though it rages at us—that conscience is not so completely seared as to be unmoved by the truth of the living God." In this way, violence is remade into an agent of remembrance, not of oneself but of enslaved others, on whose behalf the audience is reminded thereby to act.

Grimké's rhetorical authority was a function, then, not only of her experience, but of her capacity to absorb and express the full range and depth of that experience. Witnesses as such were no rarity: the land was full of them, travelers and exiles, businessmen and clergy, politicians and apologists. The fear she had earlier communicated to Garrison, that "we shall have false brethren now, just as the Apostles had, and this will be one of our greatest griefs," was not in this regard unfounded. The American Colonization Society, clearly, was not alone in bringing to Northerners reports of southern life that collided directly with antislavery narratives. Abolitionists had in turn developed a counterattack of their own, detailing the kind of fool's progress routing Northerners to the South and back home again: "they have seen slave holders and know that they are honorable customers and generous friends," explained the AASS in its fourth annual report, "they believe they have their peculiar reasons for what they do—and they know that it is hopeless to interfere." Such well-meaning visitors, "imagine themselves as much the friends of the slave as ever, and they certainly see much more to admire in the master." The consequences for northern perceptions of slavery were startling: "Now let us count the men who have direct intercourse with the South," the report concluded, "and then take into the account the circles of their northern friends—each intersecting or touching other circles, and we shall find at last that there is not an individual in the whole country whose opinion is not in a greater or lesser degree acted upon by an influence which was set in motion by a southern bribe."[26]

These false witnesses posed no small rhetorical problem for Grimké, who knew firsthand how seductive could be appearances in the slave-holding South. "Many persons go to the South for a season," she told her audience, "and are hospitably entertained in the parlor and at the table of the slaveholder." Never entering the slave huts, she continued, "they know nothing of the dark side of the picture, and they return home with praises on their lips of the generous character of those with whom they had tarried." This insensibility to the plight of the slave marked the North as equally complicitous in the system; within the terms of Grimké's reasoning, it represented a kind of moral blindness, equivalent to myopic curiosity or the delusion of mob spirit. Slavery worked these ends in several ways, to be sure; if it could not hide itself, slavery could, by its very barbarity, dull the visitor's capacity for moral judgment. Even if visitors tucked into the slave's hut, Grimké explained, "by remaining silent spectators they have naturally become callous—an insensibility has ensued which prepares them to apologize even for barbarity."

Grimké's argument underscored a widespread conviction that slavery was inherently protean, that it could never be circumscribed in place and time, and must feed itself through ever greater claims on human freedom. Numbing its victims and witnesses was one such means: it made dumb the slave, the slaveholder, the neighbor, the family, and the northern visitor. As a result, the possibilities for bearing witness against slavery effectively were severely limited: those who had never seen slavery were able only, with assistance, to imagine it; and those who had were often as not rendered mute through either complicity or denial. All the same, Grimké remained confident that while slavery had corrupted northern apologists, public opinion might still be cultivated and brought to bear against such men, and that "much will have been done for the destruction of Southern slavery when we have so reformed the North that no one here will be willing to risk his reputation by advocating or even excusing the holding of men as property."

That time must have seemed at the moment far distant. Again Grimké's speech was interrupted by an "outbreak of mobocratic spirit," and again the disturbance was thought to have spilled into the hall itself. Obviously a threat in one sense, the violence pressing close at least had the merit of assertion, at least was evidence of sensate forces and bespoke an intelligence of its own. Unlike the complacent reformer or deluded apologist, the mob expressed clearly if unintentionally its acute grasp of slavery's reach. Grimké's response to this latest push is telling and represents a pivotal moment in the speech: here she recoursed to her own story in explicit terms, bore witness to her past and progress into moral resolve. In this telling, at least, Grimké's narrative was not so much, like Birney's, a story of blindness, conversion, and rebirth of self as it was a journey from solitude to moral community, of finding there a faith to speak and the courage to act in public. The noise of the mob outside and the voices of southern intransigence were welcome contrast to the days of Grimké's youth, steeped as it was in a culture of silence about the realities of the system. "Many times have I wept in the land of my birth, over the system of slavery," Grimké recounted. " I knew of none who sympathized in my feelings—I was unaware that any efforts were made to deliver the oppressed—no voice in the wilderness was heard calling on the people and do works meet for repentance—and my heart sickened within me." Here it is not the witness who undergoes conversion—her convictions remain fixed—but the culture into which she is born. It is not yet a complete conversion, to be sure, but, "Oh, how should I have rejoiced to know that such efforts as these were being made."[27]

The real problem for Grimké and the abolitionists was not mobs. For all the rhetorical charge they were to take from them, the appeals to martyrdom, protests against violations of free speech, and calls for protection of person and property, the mob outbreaks were signs of effect and, in Grimké's speech, productive of positive change. The true problem was silence, the failure to speak, to bear witness. Slavery being what it was, there could be no easy resolution: as abolitionists stressed time and again, slavery dulled the moral imagination, eliminated the capacity for resistance before it ever had a chance to develop. Thus a writer for the *Quarterly Anti-Slavery Magazine* explained pointedly how this deadening of sensibilities worked and to what effect, stressing that "this process of hardening the heart, begins before the man is himself a slave holder. From a child he has been accustomed to see the punishment of slaves, and to see it by others as a matter of indifference. I can imagine no circumstances in which a child could be placed," he wrote, "better calculated to blunt his sensibilities. . . ."[28]

Grimké's account of her childhood in South Carolina was finely tuned to such strains. "I only wonder," she declared, "that I had such feelings. I wonder when I reflect under what influence I was brought up, that my heart is not harder than the nether millstone." Thus begins the central and controlling narrative in the speech, familiar to readers of all ages as a sojourn from the wilderness of despair, of exile into foreign lands, and of new hopes dashed; of crushing disappointment and isolation; and of final triumph in new cities of faith. Because of its importance to the speech as a whole, indeed as the chief narrative of Grimké's public life, the passage is worth quoting at some length:

> But in the midst of temptation I was preserved, and my sympathy grew warmer, and my hatred of slavery more inveterate, until at last I have exiled myself from my native land because I could no longer endure to hear the wailing of the slave. I fled to the land of Penn; for here, thought I, sympathy for the slave will surely be found. But I found it not. The people were kind and hospitable, but the slave had no place in their thoughts. Whenever questions were put to me as to his condition, I felt that they were dictated by an idle curiosity, rather than by that deep feeling which would lead to effort for his rescue.

In keeping with the general dynamics of the speech, the passage works by playing expectations off each other, sustaining forward movement as much by collapsing conventional oppositions as through the plot line itself. A ready and partial list of these binary relations so far in the speech illustrates how unstable they are made to be: speaker-audience; curiosity-sympathy; outside-inside; slavery-freedom; North-South; silence-speech; duty-dereliction; remembering-forgetting; blindness-insight; violence-quiescence. These and more will fall into each other as the speech proceeds, the effect of which is to first destroy and then reconstruct the structure of convictions that is Grimké's subject. It is not too much to say, indeed, that Grimké redirected the productive energy of the mob outdoors onto the structure of her text, wreaking violence, as it were, on such complacent and self-serving distinctions. In this passage, the tensions initially drive the story forward, where temptation gives way to resolve, sympathy and hate work to push the speaker into exile, and a measure of freedom from slavery seems briefly possible. That much is quickly dispelled, however, as the speaker comes to realize that even in the North, indeed in the land of Quakers and patriots, slavery commanded no real interest. Having fled, Grimké finds herself in precisely the same moral topography, equally isolated and the object not of genuine concern but of idle curiosity—a condition, her audience may have realized, apparently reproduced on the occasion of her speech that night.

> I remembered that I was a Carolinian, from a state which framed this iniquity by law. I knew that throughout her territory was continued suffering, on the one part, and continual brutality and sin on the other. Every Southern breeze

wafted to me the discordant tones of weeping and wailing, shrieks and groans, mingled with prayers and blasphemous curses. I thought there was no hope; that the wicked would go on his wickedness, until he had destroyed both himself and his country. My heart sunk within me at the abominations in the midst of which I had been born and educated. What will it avail, cried I in bitterness of spirit, to expose to the gaze of strangers the horrors and pollutions of slavery, when there is no ear to hear nor heart to feel and pray for the slave. The language of my soul was, "Oh tell it not in Gath, publish it not in the streets of Askelon."

Grimké's indirect allusion to Christ's "He that hath ears to hear, let him hear," reinvokes the scriptural context from Matthew with which the address began; speaker and audience are thus reminded again how tentative and vulnerable is the relationship that binds communities of faith. Grimké's momentary failure, too, is represented by reference to 2 Samuel 1:20 as a variant on that of her audience's and, for that matter, of the proslavery and antiabolitionist opposition: where they could not listen, she could not speak; where their moral capacity had been enervated by habit, creed, or mere curiosity, hers had been rendered silent through despair and fear. The crisis reaching its turning point, Grimké's despondency lifted and now, "Animated with hope," she vowed with Isaiah to "lift up my voice like a trumpet, and show this people their transgression, their sins of omission toward the slave, and what they can do towards affecting Southern mind[s], and overthrowing Southern oppression."

Although Grimké did not mention it by name, the catalyst in her transformation from silent to vocal witness had been the violence sweeping across northern reform cities. Her rhetorical work since and particularly on this night was then to bear witness to her own emergence as a witness, as if in this way of telling the audience might glimpse a better version of itself and its responsibilities. We can observe the progressive adumbration of distance between speaker and audience, from the speech's initial "you" and "I" toward more frequent references to "us" and "we." At the same time as Grimké worked to establish collective identity, however, at no time did she lose sight of that which distinguished her from others: as witness, her duty was to re-present what they could not immediately apprehend, to make sense of and apply as principle truths hidden. From such a perspective, the speaker trained her eye on the moral landscape and discerned there the terms of battle, where "there is no such thing as neutral ground." If the violence of antiabolitionist mobs clarified the limits of conflict, it also determined the degree of commitment required for entering into the battle. The lesson was plain to see: "He that is not for us is against us," Grimké declared, with Matthew's Christ in 12:30, "and he that gathereth not with us, scattereth abroad. If you are on what you suppose to be neutral ground," warned the speaker, "the South look upon you as on the side of the oppressor." There could be in any case no recourse to silence in the face of events; failing conviction, failing action, Northerners were to be reminded that "God swept Egypt with the besom of destruction, and punished Judea also with sore punishment, because of slavery. And have we any reason to believe that he is less just now?" Grimké asked, "or that he will be more favorable to us than to his own 'peculiar people?'"

With yet another volley of stones and mounting noise from without, Grimké turned for a final time to the mob at hand. Rhetorically, this has been so absorbed into the moral logic of the speech that it bears little even by way of mention. The forces of reform were seen by Grimké as already working against the opposition, its violence merely confirmation of that fact. For the remainder of the speech, Grimké's energies were devoted rather to activating what had been reconstituted; having retrieved from the circumstances a real audience, she now needed to give to it means as well as ends, encouragement as well as definition. The mob could be put to work here as well, confirming as it did that while in one regard insignificant, the abolitionists could be nonetheless effective. In short, faltering conviction or lagging enthusiasm was no excuse; true, Grimké said, the abolitionists were "nothing"— but then, as Paul once pointedly claimed, "God has chosen things that are not to bring to nought things that are." Buy books on slavery; read them; give generously and well; circulate appeals: modest beginnings, perhaps, Grimké implied, and alleged by some to be false: but then why, she asked, "do they not contradict what we say? They cannot. Moreover the South has entreated, nay commanded us to be silent; and what greater evidence of the truth of our publications could be desired?"

If Grimké's address had thus far been rhetorically effective, then the problem of violence to abolitionist efforts had been systematically eliminated. The speech worked by making violence productive, putting it to use in the transformation of audience, occasion, speaker, and movement. This much was superintended by Grimké, in and through her act of giving witness: having seen what others had not, she could, in a sense, invoke herself as testimony to the sources, meaning, and consequences of violence. On this basis, Grimké literally oversaw the symbolic process through which human beings came out of and into shared identity. Paradoxically, but no less actually, violence so reconceived produces itself out of existence: it creates those conditions of human identity and agency that must ultimately supplant mere physical force.

This realignment and final displacement of violence clears the way for Grimké's climactic appeal to women abolitionists. Here is the first direct recognition of the gendered composition of the evening's events; and while it scarcely represents a brief on behalf of women's rights, there can be no missing the special case being advanced. Coming as it does in the final moments, however, the appeal takes into itself and fully realizes the moral logic thus far set in motion by the speech generally. Its claims on the audience and women members of the audience particularly are in this sense made possible and plausible by virtue of what has come before: put another way, what Grimké said here was what could be said once the way had been made clear. What are the prospects of moral reform and abolition when violence is no longer available as a barrier, excuse, or threat? What can women, thus unfettered, accomplish? What, indeed, can they not? Within this logic, even the systematic proscriptions against certain kinds of women's activism and delimitation of opportunity can offer no retreat from the responsibility to act; in fact, they serve as warrants for specific kinds of abolition work: "Women of Philadelphia! allow me as a Southern woman, with much attachment to the land of my birth, to entreat you to come up to this work. Especially let me urge you to petition," Grimké urged, "*Men* may settle this and other questions at the ballot-box, but you have no such right; it is only through petitions that you can reach the Legislature. It is therefore peculiarly *your* duty to petition."

As specific as Grimké's case is, it is wholly in keeping with the force and direction of the argument so far: the violent reaction of the antiabolitionists had betrayed their own recognition that such measures had in fact found their mark, and it had made explicit the duties attendant to free moral beings as they act to free other moral beings. Petitioning, for half a decade now the predominate expression of women's political and social activism, the official purpose, indeed, of the sisters' New England efforts, was to be undertaken as one such duty. No resistance to it, no denial of the right to petition or intransigence on the part of public officials, could in principle represent a reason for not exercising that right. True, as Grimké observed, "Men who hold the rod over slaves, rule in the councils of the nation: and they deny our right to petition and to remonstrate against abuses of our sex and of our kind." Again, neither such violence nor violation figure here as stoppage, if only because divine right impels action where it is least welcome. "Only let us exercise them," Grimké stressed, "and though often turned away unanswered, let us remember the influence of importunity upon the unjust judge, and act accordingly. The fact that the South look with jealousy upon our measures shows that they are effectual. There is, therefore, no cause for doubting or despair, but rather for rejoicing." By way of precedent, English women petitioners offered the extraordinary example of just this process, where by importuning the Queen with their miles of petitions, serious efforts were finally made to abolish the notorious apprenticeship system. "When the women of these States," Grimké concluded, "send up to Congress such a petition, our legislators will arise as did those of England, and say, 'When all the maids and matrons of the land are knocking at our doors we must legislate.' Let the zeal and love, the faith and works of our English sisters quicken ours—that while the slaves continue to suffer, and when they shout deliverance, we may feel the satisfaction of *having done what we could.*"

Having done what she could, Angelina Grimké thus concluded her career as an abolitionist orator. "The calmness and impassioned earnestness of Angelina Grimké Weld," it was said, "speaking nearly an hour 'mid that howling mob, was not surpassed in courage and consecration even by Paul among the wild beasts at Ephesus." Still, satisfaction of any sort did not come easily to Angelina, and certainly the events of the following night must have been especially trying to the newly wed, thoroughly exhausted orator. After three years of nearly nonstop writing, speaking, and debating, she may have reflected on a career of unprecedented visibility and rhetorical acclaim, on having done what she could. More than a year after the Pennsylvania Hall address, however, Angelina continued to despair over the need for witnesses against slavery. In a letter to her English friend Elizabeth Pease, Grimké feared that slavery's end would come only "in terrible judgment," and this because, "I see not any witnesses raised up in the *midst of themselves,* who are ready to go to prison and to death, if need be, in testifying against this monarch sin," nor did she see "any Abolitionists from the North commissioned to go down and preach with all boldness against this mother of abominations."[29]

The need for such witnessing would soon result in the collaboratively composed *American Slavery As It Is,* but for now Angelina was duty-bound to offer her own brand of testimony before northern audiences. The Pennsylvania Hall speech was the greatest such effort to capitalize on what was perceived to be an anomaly: as Samuel Webb noted in his official reports on the week's proceedings and the burning of the hall, "The eloquence of this speaker, together with her thorough acquaintance with slavery from having been an eye witness of its cruelties and debasing influence, had excited much curiosity to hear her upon this subject." Grimké had dispatched the problem of idle curiosity, and the speaker had made the most of her paradoxical position as a southern woman testifying against slavery. But she knew, too, that no far-reaching advances could be had until her voice ceased being singular and became part of an overwhelming chorus. There were signs of progress in the North, Grimké told Pease, but in the South, "a sullen, death like silence prevails, save when the bursts of unholy indignation at 'Northern interference' are heard to issue from the mouths of slave holding divines and southern [de]magogues." In any case, she noted, "the reign of terror is not over and perhaps never will be until the huge bastille tumbles into ruin, and its very foundations are plowed up."[30]

The speech of 16 May was but one in a series of public performances designed to keep that apocaplyptic vision from becoming a reality. To bear witness as Grimké had done was to interpose herself between physical force and moral action, and from that stance to reinvent the rhetorical possibilities of violence. In respeaking violence into a productive agency for change, she in effect recreated one crisis as an antidote to the development of a much greater, indeed cataclysmic, eruption. The work required for this reinvention is evident in every word of the Pennsylvania Hall address, most dramatically in the way in which violence is made to rupture, expose, and reconstitute the conditions of reform, community, and collective purpose. Thus what began with a skeptical inquiry into the very identity of her listeners ends with a call to women as particular agents of social transformation. That is the work of the witness, whose task it is not only to superintend this redefinition of self and community, but to proclaim its promise to the world.

Epilogue

On the occasion of Sarah Grimké's passing at the age of eighty-one, Lydia Maria Child wondered to Angelina whether "it now sometimes seems strange to you that those exciting and eventful years, that so tried our souls and taxed our energies, have passed away into history?" Very few remained, thought Child, who had "any idea of the prayers, and tears, and inward struggles, through which you and your noble sister passed, in that arduous mission of rescuing millions of human brethren from the darkness and misery of slavery." If, in fact, as Child averred, the young of 1874 looked back on the sisters' crusade as they might recall the stoning of Stephen, then perhaps the reason lay in part with Angelina herself. For many, including Abby Kelley and Maria Weston Chapman, Grimké's marriage to Weld and subsequent retirement from public life was exasperating and, with all due sympathy for Angelina's poor health, inexplicable. Child, in her own sly way, had earlier discerned the real cause of Grimké's withdrawal; writing to Chapman in the spring of 1839, Child claimed that she did "not wonder at Angelina Grimké; for she was educated a Presbyterian, and has married a Presbyterian. I know its influences right well," Child noted, "and I love it as my eyes love smoke."[1]

Sight impaired, Child was mistaken on all three counts: Weld was not a practicing Presbyterian; Angelina had not been educated as a Presbyterian; and, more importantly, her withdrawal had nothing to do with these alleged causes. Angelina E. Grimké retired from public life because she was physically and mentally exhausted, because she looked forward to the reputed peace of quiet domestic life, and because she felt duty-bound to lavish upon her children the full extent of her love and care. If there remained any mystery as to the matter—and it is difficult to see why such reasons would not be sufficient and convincing—it may be owing to the equanimity with which Angelina so readily excused herself from the public stage at a time when the abolition of slavery and sex prejudice was anything but certain. Yet even here we have not far to seek, for Grimké had come to understand herself in a way that transcended the spheres to which others assigned her. Though not given to ironic detachment, Angelina could see that she had acted a part, an essential and genuine part, in the unfolding drama of moral reform. She had, in the process, become a model to others regardless of her particular station in life. Thus she lightly admitted to Anne Warren Weston that "our enemies [would] rejoice, could they only look in upon us from day to day and see us toiling in domestic life, instead of lecturing to *promiscuous* audiences." Still, Angelina explained, " I verily believe that we are *thus* doing *as much* for the cause of woman as we did by public speaking. For it is absolutely necessary that we should show that we are not ruined as domestic characters, but so far from it, *as soon* as duty calls us home, we can and do rejoice in the release from public service, and we are as anxious to make good bread as we ever were to deliver a good lecture."[2]

These are not words likely to satisfy Grimké's supporters—or her critics for that matter—but they do give us opportunity to reflect again on her legacy as one of America's greatest and most distinctive reform voices. By way of introduction, I had sought to raise the question of just who Grimké was, in what this "voice" consisted, and to what effect. For want of a better term, I posed the question as bearing on her *identity* as public moral actor, and advanced the several accounts of her speeches and writings as a means to answer the question. In this way, the matter of Grimké's identity was figured rhetorically, that is, it was recognizable as the process and product of symbolic action in and for the world. In this sense, identity—at least Grimké's—is better grasped as a verb than a noun, an active, creative, changing force, a self that is coherent on its own terms but finds its fullest realization as it is exercised in building and transforming human community.

Identity thus formulated bears directly on the more specific issue of how "the public" may be seen at work in her reform career and rhetorical efforts; it gives us reason, moreover, to think of her as "radical" in the most productive sense. Grimké's public activity, it should be clear by now, was never motivated by a will to public life, and certainly not to the "sphere" of politics, business, and other typically masculine activities in antebellum America. It is equally clear, however, that she early on cast a very sharp eye to what certain features of public life might yield in the way of advantage, power, and access to organized opinion. To this end, she developed and exercised her talent for those arts likely to extract what she and her associates needed most: concerted, directed, and effective moral action against race and sex prejudice. That talent was rhetorical, and with it she produced a vision of change that was beholden to neither public nor private domains, but to a boundless conviction that the good must prevail; and that conviction, that commitment to act through oneself for others, could know no boundaries, indeed must not. The result of her public toil is not to be measured by immediate gain, but appreciated in the fact: that in so crafting herself and thus the communities to which she spoke, Grimké unshackled virtue from the false imprisonment to which it had been so long subjected. To thus stress the public career of Grimké as

I have done is not to imply that she found the fullest realization of herself in such a career; it is rather to emphasize how she used the medium of the public to radically transform its own claim to being a separate and superior domain of human activity. This is, I think, the only way that we can make sense of her insistence to Anne Warren Weston: as anxious to make a good loaf of bread as to deliver a good lecture, Angelina, far from abdicating her responsibilities, was in fact asserting the most radical of truths—that at some point, the public and private just do not matter *as* public and private. In demonstrating that claim, in demanding that "it is absolutely necessary that we should show that we are not ruined as domestic characters," Grimké sought to bring into herself and reveal to others a new and drastic reality. *That* was Angelina E. Grimké.

Angelina died on 26 October 1879, at the age of seventy-four. The years since her triumphant entry and exit from public life had not been easy ones: the hardships of domestic labor, complicated births, and sickness conspired to keep Grimké from returning, even if she had so desired, to sustained work in the fields of antislavery and women's rights. She had, of course, been instrumental in the research and publication of *American Slavery As It Is,* the largest selling antislavery tract of its time; had attended Rochester's Women's Rights Convention in 1851; had sent words of support to the Women's Rights Convention in Syracuse a year later; had spoken before the National Equal Rights Association in New York City during the war; and had actually "voted" in a local election in 1870. These were busy years, but we are often left with the impression that Grimké's personal commitment to public speaking and disputation had exhausted itself finally with the destruction of Pennsylvania Hall.

Perhaps that is true, but we know in any case that the brief time Angelina spent on the public stage catalyzed the moral imagination of her generation. Some of the reasons for this have been suggested in the preceding chapters. Then, too, we have the testimony of those who had worked with her in those days, when the battles were undertaken with such confidence, the issues proved so starkly clear, before the complications, jealousies, and ultimate disintegration of organized moral suasion had changed the reform scene almost beyond recognition. For some, like Elizur Wright, Grimké's distinctive trait was courage, courage born not only of experience, but of the moral imperative to communicate that experience to all who would—and would not—listen. "She not only faced death at the hands of stealthy assassins and howling mobs," Wright remembered, "but she encountered unflinchingly the awful frowns of the mighty consecrated leaders of society, the scoffs and sneers of the multitude, the outstretched finger of scorn, and the whispered mockery of pity, standing up for the lowest of the low." Grimké's conviction that slavery was profoundly evil was unmovable, he concluded, and "Neither wealth, nor fame, nor tyrant fashion, nor all that the high position of her birth had to offer, could bribe her to bate one syllable of her testimony against the seductive system."[3]

To Wendell Phillips, who along with Grimké and Frederick Douglass may be considered one of the most accomplished orators of the movement, Angelina's unique contribution was to have used language not as a barrier but as a medium for the contact of consciousness. "Her own hard experience, the long, lonely, intellectual, and moral struggle from which she came out conqueror, had ripened her power," Phillips recalled, "and her wondrous faculty of laying bear her own heart to reach the hearts of others shone forth till she carried us all captive." Phillips, who knew the dynamics of audience response as well as anyone, remained late in life deeply impressed by the effect of Grimké's words: "It was when you saw she was opening some secret record of her own experience that the painful silence and breathless interest told the deep effect and lasting impression her words were making on minds that afterwards never rested in their work."[4]

Lucy Stone, who had heard Grimké speak during the tour of New England, was later to assume Grimké's mantle of eloquence and carry it into the suffrage movement. Still, Stone reflected, "It is impossible for those who to-day see and hear women as ministers and lecturers to understand the state of mind and feeling forty-three years ago, when no woman's voice was heard in public, and when the injunction for her to "keep silence" in the church was held to be as sacred as the commandment, 'Thou shalt not steal.'" When all was said, Stone reminded her fellow reformers on this day, "The women of to-day owe more than they will ever know to the high courage, the rare insight, and fidelity to principle of this woman, by whose suffering easy paths have been made for them."[5]

Kind words for a sad occasion, and we would be surprised at anything less on the day of Grimké's passing. The reflections of Wright, Phillips, and Stone nevertheless alert us again to an irony deeply laid in the foundation of Grimké's rhetorical career. She was remarkable, as I have tried to suggest and as her friends appreciated, for her ability to bring into productive alliance forces—ideas, people, possibilities—that might otherwise have remained distant and, if not mute, unheard. At the center of these forces, and by virtue of the rhetorical art she exercised in bringing them into proximity, stood the writer and speaker herself. The irony, in one sense, was that there seemed so little of "Angelina Grimké" to be actually heard; she was, as others remarked, the most selfless person many had ever encountered, a vessel simply for carrying the Word of God and the abolitionist's message to the world. Hers was in this respect the office of the witness, the martyr and prophet, the self who is no Self. This much is readily evident in her public address and in responses to them; indeed, she was wholly recognizable to a culture whose stages were crowded with what Robert Abzug has called the religious "virtuoso." Thus in 1880 Oliver Johnson, in a telling bit of recollection, wrote that Grimké "was then in her womanly prime, handsome in person and graceful in manner, with a musical and singing voice, as penetrating as it was pleasant. In her simple Quaker garb, her intelligent face lighted up with animation, as she stood before an audience, she presented a most lovely picture of womanhood. She was entirely self-preserved," Johnson noted, "without a suggestion of masculine assurance, and mistress of her facts and of all the questions to which they were related." Unable to conceive of Grimké in other than overtly gendered and aestheticized terms, Johnson, like others, could nevertheless make sense of her within the dramaturgy of antebellum reform.[6]

Part of the burden of the essays comprising this study has been to show that Angelina played a definitive role in the crafting of *herself* within this dramaturgy. The interplay of individual will and public reception is always a complex and ultimately mysterious process, the more so under such proscriptive conditions as pressed against a young southern woman of the 1830s. Still, we can trace in fairly explicit terms the ways in which Angelina labored first to transform and strengthen herself, as if by doing so she would more effectively transform and strengthen the world she so memorably entered. The early phases of this process are evident in her diary. There we have found a record of how one's identity can be self-consciously altered, radicalized as we might say now, as propaedeutic to the work of reform. In her efforts to confront brother Henry over his treatment of the family slave John, she demonstrated early her faith in the power of persuasion to right what was known to be wrong; in her defense of herself before the Presbyterian Session, she showed that principle, effectively expressed, could supersede disparities of power and numbers; and in the self-persuasion required to rationalize her move from Charleston, Angelina revealed to herself resources of courage and conviction that would stand her in good stead in the years to come.

The letter to William Lloyd Garrison could not offer a more dramatic illustration of the symbolic process through which this identity-formation is made possible. It is not enough to say that the medium of the public letter suited her purposes nicely (indeed, it was only retroactively posed as a public letter by the ambitious Garrison); the more important point directs us to how and to what effect she utilized the letter as an entrée into public life. In going public, Grimké said nothing about private life, repudiated no part of herself; she aimed rather to recreate from the violence of Garrison's world a rationale for her own claim on that world and on the work required to change it. The result was to exemplify the possibilities of free choice, public responsibility, and shared moral action. The letter was a means to stage and orchestrate this process, as if in its disclosure could be read not only a ritualized passage from one sphere to the next, but the very process through which the self is integrated into community; here the aim is met not by dissolving the one into the other, but, by virtue of the very encounter, effecting a transformation in both.

Grimké lived her public career, as most of us do, with both eyes on the future. That was what abolitionists and women's rights activists did; they were futurists of a kind, forever anticipating, hoping, calculating, knowing that however fatalistic they might be, theologically, they were nonetheless bound to act now for tomorrow. To dwell on anything else would be to despair of the prospects for meaningful change. It would be naive, however, to think that Grimké's own past did not in some significant ways bear discernibly on her public conduct and identity. As with most other members of the immediatist community, Grimké's commitments required that she break decisively with her past and the cluster of traditions, values, and kinship systems by which it was defined. In several cases these breaks were severe, as they were for Phillips and Child, Birney and Weld; and like these leaders, Angelina and Sarah turned their experience to productive ends in the form of conversion narratives. Grimké was especially concerned, however, not simply to leave behind her past but in some sense to reconstitute it, to make of it something more than a regrettable fact of life. Who she was, privately and publicly, depended on her ongoing relationship with those whom she had left behind; she needed, then, to literally (and symbolically) recreate from her southern heritage a rationale for moral action that would embrace, rather than repudiate, her past.

To this end, the *Appeal to the Christian Woman of the South* was devoted to the work of reparation, to rewriting for her readers a story they had forgotten. The *Appeal* advances the process through which Grimké came to public identity by reminding her southern sisters of who they truly are; it is an act of remembrance, an effort to put back together what had been rent through the ravages of history, slavery, and moral forgetfulness. Whether or not it was read by a single southern woman is not, in this analysis, of particular concern. It was a gesture in one direction that worked in another: with it, Grimké extended a hand to the South even as she offered to the North a model of moral generosity and accommodation without compromise.

Grimké came to public recognition by virtue of the letter to Garrison and the *Appeal*. They marked, indeed introduced and established, her credentials as an authentic force in the abolitionist community, and would perhaps have been enough to keep her there for some time. The years 1835–36 were, as it turned out, but the early stages in a rapidly developing consciousness, when fundamental convictions were finally arrived at, publicly announced, and awaited fuller realization. Certainly Grimké seems never to have settled comfortably on her laurels; she was, indeed, constitutionally incapable of settling comfortably on much of anything, and the press of people, events, and circumstances demanded that whatever momentum she had built be increased and exploited. Within a year after the publication of her *Appeal,* Grimké entered into the most active, trying, and productive period of her public life. Disciplined and invigorated by the training sessions in New York City, she and sister Sarah soon encountered more than they had ever reckoned for, either in the way of applause or criticism.

Angelina's debate with Catharine Beecher in the summer of 1837, crowded though it was by her speaking schedule, gives us a striking record of how direct was the route she was then taking from the logic of immediate abolitionism to the case for women's rights. Underrated and underread, the debate remains one of the most revealing instances of early feminist argumentation extant. In it, Grimké comes to as explicit and forceful an articulation of woman's rights as can be found in the decade. It is especially revealing not only as a defense of her own public identity, but of *what it means to have an identity as such.* At the very heart of her argument was the claim that one literally has no identity without a corresponding principle of rights—not duty, not negotiable or positive rights, not rights as given by man or God, but rights as rights, universal, absolute, and enduring. To constitute one's identity in public therefore was to assert what was already provided; the rhetoric required for such work was designed then to make others see, paradoxically, the self-evident. As a public advocate, Grimké labored throughout her career to just these ends. A decade and more later, it was a task that would exasperate Frederick Douglass, who finally refused in a parallel case to argue systematically for the manhood of African Americans. In 1837, Grimké was still struggling to convince her opponent that women's rights were "an integral part of her moral being; they cannot be withdrawn; they must live with her forever." To ask after Grimké's identity, then, is to consider not only who she was publicly, but what she said in public about the sources and constitution of identity as such.[7]

If Beecher's challenge was a disappointing surprise to Grimké, Weld's nearly mortified. Of all people, Grimké must have thought, to check her public activities on behalf of the enslaved, Weld would surely be thought the last. In truth he posed a serious and predictable objection to his friend respecting the course of her speaking agenda—which, as it turned out, he knew rather little about. Weld's position will not strike us as deserving much credit, and perhaps it does not; in context, however, he simply expressed the abiding and perfectly reputable view that revolutions need to come one at a time. The more interesting lesson for our purposes rests in Grimké's several responses to that challenge. One way of approaching it is to read Weld as asking, in effect, "Who do you think you are?" Grimké's answer is represented in the "private" exchange with Weld during the month of August 1837, where she elaborates on the principle of universal rights presented in the Beecher debate. There she had argued that one's being, one's *moral* being, was incoherent without an attending conception of rights. The two could not legitimately be rendered independent of each other, indeed, were defined precisely by their relationship as mutually constitutive. Under fire from Weld for allegedly introducing onto the abolitionists platform the subsidiary issue of women's rights, Grimké was prompted to further reflection on the responsibilities attendant to the possession of such rights. In the process, she responds to the question "who are you?" by stressing that we are who we are not only by the possession of rights, but by their exercise for the common good. That much is to say that our identity is a function not simply of moral being, but of moral action. And to the extent that the effectiveness of such action presumes access to the resources of public life, then it is immoral to withhold that access from human beings. Such a view comes close to what contemporary thinkers like Thomas Benson have referred to as rhetoric as a way of being; that is, a way of understanding oneself and others as they are publicly constituted, recognized, and respected. Grimké's appropriation of a Protestant and republican vocabulary of rights is thus put to work as a rationale for the full realization of the self as an individual—and as a warrant for asserting rights as those rights are required for collective moral action.[8]

No more conspicuous example of Grimké's principles in action can be found than in the speaking tour of 1837–38. Whether at work drafting statements for the first Anti-Slavery Convention of American Women, speaking before crowds throughout Boston and its regions, addressing the Massachusetts Legislature, lecturing at the Odeon, or, finally, at the ill-fated Pennsylvania Hall, Grimké seems literally to have embodied and voiced the ideal to which she lay claim. The speech of 16 May 1838 is perhaps too readily invoked for dramatic purposes as the culmination of that ideal, with all its drama, irony, momentary tragedy, and ultimate triumph. Still, we should not ignore the obvious: there, before the assembled abolitionist host, she seems to have brought to full issue all the energies, arguments, and implications that she had been professing since the summer of 1835. Among its many dimensions, the speech is remarkable for the way in which it takes from the world that which the world gives; transforms constraint into possibility; and gives back to her audience a reason for believing—and for acting. The authority for this work she finds neither in herself alone, nor in those before only; but in the "concatenation of circumstances" she so perceptively managed. Grimké was there as a witness—for that was who she was—and to bear testimony—for that was what she had to do.

If it is at all wise to draw a line from 1835 to 1838, it follows from the realization that the public must be pursued; that to do so Angelina must become public herself; that in being herself she had certain rights to which she and all others were entitled; that those rights were to be exercised in public or in private to the common good; and that to proclaim the rights of others was the fullest expression of herself as a free moral being.

Notes

Introduction

1. Angelina Emily Grimké Weld, Speech at Pennsylvania Hall, in Larry Ceplair, ed., *The Public Years of Sarah and Angelina Grimké: Selected Writings, 1835–1839* (New York: Columbia University Press, 1989), 321.

2. Catherine H. Birney, *Sarah and Angelina Grimké: The First American Women Advocates of Abolition and Woman's Rights* (Boston: Lee and Shappard, 1885; reprint, Westport, Conn.: Greenwood, 1969); Gerda Lerner, *The Grimké Sisters From South Carolina: Pioneers for Woman's Rights and Abolition* (New York: Schocken Books, 1974); Katharine Du Pre Lumpkin, *The Emancipation of Angelina Grimké* (Chapel Hill, N.C.: University of North Carolina Press, 1974). Lerner's biography remains the definitive treatment of the Grimké sisters; as with anyone working on the subject generally, I am deeply indebted to Lerner's scholarship, and her influence in the following chapters is unapologetically evident.

3. Angelina Grimké, *Letters to Catherine [sic] E. Beecher*, in Ceplair, *Public Years*, 197; Diary of Angelina Grimké, 14 July 1829, Weld Manuscripts, Clements Library, University of Michigan.

4. James Brewer Stewart, *Holy Warriors: The Abolitionists and American Slavery* (New York: Hill and Wang, 1996), 35–74.

5. Maria Chapman, "To Female Anti-Slavery Societies throughout New England," in *Letters of Theodore Dwight Weld, Angelina Grimké Weld and Sarah Grimké, 1822–1844*, ed. G. H. Barnes and D. L. Dummond (Gloucester, Mass.: Peter Smith, 1965), 1:396. Hereafter cited as *Weld-Grimké Letters*.

6. William Lloyd Garrison, quoted in Samuel Webb, *History of Pennsylvania Hall* (Philadelphia: Merrihew and Gunn, 1838), 118, 120.

7. John Greenleaf Whittier to Harriet Minot, 5 July, 1837, in John B. Pickard, ed., *The Letters of John Greenleaf Whittier* (Cambridge: Harvard University Press, 1975), 1:243. Minot confirmed Whittier's sentiments later in the month by observing of Angelina that "She is the most eloquent, and I think the most beautiful creature I ever saw . . . when she became interested in her subject, when her soul beamed brightly in her eye, and her whole countenance became radiant with emotion, she seemed transcendentally beautiful." Quoted in Whittier, *Letters*, 1:244, n. 2.

8. Lucretia Mott, quoted in Webb, *Pennsylvania Hall*, 127.

9. Whittier, *Letters*, 1:243; Sarah Grimké to Theodore Weld, 12 February 1838, *Weld-Grimké Letters*, 1:541; Sarah's true talents may not have rested in public specifying as

such, but her contributions to the theoretical basis of feminist thought were at once original and profound. See especially Lerner, *The Feminist Thought of Sarah Grimké* (New York: Oxford University Press, 1998).

10. Theodore Weld to Sarah and Angelina Grimké, 26 August 1837, *Weld-Grimké Letters,* 1:433.

11. Angelina Grimké, *Appeal to the Christian Women of the South,* in Ceplair, *Public Years,* 60.

12. Ibid., 37.

13. Angelina Grimké, *Speech at Pennsylvania Hall,* 318–19.

Chapter 1

1. Diary of Angelina Grimké, 10 January 1828, Weld Manuscripts, Clements Library, University of Michigan, Ann Arbor, Michigan. All citations are to the microfilm edition.

2. Howard Brinton, *Quaker Journals: Varieties of Religious Experience Among Friends* (Wallingford, Penn.: Pendle Hill, 1972), 1–5. For women's diary writing see Margo Culley, "I Look at Me: Self as Subject in the Diaries of American Women," *Women's Studies Quarterly* 17 (1989): 15–22; Penelope Franklin, ed., *Private Pages: Diaries of American Women, 1830–1870* (New York: Ballantine, 1986); and Valerie Raoul, "Women and Diaries: Gender and Genre," *Mosaic* 22 (1989): 57–65.

3. Throughout I rely on Gerda Lerner, *The Grimké Sisters from South Carolina: Pioneers for Woman's Rights and Abolitionism* (New York: Schocken Books, 1974), 1–86 for biographical details. See also Diary, 10 January 1828.

4. On conventions of Quaker writing in particular, see especially Howard Beeth, "Among Friends: Epistolary Correspondence Among Quakers in the Emergent South," *Quaker History* 76 (1987): 108–27; Brinton, *Quaker Journals;* Elizabeth Potts Brown and Susan M. Stuard, eds., *Witnesses for Change: Quaker Women Over Three Centuries* (New Brunswick, N.J.: Rutgers University Press, 1989); and Carol Edkins, "Quest for Community: Spiritual Autobiographies of Eighteenth-Century Quaker and Puritan Women in America," in Estelle C. Jelling, ed., *Women's Autobiography* (Bloomington: Indiana University Press, 1980): 39–52.

5. "Testimony of Angelina Grimké Weld," in Larry Ceplair, ed., *The Public Years of Sara and Angelina Grimké: Selected Writings, 1835-1839* (New York: Columbia University Press, 1989), 338–49.

6. Diary, 31 October 1828; 30 November 1828.

7. Ceplair, *Public Years,* 344; Diary, 1 November 1828.

8. Diary, 29 January 1829.

9. Ibid.

10. Diary, 7 February 1829; 8 February 1829.

11. Diary, 8 April 1929.

12. Diary, 27 April 1829.

13. Quoted in Lerner, *Grimké Sisters,* 83.

14. Diary, 15 May 1829.
15. Diary, 26 May 1829.
16. Diary, 17 April 1829.
17. Diary, 17 April 1829.
18. Ibid.
19. Ibid.
20. Ibid.
21. Diary, 29 July 1828.
22. Diary, 3 August 1828.
23. Ibid.
24. Diary, 30 November 1828.
25. Diary, 19 December 1928; 9 February 1829; 23 April 1829.
26. Diary, 23 April 1829.
27. Diary, 23 July 1829.
28. Diary, 23 September 1829.
29. Diary, 5 October 1829.

Chapter 2

1. Richard Maxwell Brown, *Strain of Violence: Historical Studies of American Violence and Vigilantism* (New York: Oxford University Press, 1975), 29; *New York Herald,* "State of the Country," 1 September 1835, p. 2; George Thompson, quoted in Louis Ruchames, ed., *The Abolitionists: A Collection of Their Writings* (New York: G. P. Putnam, 1963), 20.
2. For general studies of violence in American culture, see Brown, *Strains of Violence;* Hugh Davis Graham and Theodore Robert Gurr, eds., *The History of Violence in America* (New York: Praeger, 1969); Richard Hofstadter and Michael Wallace, eds., *American Violence: A Documentary History* (New York: Knopf, 1970); and Thomas Rose, *Violence in America: A Historical and Contemporary Reader* (New York: Random House, 1969). For period studies see especially Michael Feldberg, *The Turbulent Era: Riot and Disorder in Jacksonian America* (New York: Oxford University Press, 1980); Roger Lane, *Policing the City: Boston, 1822–1885* (Cambridge: Harvard University Press, 1967); Leonard L. Richards, *"Gentlemen of Property and Standing": Antiabolition Mobs in Jacksonian America* (New York: Oxford University Press, 1970); and Sam Bass Warner Jr., *The Private City: Philadelphia in Three Periods of its Growth,* 2d ed. (Philadelphia: University of Pennsylvania Press, 1987). For the relationship between violence, culture, and language, see especially Dickson D. Bruce Jr., *Violence and Culture in the Antebellum South* (Austin: University of Texas Press, 1979).
3. Bruce, *Violence and Culture,* 211; Robert L. Scott and Donald K. Smith, "The Rhetoric of Confrontation," *Quarterly Journal of Speech* 55 (1969): 7; Donald G. Mathews, "The Radicalism of the Abolitionists," in *Agitation for Freedom: The Abolitionist Movement* (New York: John Wiley and Sons, 1972), 11.

4. Richard W. Leeman, *The Rhetoric of Terrorism and Counterterrorism* (New York: Greenwood Press, 1991), 18–19.

5. On the relationship between the sacred, the symbolic, and violence, see especially Rene Girard, *Violence and the Sacred*, trans. Patrick Gregory (Baltimore: Johns Hopkins University Press, 1977); and James M. I. Williams, *The Bible, Violence, and the Sacred: Liberation From the Myth of Sanctioned Violence* (San Francisco: Harper San Francisco, 1991).

6. Diary of Angelina Grimké, 30 September 1835. Weld Manuscripts, Clements Library, University of Michigan. All diary references are to this collection.

7. The text of Grimké's letter appeared first as a published letter in the *Liberator*, 19 September 1835; Garrison eventually had the letter printed as a broadside under the heading *Slavery and the Boston Riot*. It is reprinted in Larry Ceplair, ed., *The Public Years of Angelina and Sarah Grimké: Selected Writings, 1835–1839* (New York: Columbia University Press, 1989). For background and biographical treatment, see especially Gerda Lerner, *The Grimké Sisters from South Carolina: Pioneers for Women's Rights and Abolition* (New York: Schocken Books, 1974), 112–28. See also Robert Abzug, *Cosmos Crumbling: American Reform and the Religious Imagination* (New York: Oxford University Press, 1994), 209–10; and Katharine Du Pre Lumpkin, *The Emancipation of Angelina Grimké* (Chapel Hill: University of North Carolina Press, 1974), 78–87. For rhetorical studies, see especially Ellen Reid Gold, "The Grimké Sisters and the Emergence of the Women's Rights Movement," *Southern Speech Communication Journal* 46 (1981): 341–60; and Phyllis M. Japp, "Esther or Isaiah?: The Abolitionist-Feminist Rhetoric of Angelina Grimké," *Quarterly Journal of Speech* 71 (1985): 335–48.

8. Recent studies examining the status and role of language in the antebellum era include Thomas Gustafson, *Representative Words: Politics, Literature, and the American Language, 1776–1865* (New York: Cambridge University Press, 1992); Daniel J. McInerney, *The Fortunate Heirs of Freedom: Abolition and Republican Thought* (Lincoln: University of Nebraska Press, 1994); and David Reynolds, *Beneath the American Renaissance: The Subversive Imagination in the Age of Emerson and Melville* (Cambridge: Harvard University Press, 1988).

9. Elizabeth Fox-Genovese, *Within the Plantation Household: Black and White Women of the Old South* (Chapel Hill: University of North Carolina Press, 1988), 308. See also William H. and Jane H. Pease, *The Web of Progress: Private Values and Public Styles in Boston and Charleston, 1828–1843* (New York: Oxford University Press, 1985) 153–70; Grimké's childhood and early adulthood are extensively treated in Lerner, *Grimké Sisters*, 1–111.

10. William Lloyd Garrison, "Appeal to Our Fellow Citizens," *Liberator*, 22 August 1835.

11. Ibid.

12. Ibid.

13. Ibid.

14. Angelina Grimké to Thomas Smith Grimké, 3 June 1832, Weld Manuscripts.

15. Angelina Grimké diary, June 1830, Weld Manuscripts.

16. Lerner, *Grimké Sisters*, 125.

17. For important studies relating issues of gender, epistolary conventions, and Quaker activism, see Richard Bauman, *Let Your Words Be Few: Symbolism of Speaking and Silence Among Seventeenth-Century Quakers* (New York: Cambridge University Press, 1983); Howard H. Brinton, *Quaker Journals: Varieties of Religious Experience Among Friends* (Wallingford, PA: Pendle Hill, 1972); Elizabeth Potts Brown and Susan Mosher Stuard, eds., *Witnesses for Change: Quaker Women Over Three Centuries* (New Brunswick, N.J.: Rutgers University Press, 1989), esp. Nancy A. Hewitt, "The Fragmentation of Friends: The Consequences for Quaker Women in Antebellum America," 93–108; and Carol Edkins, "Quest for Community: Spiritual Autobiographies of Eighteenth-Century Quaker and Puritan Women in America," in *Women's Autobiography: Essays in Criticism,* ed. Estelle C. Jelinek (Bloomington: Indiana University Press, 1980), 39–52.

18. Grimké, letter to Garrison, *Liberator,* 19 September 1835. All citations sequential.

19. See Acts 7:33

20. See Luke 12:4

21. Acts 20:24

22. For more detailed examinations of this function in rhetorical discourse, see James Darsey, "The Legend of Eugene Debs: Prophetic Ethos as Radical Argument," *Quarterly Journal of Speech* 74 (1988): 434–52; Japp, "Esther or Isaiah?"; and Margaret Zulick, "The Agon of Jeremiah: On the Dialogic Invention of Prophetic Ethos," *Quarterly Journal of Speech* 78 (1992): 125–48.

23. Exodus 10:21–22.

24. Angelina Grimké diary, 11 June 1829, Grimké-Weld Manuscripts.

25. Abzug, *Cosmos Crumbling,* 97; William W. Freehling, *Prelude to Civil War: The Nullification Controversy in South Carolina, 1816–1836* (New York: Harper & Row, 1966).

26. *Boston Daily Evening Transcript,* 18 August 1835, p. 1.

27. Garrison, "Appeal."

28. Ezekiel 8:16.

29. Ephesians 6:11.

30. Matthew 5:11–12.

31. Grimké, diary, September 1835; Grimké to Theodore Dwight Weld, 11 February 1838 *Weld-Grimké Letters,* 2:536–37.

32. Garrison, *Liberator,* 7 November 1835.

33. Weld to Angelina Grimké, 8 February 1838 *Weld-Grimké Letters,* 2:533–34.

Chapter 3

1. *Liberator,* 7 November 1835, 179; Garrison's treatment at the hands of the mob quickly became—and remains—a set piece for sympathetic accounts of abolitionism; that Garrison was more than up to the task of assisting in this bit of public apotheosis is evident in the *Liberator* accounts. For more detailed descriptions, see especially Walter M. Merrill and Louis Ruchames, eds., *Letters of William Lloyd Garrison* (Cambridge:

Harvard University Press, 1971), 1:541–45; John L. Thomas, *The Liberator: William Lloyd Garrison* (Boston: Little, Brown, 1963), 198–206; and Ralph Korngold, *Two Friends of Man* (Boston: Little, Brown, 1950), 96–104.

2. Garrison, *Liberator,* 1 January 1831, 1; Robert Abzug, *Cosmos Crumbling: American Reform and the Religious Imagination* (New York: Oxford University Press, 1994), 30.

3. The best and most systematic study of the background, sources, and reception of *Appeal* is to be found in Susan Zaeske, "Angelina Grimké's *Appeal to the Christian Women of the South*: Characterizing the Female Citizen in Jacksonian America," forthcoming.

4. For Grimké's arrival and early experiences in Philadelphia, see Gerda Lerner, *The Grimké Sisters from South Carolina: Pioneers for Woman's Rights and Abolitionism* (New York: Schocken Books, 1967), 126–45; for an excellent and provocative history of the PFASS, see Jean R. Soderlund, "Priorities and Power: The Philadelphia Female Anti-Slavery Society, in Jean Fagan Yellin and John C. Van Horne, eds., *The Abolitionist Sisterhood: Women's Political Culture in Antebellum America* (Ithaca: Cornell University Press, 1994), 67–88; for The Grimké sisters' involvement with African-American women in PFASS, see Carolyn Williams, "The Female Antislavery Movement: Fighting against Racial Prejudice and Promoting Women's Rights in Antebellum America," in Yellin and Van Horne, *Sisterhood,* 167–68.

5. Quoted in Catherine Birney, *The Grimké Sisters: Sarah and Angelina Grimké , the First American Women Advocates of Abolition and Woman's Rights* (Westport, Conn.: Greenwood Press, 1969), 137–38; Angelina Grimké diary, 18 July 1829, Weld Manuscripts, Clements Library, University of Michigan.

6. Quoted in Birney, *Grimké Sisters,* 138.

7. Angelina Grimké to Sarah Grimké, 19 July 1836, Weld Manuscripts.

8. Ibid.; Lerner, *Grimké Sisters,* 141; Zaeske, "Grimké's *Appeal*"; Abzug, *Cosmos Crumbling,* 210.

9. Angelina E. Grimké, *Appeal to the Christian Women of the South,* in Larry Ceplair, ed., *The Public Years of Sarah and Angelina Grimké: Selected Writings, 1835-1839* (New York: Columbia University Press, 1989), 37.

10. Lerner, *Grimké Sisters,* 141.

11. For incisive studies in the historical formation of southern gender relations, see especially Virginia Bernhard et al., eds., *Southern Women: Histories and Identities* (Columbia: University of Missouri Press, 1992).

12. Zaeske, "Grimké's *Appeal.*"

13. David Walker, *David Walker's Appeal in Four Articles* (Boston: Walker, 1829), 40; Lundy, quoted in *Walker's Appeal* (New York: Arno Press, 1969), vi; Garrison, quoted in Abzug, *Cosmos Crumbling,* 147.

14. Daniel J. McInerney, *The Fortunate Heirs of Freedom: Abolition and Republican Thought* (Lincoln: University of Nebraska Press, 1994), 27

15. Carolyn L. Karcher, *The First Woman of the Republic: A Cultural Biography of Lydia Maria Child* (Durham, N.C.: Duke University Press, 1994), 183.

16. Lydia Maria Child, *An Appeal in Favor of that Class of Americans Called Africans* (Boston: Allen and Tichnor, 1833), 150.

17. Ibid., 231–32.
18. Benjamin Lundy, ed., *Elizabeth Margaret Chandler, Essays, Philanthropic and Moral* (Philadelphia: L. Howell, 1836), 12–13.
19. Ibid., 45.
20. Ibid., 50, 49.
21. Ibid., 48.
22. Angelina Grimké, *Appeal*, in Ceplair, *Public Years*, 37. All citations seriatim.
23. Grimké, *Appeal*, 222–23.
24. McInerney, *Fortunate Heirs of Freedom*; for the interplay of republican and scriptural traditions, see also Abzug, *Cosmos Crumbling*, and Nathan O. Hatch, *The Democratization of American Democracy* (New Haven, Conn.: Yale University Press, 1989).
25. Zaeske, "Grimké's *Appeal*."
26. The appeal to maternal sentiments is found as well in Child, *Appeal*, and Lundy, *Essays*.
27. Lerner, *Grimké Sisters*, 147.
28. Margaret Fell, *Womens Speaking Justified by the Scriptures* (London: Augustan Reprint Society, 1979); Zaeske, "Grimké's *Appeal*." For the prominent role of Quaker women in Western antislavery, see Margaret Hope Bacon, *Mothers of Feminism: The Story of Quaker Women in America* (San Francisco: Harper and Row, 1986); and especially Jean R. Soderlund, *Quakers and Slavery: A Divided Spirit* (Princeton, N.J.: Princeton University Press, 1985).
29. On the background, purpose, and effects of women's petitioning, see Deborah Bingham Van Broekhoven, "'Let Your Names Be Enrolled': Method and Ideology in Women's Antislavery Petitioning," in Jean Fagan Yellin and John C. Van Horne, eds., *The Abolitionist Sisterhood: Women's Political Culture in Antebellum America* (Ithaca: Cornell University Press, 1994), 179–99.
30. Angelina Grimké to Sarah Grimké, 31 September 1836, Weld Manuscripts; *Quarterly Anti-Slavery Magazine* 2 (1836): 112.
31. Angelina Grimké to Sarah Grimké, 31 September 1836, Weld Manuscripts.

Chapter 4

1. Angelina Grimké to Theodore Weld, 12 August 1837, in G. H. Barnes and D. L. Dummond, eds., *Letters of Theodore Dwight Weld, Angelina Grimké Weld, and Sarah Grimké , 1822-1844* (Gloucester, Mass.: Peter Smith, 1965), 1:414. Hereafter cited as *Weld-Grimké Letters*.
2. Kathryn Kish Sklar, *Catharine Beecher: A Study in American Domesticity* (New Haven, Conn.: Yale University Press, 1973), 132; Angelina Grimké to Theodore Weld, 12 August, 1837, *Weld-Grimké Letters*, 1:415.
3. Catharine Beecher, *An Essay on Slavery and Abolition, with Reference to the Duty of American Females* (Philadelphia: Henry Perkins, 1837); Angelina E. Grimké, *Letters to Catherine [sic] E. Beecher, in reply to An Essay on Slavery and Abolitionism*, in Larry

Ceplair, ed., *The Public Years of Sarah and Angelina Grimké: Selected Writings, 1835-1839* (New York: Columbia University Press, 1989), 146–204. See also Catherine Birney, *The Grimké Sisters: Sarah and Angelina Grimké , the First American Women Advocates of Abolition and Woman's Rights* (Westport, Conn.: Greenwood Press, 1969), 197–201; Jeanne Boydston, Mary Kelley, and Anne Margolis, eds., *The Limits of Sisterhood: The Beecher Sisters on Women's Rights and Woman's Sphere* (Chapel Hill, N.C.: University of North Carolina Press, 1988), 114–29; Gerda Lerner, *The Grimké Sisters from South Carolina: Pioneers for Woman's Rights and Abolitionism* (New York: Schocken Books, 1967), 183–87; and Milton Rugoff, *The Beechers: An American Family in the Nineteenth Century* (New York: Harper and Row, 1981).

4. Birney, *Grimké Sisters*, 197.

5. Catharine Beecher, *Letters on the Difficulties of Religion* (Hartford, Conn.: Belknap and Hamersley, 1836), 23. For an incisive account of Wright's public reception and reputation in America, see Lori D. Ginzberg, "'The Hearts of Your Readers Will Shudder': Fanny Wright, Infidelity, and American Free Thought," *American Quarterly* 46 (1994): 195–226.

6. Robert Abzug, *Cosmos Crumbling: American Reform and the Religious Imagination* (New York: Oxford University Press, 1994), 214.

7. Catharine Beecher, *An Essay on the Education of Female Teachers, Written at the Request of the American Lyceum* (New York, 1835), 2; Sklar, *Beecher,* 113.

8. For the best and most comprehensive treatment of Beecher's views on education and female teaching, see Sklar, *Beecher,* esp. 113–15, 168–83, 220–22.

9. Beecher, *Female Teachers,* 4, 5.

10. Ibid., 5, 6.

11. Ibid., 6, 10.

12. Sklar, *Beecher,* 113; Beecher, *Female Teachers,* 22.

13. Sklar, *Beecher,* 124, 129.

14. Beecher, *Religion,* v-vi.

15. Ibid., vi.

16. Ibid.

17. Ibid., 17.

18. Sklar, *Beecher,* 135–36, 138.

19. Beecher, *Essay on Slavery,* 4.

20. Ibid., 6.

21. Ibid., 7–8.

22. Ibid., 13–14.

23. Ibid., 14, 25.

24. Ibid., 40.

25. Ibid., 46–47.

26. Ibid., 55.

27. Ibid., 100, 101.

28. As to the question of who might—or might not—stand as the appropriate role model for American women, Beecher was characteristically blunt. Certainly she proved unimpressed by the appeal to Esther so favored by women abolitionists. It is

interesting to note Beecher's observation that "when a woman is asked to join an Abolitionist Society, or to put her name to a petition to congress, for the purpose of contributing her measure of influence to keep up agitation in Congress, to promote the excitement of the North against the iniquities of the South, to coerce the South by fear, shame, anger, and a sense of odium, to do what she has determined not to do, the case of Queen Esther is not at all to be regarded as a suitable example for imitation." Beecher, *Essay on Slavery*, 104.

29. Angelina Grimké to Theodore Weld, 12 August 1837, *Weld-Grimké Letters, vol. I*, 415.
30. Ibid., 418.
31. Grimké, *Letters to Catherine Beecher*, 146. Hereafter cited parenthetically within the text.
32. Angelina Grimké to Theodore Weld, 27 August, 1827, *Weld-Grimké Letters*, 441.
33. Barbara Welter, *Dimity Convictions: The American Woman in the Nineteenth Century* (Athens: Ohio University Press, 1976). But see also Aileen Kraditor, *Up From the Pedestal: Selected Writings in the History of American Feminism* (Chicago: Quadrangle Books, 1968), esp. the author's introduction; and Linda Kerber, *Toward an Intellectual History of Women* (Chapel Hill, N.C.: University of North Carolina Press, 1997); Boydston, Kelley, and Margolis, *Limits of Sisterhood*, 13.
34. For treatments stressing the intimate relationship between feminism and abolitionism, see especially Ellen DuBois, *Feminism and Suffrage: The Emergence of an Independent Women's Movement in America, 1848–1869* (Ithaca: Cornell University Press, 1978); Blanch Glassman Hersh, *The Slavery of Sex: Feminist Abolitionists in America* (Urbana: University of Illinois Press, 1978); Gerda Lerner, "The Political Activities of Antislavery Women," in *The Feminist Thought of Sarah Grimké* (New York: Oxford University Press, 1998), 175–93; and Alma Lutz, *Crusade for Freedom: Women of the Antislavery Movement* (Boston: Beacon Press, 1968).
35. Angelina Grimké to Jane Smith, 26 June, 1837 Weld Manuscripts.

Chapter 5

1. Gerda Lerner, *The Grimké Sisters from South Carolina: Pioneers for Woman's Rights and Abolitionism* (New York: Schocken Books, 1967), 227; for additional coverage of the tour, see Catherine Birney, *The Grimké Sisters: Sarah and Angelina Grimké, the First American Women Advocates of Abolition and Woman's Rights* (Westport, Conn.: Greenwood Press, 1969), 175–90; Keith Melder, "Forerunners of Freedom: The Grimké Sisters in Massachusetts, 1837–38, "*Essex Institute Historical Collections* 103 (1967): 223–49; "Essay on Eloquence," *The Visitor, or Ladies' Monthly, vol. 20* (1808), 133.
2. Frances Trollope, *Domestic Manners of the Americans* (New York: Vintage, 1949), 328; Frederick Raumer, *America and the American People*, trans. William W. Turner (New York: J. & H. G. Langley, 1846), 310; Thomas Hamilton, *Men and Manners in America* (Philadelphia: Carey, Lea, and Blanchard, 1833); Isabella Lucy Bird (Bishop), *The Englishwoman in America*, ed., Andrew Hill Clark (Madison: University of Wisconsin Press, 1966), 416.

3. For studies addressing women and public life specifically, see especially Susan Phinney Conrad, *Perish the Thought: Intellectual Women in Romantic America, 1830–1860* (Seacaucus, N.J.: Citadel, 1976); Lori D. Ginzberg, *Women and the Work of Benevolence: Morality, Politics, and Class in Nineteenth-Century America* (New Haven, Conn.: Yale University Press, 1990); Deborah Gold Hansen, *Strained Sisterhood: Gender and Class in the Boston Female Anti-Slavery Society* (Amherst: University of Massachusetts Press, 1993); Nancy Hewitt, *Women's Activism and Social Change: Rochester, New York, 1822–1872* (Ithaca, N.Y.: Cornell University Press, 1984); Linda Kerber, *Women of the Republic: Intellect and Ideology in Revolutionary America* (Chapel Hill: University of North Carolina Press, 1980); and Glenna Mathews, *The Rise of Public Woman: Woman's Power and Woman's Place in the United States, 1630–1970* (New York: Oxford University Press, 1992).

4. Angelina Grimké to Jane Smith, 17 December 1837, Weld Manuscripts, Clements Library, University of Michigan.

5. *Liberator,* 17 December 1836, 202; *Liberator,* 5 November 1836; *Liberator,* 10 December 1836, 200; *Liberator,* 17 December 1836, 202; on Garrison's support for women abolitionists, see especially Suzanne M. Marilley, *Woman Suffrage and the Origins of Liberal Feminism in the United States, 1820–1920* (Cambridge, Mass.: Harvard University Press, 1996), 22–42.

6. G. H. Barnes and D. L. Drummond, eds. *Letters of Theodore Dwight Weld, Angelina Grimké Weld, and Sarah Grimké, 1822–1844* (1934 reprint, Gloucester, Mass.: Peter Smith, 1965) 1:374–75.

7. Angelina Grimké to Sarah Douglass, 3 April 1837, *Black Abolitionist Papers,* reel 2; Angelina Grimké to Jane Smith 29 May, 1837, Weld Manuscripts.

8. Angelina Grimké to Jane Smith 29 May, 1837, Weld Manuscrtipts; *Weld-Grimké Letters,* 1:396.

9. Hubbard Winslow, *Woman As She Should Be* (Boston: T. H. Carter, 1838), 30–31.

10. Sarah Grimké and Angelina Grimké to 'Clarkson,' *Weld-Grimké Letters,* 1:365–72; on the Amesbury debate, see Lerner, *Grimké Sisters,* 178–80.

11. Angelina Grimké to Weld, 12 August 1837, *Weld-Grimké Letters,* 1:414–19.

12. Ibid.; *Liberator,* "To the Public," 1 September 1837, 1.

13. Angelina Grimké to Weld, 12 August 1837, *Weld-Grimké Letters,* 1:414–15.

14. Ibid., 1:415.

15. Ibid.

16. Ibid. 1:416.

17. Angelina Grimké to Jane Smith, 19 November 1836, Weld Manuscripts; on the Grimké-Weld courtship, see Robert Abzug, *Passionate Liberator: Theodore Dwight Weld and the Dilemma of Reform* (New York: Oxford University Press, 1980), 165–218; and Lerner, *Grimké Sisters,* 205–25;

18. Weld's leadership for the agency system is detailed in Abzug, *Passionate Liberator,* 150–52; and especially Gilbert H. Barnes, *The Antislavery Impulse, 1830–1844* (New York: Harcourt, Brace, and World, 1964), 79–87.

19. Theodore Weld to Angelina Grimké, 15 August 1837, *Weld-Grimké Letters,* 1:425.

20. Ibid., 1:426.

21. Ibid., 1:427.
22. Ibid.
23. Samuel Philbrick, Diary, 1837, Weld Manuscripts.
24. Angelina Grimké to Theodore Weld and John Greenleaf Whittier, 20 August, 1837, *Weld-Grimké Letters,* 1:427–32.
25. Angelina Grimké to George M. Chase, 20 August 1837, Weld Manuscripts.
26. Ibid.
27. Angelina Grimké to Weld and Whittier, 20 August 1837, *Weld-Grimké Letters,* 1:428; the *Pastoral Letter* is reprinted in full in Ronald F. Reid, *American Rhetorical Discourse* (Prospect Heights, Ill.: Waveland Press, 1995), 363–67.
28. *Pastoral Letter,* 365.
29. Ibid., 366; Sarah M. Grimké, "Letters on the Equality of the Sexes and the Condition of Woman,"in Ceplair, *Public Years,* 204.
30. Angelina Grimké to Weld and Whittier, *Weld-Grimké Letters,* 1:428.
31. *Pastoral Letter,* 366.
32. Ibid., 367.
33. Angelina Grimké to Weld and Whittier, *Weld-Grimké Letters,* 1:428.
34. Ibid., 1:429.
35. Ibid.
36. Ibid., 1:429–30.
37. Ibid., 1:431.
38. Ibid.
39. Ibid., 1:431–32.
40. Theodore Weld to Sarah and Angelina Grimké, 26 August 1837, *Weld-Grimké Letters,* 1:434.
41. Ibid., 1:435.
42. Sarah and Angelina Grimké to Henry C. Wright, 27 August 1837, *Weld-Grimké Letters,* 1:440.
43. Theodore Weld to Sarah and Angelina Grimké, 10 October 1837, *Weld-Grimké Letters,* 1:453.
44. Angelina Grimké to Theodore Weld, 20 September 1837, *Weld-Grimké Letters,* 1:450; Grimké to Jane Smith, 26 October 1837, Weld Manuscripts.

Chapter 6

1. Angelina Grimké to William Lloyd Garrison, 30 August, 1835, in Larry Ceplair, ed., *The Public Years of Sarah and Angelina Grimké: Selected Writings, 1835–1839* (New York: Columbia University Press, 1989), 26.
2. Gerda Lerner, The *Grimké Sisters from South Carolina: Pioneers for Women's Rights and Abolition* (New York: Schockeu Books, 1974), 245; Karlyn Kohrs Campbell, *Man Cannot Speak For Her: A Critical Study of Early Feminist Rhetoric* (New York: Praeger, 1989), vol. 1, 29; Garrison to Sarah Benson, 19 May 1838, in *Letters of William Lloyd Garrison,* II, 363. Angelina married Theodore Weld several days before the

Pennsylvania Hall address and took his name as her last; I retain her birth name because, in effect, this is an analysis of Grimké as a single woman.

3. Catherine Birney, *The Grimke Sisters: Sarah and Angelina Grimké: The First American Women Advocates of Abolition and Women's* Rights (Westport, Conn.: Greenwood Press, 1969), 240; Elizabeth Cady Stanton, Susan B. Anthony, and Metilda Joslyn Gage, eds., *History of Woman Suffrage, 1848–1851* (New York: Arnow Press, 1969), vol. 1:343.

4. Jean Fagan Yellin, *Women and Sisters: The Anti-Slavery Feminists in American Culture* (New Haven, Conn.: Yale University Press, 1989), 48; Campbell, *Man Cannot Speak For Her,* I, 34.

5. For systematic examination of the Pennsylvania Hall address, see especially Suzanne M. Daughton, "'The Fine Texture of Enactment': Iconicity as Empowerment in Angelina Grimké's Pennsylvania Hall Address," *Women's Studies in Communication* 18 (1995): 19–43; Campbell, *Man Cannot Speak For Her,* 1:29–36; and Phyllis M. Japp, "Esther or Isaiah? The Abolitionist-Feminist Rhetoric of Angelina Grimké," *Quarterly Journal of Speech* 71 (1985): 335–48. See also Kathrine Henry, "Angelina Grimké's Rhetoric of Exposure," *American Quarterly* 49 (1997): 328–55.

6. *Boston Quarterly Review* 1(1838): 475; James K. Paulding, *Slavery in the United States* (New York, 1836), 281–82.

7. *New England Magazine* 8 (1835): 144; *Literary and Theological Review* (1839) 9:42.

8. *Boston Recorder,* quoted in Maria Weston Chapman, *Right and Wrong in Boston* (Boston: Boston Female Anti-Slavery Society, 1835), 66; Linda Kerber, "Separate Spheres, Female Worlds, Woman's Place: The Rhetoric of Women's History," in Kerber, *Toward an Intellectual History of Women* (Chapel Hill, N.C.: University of North Carolina Press, 1997), 159–99; *Boston Centennial and Gazette,* quoted in Chapman, *Right and Wrong in Boston* (Boston: Boston Female Anti-Slavery Society, 1836), 61; Ibid., 62; *Boston Transcript,* quoted in ibid., 62–63; *Boston Atlas,* quoted in ibid., 63.

9. Quoted in *Boston Female Anti-Slavery Society Annual Report,* 14; ibid., 17.

10. *Boston Quarterly Review* 1 (1838): 381.

11. Chapman, *Right and Wrong in Boston,* 81; Garrison, et al., "Declaration of Sentiments,"quoted in Reid, *American Rhetorical Discourse,* 362.

12. [Chapman], *Annual Report* (1835), 21; Child, ibid., 91; Jackson, ibid., 99.

13. *Liberator,* 5 January 1838, 1.

14. For one suggestion, see Stephen H. Browne, "'Like Gory Spectres': Representing Evil in Theodore Weld's *American Slavery As It Is*," *Quarterly Journal of Speech* 80 (1994): 277–92.

15. Theodore Weld to Sarah and Angelina Grimké, 15 August 1837, *Weld-Grimké Letters,* 1:426; *American Quarterly Observer* 2 (1834): 267.

16. Stanley Harrold, *The Abolitionists and the South, 1831–1861* (Lexington: University Press of Kentucky, 1995), 43.

17. James Birney, *Letter on Colonization, Addressed to the Rev. Thomas J. Mills, Corresponding Secretary of the Kentucky Colonization Society* (New York: American Anti-Slavery Society, 1834), 45; Theodore Weld to James Birney, 28 May 1834, in Dwight L. Dumond, ed., *Letters of James Gillespie Birney, 1831–1857* (New York: Appleton-Century), 1:112; Birney, *Letter on Colonization,* 45.

18. Weld to Birney, 17 June 1836, *Letters of James Gillespie Birney*, 1:120; Weld quotes Tappan in ibid., 130; and Wright, in ibid., 131.

19. John G. Fee, *Autobiography of John Fee* (Chicago: National Christian Association, 1891), 14.

20. Editor's note, in David Nelson, *David Nelson's Lecture on Slavery* (New York: American Anti-Slavery Society, 1839), 16; Nelson, *Lecture*, 6–7.

21. For a brilliant treatment of the rhetorical work of testimony, witnessing, and autobiography by African Americans, see William L. Andrews, *To Tell a Free Story: The First Century of African-American Autobiography, 1760–1865* (Urbana: University of Illinois Press, 1988).

22. Angelina Grimké, letter to Garrison, in Ceplair, *Public Years*, 26; Grimké, *Appeal*, ibid., 55, 70; "Speech to a Committee of the Massachusetts House of Representatives, February 21, 1838," Ceplair, *Public Years*, 312.

23. Isocrates, *Antidosis*, in Patricia Bizzell and Bruce Herzberg, eds., *The Rhetorical Tradition: Readings from Classical Times to the Present* (Boston: St. Martin's, 1990), 50; Cicero, *De oratore*, bk. 1, in ibid., 204; Thomas Wilson, *Arte of Rhetorique*, in ibid., 588.

24. Angelina Grimké to Sarah M. Douglass, 25 February 1838, *Weld-Grimké Letters*, 2:574.

25. Angelina Grimké Weld, "Speech at Pennsylvania Hall, May 16, 1838," in Ceplair, *Public Years*, 318; Samuel Danforth, "Errand into the Wilderness," in Ronald F. Reid, *American Rhetorical Discourse* (Prosect Heights, Ill.: Waveland Press, 1995), 38–39.

26. Angelina Grimké, letter to Garrison, in Ceplair, *Public Years*, 27; *Quarterly Anti-Slavery Magazine* 2 (1837): 372–73.

27. Editorial allusions to the mob are presumably by Samuel Webb, as recorded in his *History of Pennsylvania Hall* (Philadelphia: Merrihew and Gunn, 1838).

28. *Quarterly Anti-Slavery Magazine* 1 (1836): 320.

29. Stanton et al., *History of Woman Suffrage*, 1:343; Angelina Grimké Weld to Elizabeth Pease, 14 August 1839, *Weld-Grimké Letters*, 2:784–85.

30. Webb, *Pennsylvania Hall*, 123; Angelina Grimké Weld to Elizabeth Pease, 14 August 1839, *Weld-Grimké Letters*, 2:785.

Epilogue

1. Lydia Maria Child to Angelina Grimké, 4 February 1874, Weld Manuscripts; Child to Maria Weston Chapman, 10 April 1839, Lydia Maria Child Papers.

2. Angelina Grimké Weld to Anne Warren Weston, 15 July, 1838, in Larry Ceplair, ed., *The Public Years of Sarah and Angelina Grimké: Selected Writings, 1835–1839* (New York: Columbia University Press, 1989), 326.

3. Elizur Wright Jr., in Theodore Dwight Weld, *In Memory. Angelina Grimké Weld* (Boston: G. H. Ellis, 1880), 21.

4. Wendell Phillips, in Weld, *In Memory*, 28–29.

5. Lucy Stone, in Weld, *In Memory*, 26.

6. Oliver Johnson, *William Lloyd Garrison and His Times* (Boston: B. B. Russell, 1880), 259–60.

7. Angelina Grimké, Letters, in Ceplair, *Public Years*, 191; Grimké diary, 14 July 1829, Weld Manuscripts, Clements Library, University of Michigan.

8. Thomas W. Benson, "Rhetoric as a Way of Being," in Thomas W. Benson, ed., *American Rhetoric: Context and Criticism* (Carbondale, Ill.: Southern Illinois University Press, 1989), 293–322.

Bibliography

Primary Source Materials

Manuscript Collections

Blackwell Family Papers
Elizabeth Cady Stanton Papers, Manuscripts Division, Library of Congress
Weld Manuscripts, William C. Clements Library, University of Michigan

Newspapers

American Quarterly Observer
Boston Quarterly Review
Liberator
Literary and Theological Review
New England Magazine
New York Herald
Quarterly Anti-Slavery Magazine

Published Collections

Angelina Grimké to Sarah Douglass, 3 April 1837, *Black Abolitionist Papers*, reel 2; Angelina Grimké to Jane Smith 29 May, 1837, Weld Manuscripts.

Barnes, G. H., and D. L. Dummond, eds. 1934; rpt. 1965. *Letters of Theodore Dwight Weld, Angelina Grimké Weld, and Sarah Grimké, 1822–1844.* 2 vols. Gloucester, Mass.: Peter Smith.

Campbell, Karlyn Kohrs. 1989. *Man Cannot Speak For Her.* 2 vols.: 1. *A Critical Study of Early Feminist Rhetoric*; 2 *Key Texts of the Early Feminists.* New York: Praeger.

Ceplair, Larry, ed. 1989. *The Public Years of Sarah and Angelina Grimké: Selected Writings, 1835-1839.* New York: Columbia University Press.

Dummond, Dwight L., ed. 1938. *Letters of James Gillespie Birney, 1831–1857.* 2 Vols. New York: Appleton-Century.

Merritt, Walter, ed. 1971–1981. *The Letters of William Lloyd Garrison*. Cambridge: Belknap Press of Harvard University Press.

Pickard, John B., ed. 1975. *The Letters of John Greenleaf Whittier*. Cambridge: Harvard University Press. 3 vols.

Ripley, Peter. 1985. *The Black Abolitionist Papers*. Vols. 1–5. Chapel Hill: University of North Carolina Press.

Stanton, Elizabeth Cady, Susan B. Anthony, and Matilda Joslyn Gage, eds. *History of Woman Suffrage*, 1848–1851. Vols. 1–3. 1881–87. New York: Fowler and Wells.

Books and Articles

Abzug Robert. 1980. *Passionate Liberator: Theodore Dwight Weld and the Dilemma of Reform*. New York: Oxford University Press.

Abzug, Robert. 1994. *Cosmos Crumbling: American Reform and the Religious Imagination*. New York: Oxford University Press.

Andrews, William L. 1988. *To Tell a Free Story: The First Century of African-American Autobiography, 1760–1865*. Urbana: University of Illinois Press.

Bacon, Margaret Hope. 1986. *Mothers of Feminism: The Story of Quaker Women in America*. San Francisco: Harper and Row.

Barbour, Hugh. 1986. "Quaker Prophetesses and Mothers in Israel." In Stoneburner, *Influence*, 57-80.

Barnes, Gilbert H. 1964. *The Antislavery Impulse, 1830–1844*. New York: Harcourt, Brace, and World.

Bartlett, Elizabeth Ann, ed. 1988. *Sarah Grimké: Letters on the Equality of the Sexes and Other Essays*. New Haven, Conn.: Yale University Press.

Bauman, Richard. 1983. *Let Your Words Be Few: Symbolism of Speaking and Silence Among Seventeenth-Century Quakers*. New York: Cambridge University Press.

Beecher, Catharine. 1835. *An Essay on the Education of Female Teachers, Written at the Request of the American Lyceum*. New York: Van Nostrand and Dwight.

Beecher, Catharine. 1836. *Letters on the Difficulties of Religion*. Hartford, Conn.: Belknap and Hamersley.

Beecher, Catharine. 1837. *An Essay on Slavery and Abolition with Reference to the Duty of American Females*. Philadelphia: Henry Perkins.

Beeth, Howard. 1987. Among Friends: Epistolary Correspondence Among Quakers in the Emergent South. *Quaker History* 76: 108–27.

Benson, Thomas W. 1989. "Rhetoric as a Way of Being." In Thomas W. Benson, ed., *American Rhetoric: Contexts and Criticism*. Carbondale, Ill.: Southern Illinois University Press.

Berg, Barbara. 1978. *The Remembered Gate: Origins of American Feminism, The Woman and the City, 1800–1860*. New York: Oxford University Press.

Bernhard, Virginia, ed. 1992. *Southern Women: Histories and Identities* Columbia: University of Missouri Press.

Bird, Isabella Lucy (Bishop). 1966. *The Englishwoman in America,* ed. Andrew Hill Clark. Madison: University of Wisconsin Press.

Birney, James. 1834. *Letter on Colonization, Addressed to the Rev. Thomas J. Mills, Corresponding Secretary of the Kentucky Colonization Society.* New York: American Anti-Slavery Society.

Birney, Catherine. 1885; rpt., 1969. *The Grimké Sisters: Sarah and Angelina Grimké, the First American Women Advocates of Abolition and Woman's Rights.* Westport, Conn.: Greenwood Press.

Bizzell, Patricia, and Bruce Herzberg, eds. 1990. *The Rhetorical Tradition: Readings From Classical Times to the Present.* Boston: St. Martin's.

Boydston, Jean, Mary Kelley, and Anne Margolis, eds. 1988. *The Limits of Sisterhood: The Beecher Sisters on Women's Rights and Woman's Sphere.* Chapel Hill: University of North Carolina Press.

Brinton, Howard H. 1972. *Quaker Journals: Varieties of Religious Experience Among Friends.* Wallingford, Penn.: Pendle Hill.

Broekhoven, Deborah Bingham Van. "'Let Your Names Be Enrolled': Method and Ideology in Women's Antislavery Petitioning," in Yellin and Van Horne, *Sisterhood,* 179–99.

Brown, Elizabeth Potts, and Susan Mosher Stuard, eds. 1989. *Witnesses for Change: Quaker Women Over Three Centuries.* New Brunswick, N.J.: Rutgers University Press.

Brown, Richard Maxwell. 1975. *Strain of Violence: Historical Studies of American Violence and Vigilantism.* New York: Oxford University Press.

Browne, Stephen H. 1994. "'Like Gory Spectres': Representing Evil in Theodore Weld's *American Slavery As It Is.*" *Quarterly Journal of Speech* 80:277–92.

Bruce Jr., Dickson. 1979. *Violence and Culture in the Antebellum South.* Austin: University of Texas Press.

Chapman, Maria Weston. 1835. *Right and Wrong in Boston.* Boston: Boston Female Anti-Slavery Society.

Chapman, Maria Weston. 1836. *Right and Wrong in Massachusetts.* Boston: Boston Female Anti-Slavery Society.

Child, Lydia Maria. 1833. *An Appeal in Favor of that Class of Americans Called Africans.* Boston: Allen and Tichnor.

Child, Lydia Maria. 1839. Child to Maria Weston Chapman, 10 April 1839, Lydia Maria Child Papers.

Cicero, Marcus Tullius. *De Oratore.* 1990. In Bizzell and Herzberg, *Rhetorical Tradition,* 200–250.

Conrad, Susan Phinney. 1976. *Perish the Thought: Intellectual Women in Romantic America, 1830–1860*. Secaucus, N.J.: Citadel Press.

Cott, Nancy F. 1977. *The Bonds of Womanhood: 'Woman's Sphere' in New England, 1780-1835*. New Haven, Conn.: Yale University Press.

Culley, Margo. 1989. "I Look at Me: Self as Subject in the Diaries of Women." *Women's Studies Quarterly* 17:15–22.

Danforth, Samuel. 1995. "Errand into the Wilderness," in Reid, *American Rhetorical Discourse*, 39–53.

Darsey, James. 1988. "The Legend of Eugene Debs: Prophetic Ethos as Radical Argument." *Quarterly Journal of Speech* 74:434–52.

Darsey, James. 1997. *The Prophetic Tradition and Radical Rhetoric in America*. New York: New York University Press.

Daughton, Suzanne M. 1995. "'The Fine Texture of Enactment': Iconicity as Empowerment in Angelina Grimké's Pennsylvania Hall Address." *Women's Studies in Communication* 18:19–43.

Dubois, Ellen Carol. 1978. *Feminism and Suffrage: The Emergence of an Independent Women's Movement in America, 1848–1869*. Ithaca, N.Y.: Cornell University Press.

Edkins, Carol. 1980. "Quest for Community: Spiritual Autobiographies of Eighteenth-Century Quaker and Puritan Women in America." In Jelinek, *Women's Autobiography*, 39-52.

"Essay on Eloquence." 1808. *The Visitor, or Ladies' Monthly* 20:133–35.

Fee, John G. 1891. *Autobiography of John Fee* . Chicago: National Christian Association.

Feldberg, Michael. 1980. *The Turbulent Era: Riot and Disorder in Jacksonian America*. New York: Oxford University Press.

Fell, Margaret. 1667; rpt. 1979. *Womens Speaking Justified*. In *Womens Speaking Justified*, intro. David J. Latt. Los Angeles: Augustan Reprint Society.

Flexnor, Eleanor. 1959; rpt., 1974. *Century of Struggle: The Woman's Rights Movement in the United States*. New York: Athenaeum.

Fox-Genovese, Elizabeth. 1988. *Within the Plantation Household: Black and White Women of the Old South*. Chapel Hill: University of North Carolina Press.

Franklin, Penelope, ed. 1986. *Private Pages: Diaries of American Women, 1830–1870*. New York: Balantine Books.

Freehling, William W. 1966. *Prelude to Civil War: The Nullification Controversy in South , Carolina, 1816–1836*. New York: Harper and Row.

Garrison, William Lloyd. Garrison to Sarah Benson, 19 May 1838, in *Letters of William Lloyd Garrison*, II, 363.

Ginzberg, Lori D. 1990. *Women and the Work of Benevolence: Morality, Politics, and Class in Nineteenth-Century America*. New Haven, Conn.: Yale University Press.

Ginzberg, Lori D. 1994. "'The Hearts of Your Readers Will Shudder': Fanny Wright, Infidelity, and American Free Thought." *American Quarterly* 46:195–226.

Girard, Rene. 1977. *Violence and the Sacred*. Trans. Patrick Gregory. Baltimore: Johns Hopkins University Press.

Gold, Ellen Reid. 1981. "The Grimké Sisters and the Emergence of the Woman's Rights Movement." *Southern Speech Communication Journal* 46:341–60.

Graham, Hugh Davis, and Theodore Robert Gurr, eds. 1969. *The History of Violence in America*. New York: Praeger.

Gustafson, Thomas. 1992. *Representative Words: Politics, Literature, and the American Language, 1776–1865*. New York: Cambridge University Press.

Hamilton, Thomas. 1833. *Men and Manners in America*. Philadelphia: Carey, Lea, and Blanchard.

Hansen, Deborah Gold. 1993. *Strained Sisterhood: Gender and Class in the Boston Female Anti-Slavery Society*. Amherst: University of Massachusetts Press.

Harrold, Stanley. 1995. *The Abolitionists and the South, 1831–1861*. Lexington: University Press of Kentucky.

Hatch, Nathan O. 1989. *The Democratization of American Democracy*. New Haven, Conn.: Yale University Press.

Henry, Katherine. 1997. "Angelina Grimké's Rhetoric of Exposure." *American Quarterly* 49:328-55.

Hersh, Blanch Glassman. 1978. *The Slavery of Sex: Feminist Abolitionists in America*. Urbana: University of Illinois Press.

Hewitt, Nancy. 1984. *Women's Activism and Social Change: Rochester, New York, 1822–1872*. Ithaca, N.Y.: Cornell University Press.

Hewitt, Nancy A. 1989. "The Fragmentation of Friends: The Consequences for Quaker Women in Antebellum America." In Brown and Stuard, *Witnesses*, 93-108.

Hofstadter, Richard, and Michael Wallace., eds. 1970. *American Violence: A Documentary History*. New York: Knopf.

Isocrates. 1990. *Antidosis*. In Bizzell and Herzberg, *The Rhetorical Tradition*, 50–54.

Japp, Phyllis M. 1985. "Esther or Isaiah? The Abolitionist-Feminist Rhetoric of Angelina Grimké." *Quarterly Journal of Speech* 71:335–48.

Jelinek, Estelle C., ed. 1980. *Women's Autobiography: Essays in Criticism*. Bloomington: Indiana University Press.

Johnson, Oliver. 1880. *William Lloyd Garrison and His Times*. Boston: B. B. Russell.

Karcher, Carolyn L. 1994. *The First Woman of the Republic: A Cultural Biography of Lydia Maria Child*. Durham, N.C.: Duke University Press.

Kerber, Linda. 1980. *Women of the Republic: Intellect and Ideology in the American Revolution*. Chapel Hill: University of North Carolina Press.

Kerber, Linda. 1997. *Towards an Intellectual History of Women.* Chapel Hill: University of North Carolina Press.

Korngold, Ralph. 1950. *Two Friends of Man.* Boston: Little, Brown.

Kraditor, Aileen. 1967. *Means and Ends in American Abolitionism.* New York: Pantheon.

Kraditor, Aileen. 1968. *Up From the Pedestal: Selected Writings in the History of American Feminism.* Chicago: Quadrangle Books.

Lane, Roger. 1967. *Policing the City: Boston, 1822–1885.* Cambridge: Harvard University Press.

Leeman, Richard. 1991. *The Rhetoric of Terrorism and Counterterrorism.* New York: Greenwood Press.

Lerner, Gerda. 1967. *The Grimké Sisters from South Carolina: Pioneers for Woman's Rights and Abolitionism.* New York: Schocken Books.

Lerner, Gerda. 1998. *The Feminist Thought of Sarah Grimké.* New York: Oxford University Press.

Lumpkin, Katharine Du Pre. 1974. *The Emancipation of Angelina Grimké.* Chapel Hill: University of North Carolina Press.

Lundy, Benjamin, ed., 1836. *Elizabeth Margaret Chandler, Essays, Philanthropic and Moral.* Philadelphia: L. Howell.

Lutz, Alma. 1968. *Crusade for Freedom: Women of the Anti-Slavery Movement.* Boston: Beacon Press.

McInerney, Daniel J. 1994. *The Fortunate Heirs of Freedom: Abolition and Republican Thought.* Lincoln: University of Nebraska Press.

Marilley, Suzanne M.1996. *Woman Suffrage and the Origins of Liberal Feminism in the United States, 1820–1920.* Cambridge, Mass.: Harvard University Press.

Matthews, Glenna. 1992. The *Rise of Public Woman: Woman's Power and Woman's Place in the United States, 1630–1970.* New York: Oxford University Press.

Melder, Keith. 1967. "Forerunners of Freedom: The Grimké Sisters in Massachusetts, 1837–1838." *Essex Institute Historical Collections* 103:223–49.

Melder, Keith. 1977. *Beginnings of Sisterhood: The American Woman's Rights Movement, 1800–1850.* New York: Schoken Books.

Merrill, Walter M. 1963. *Against Wind and Tide: A Biography of William Lloyd Garrison.* Cambridge: Harvard University Press.

Merrill, Walter M., and Louis Ruchames, eds. 1971. *Letters of William Lloyd Garrison.* Vol. 1. Cambridge: Harvard University Press.

Nelson, David. 1839. *David Nelson's Lecture on Slavery.* New York: American Anti-Slavery Society.

Paulding, James K. 1836. *Slavery in the United States.* New York: Harper and Brothers.

Pease, William H., and Jane H. Pease. 1985. *The Web of Progress: Private Values and Public Styles in Boston and Charleston, 1828–1843.* New York: Oxford University Press.

Raoul, Valerie. 1989. "Women and Diaries: Gender and Genre." *Mosaic* 22:57–65.

Raumer, Frederick. 1846. *America and the American People.* Trans. William W. Turner. New York: J. & H. G. Langley.

Reid, Ronald F. 1995. *American Rhetorical Discourse.* Prospect Heights, Ill.: Waveland Press.

Reynolds, David. 1988. *Beneath the American Renaissance: The Subversive Imagination in the Age of Emerson and Melville.* Cambridge: Harvard University Press.

Rose, Thomas. 1969. *Violence in America: A Historical and Contemporary Reader.* New York: Random House.

Rugoff, Milton. 1981. *The Beechers: An American Family in the Nineteenth Century.* New York: Harper and Row.

Ruchames, Louis. 1963. *The Abolitionists: A Collection of Their Writing.* New York: Harper and Row.

Ryan, Mary P. 1990. *Women in Public: Between Banners and Ballots, 1825–1880.* Baltimore: Johns Hopkins University Press.

Scott, Ann Firor. 1970. *The Southern Lady: From Pedestal to Politics, 1830–1930.* Chicago: University of Chicago Press.

Scott, Robert L., and Donald K. Smith. 1969. "The Rhetoric of Confrontation." *Quarterly Journal of Speech* 55:1–8.

Sklar, Kathryn Kish. 1973. *Catharine Beecher: A Study in American Domesticity.* New York: Norton.

Soderlund, Jean R. 1985. Quakers and Slavery: A Divided Spirit. Princeton, N.J.: Princeton University Press.

Soderlund, Jean R. 1987. "Women's Authority in Pennsylvania and New Jersey Quaker Meetings, 1680–1760." *William and Mary Quarterly,* 3d ser., 44:722–49.

Soderlund, Jean R. 1994. "Priorities and Power: The Philadelphia Female Anti-Slavery Society," in Yellin and Van Horne, *Abolitionist Sisterhood,* 67–88.

Stewart, James Brewer. 1996. *Holy Warriors: Abolitionists and American Slavery.* New York: Hill and Wang.

Stoneburner, Carol, and John Stoneburner. 1986. *The Influence of Quaker Women on American History.* Lewiston, N.Y.: Edwin Mellon.

Thomas, John L. 1963. *The Liberator: William Lloyd Garrison.* Boston: Little, Brown.

Trollope, Frances.1849. *Domestic Manners of the Americans.* New York: Vintage.

Walker, David. 1969. *David Walker's Appeal in Four Articles.* New York: Arno Press.

Warner Jr., Sam Bass. 1987. *The Private City: Philadelphia in Three Periods of its Growth.* 2d ed. Philadelphia: University of Pennsylvania Press.

Webb, Samuel. 1838. *History of Pennsylvania Hall.* Philadelphia: Merrihew and Gunn.

Weld, Theodore Dwight. 1839. *American Slavery As It Is: Testimony of a Thousand Witnesses.* New York: American Anti-Slavery Society.

Weld, Theodore Dwight. 1880. *In Memory: Angelina Grimké Weld.* Boston: G. H. Ellis.

Welter, Barbara. 1976. *Dimity Convictions: The American Woman in the Nineteenth Century.* Athens: Ohio University Press.

Williams, Carolyn. 1994. "The Female Antislavery Movement: Fighting against Racial Prejudice and Promoting Women's Rights in Antebellum America." In Yellin and Van Horne, *Abolitionist Sisterhood,* 167–68.

Williams, James M. I. 1991. *The Bible, Violence, and the Sacred: Liberation From the Myth of Sanctioned Violence.* San Francisco: Harper Torchbooks.

Wilson, Thomas. 1990. *Arte of Rhetorique.* In Bizzell and Herzberg, *Rhetorical Tradition,* 587-621.

Winslow, Hubbard. 1838. *Woman As She Should Be.* Boston: T. H. Carter.

Yellin, Jean Fagan. 1989. *Women and Sisters: The Anti-Slavery Feminists in American Culture.* New Haven, Conn.: Yale University Press.

Yellin, Jean Fagan, and John C. Van Horne, eds. 1994. *The Abolitionist Sisterhood: Women's Political Culture in Antebellum America.* Ithaca, N.Y.: Cornell University Press.

Zaeske, Susan. 1995. "The 'Promiscuous Audience' Controversy and the Emergence of the Early Woman's Rights Movement." *Quarterly Journal of Speech* 81:191–207.

Zaeske, Susan. Forthcoming. "Angelina Grimké's *Appeal to the Christian Women of the South*: Characterizing the Female Citizen in Jacksonian America" in Stephen H. Browne, ed., *Rhetoric and Identity in the Early Republic.* East Lansing, Mich.: Michigan State University Press.

Zulick, Margaret. 1992. "The Agon of Jeremiah: On the Dialogic Invention of Prophetic Ethos." *Quarterly Journal of Speech* 78:125–48.

Index